Words of Intelligence

A Dictionary

Jan Goldman

The Scarecrow Press, Inc.
Lanham, Maryland • Toronto • Oxford
2006

SCARECROW PRESS, INC.

Published in the United States of America
by Scarecrow Press, Inc.
A wholly owned subsidiary of
The Rowman & Littlefield Publishing Group, Inc.
4501 Forbes Boulevard, Suite 200, Lanham, Maryland 20706
www.scarecrowpress.com

PO Box 317
Oxford
OX2 9RU, UK

British Library Cataloguing in Publication Information Available

Library of Congress Cataloging-in-Publication Data

Goldman, Jan.
  Words of intelligence : a dictionary / Jan Goldman.
     p.   cm.
  Includes bibliographic references.
  ISBN-13: 978-0-8108-5641-7 (pbk. : alk. paper)
  ISBN-10: 0-8108-5641-7 (pbk. : alk. paper)
  1. Intelligence service—Dictionaries.   2. Military intelligence—Dictionaries.
I. Title.
UB250.G65   2006
327.1203—dc22   2006004627

The difference between the right word and the almost right word is the difference between lightning and a lightning bug.

—Mark Twain

We are struggling, above all, to find adequate words of condemnation for those who planned and carried out these abominable attacks. In truth, no such words can be found. And words, in any case, are not enough.

—Secretary-General Kofi Annan to the UN General Assembly,
September 12, 2001

Contents

Foreword

Words of Intelligence presents the operational vocabulary of the enigmatic and secretive Intelligence Community (IC), and the evolving vocabulary of the post 9/11 world of homeland security. At the core of the IC and homeland security worlds are those theoretical and analytical practices that forge intelligence, threat, and warning in protection of national security.[1] So much so that in a 2002 publication entitled *The National Strategy for Homeland Security,* intelligence and warning are considered critical mission areas for homeland security.[2] *Words of Intelligence*, a worthy contribution to this literature, elucidates the context, practice and machinations of these specialized vocabularies.

Words of Intelligence is also an effort to consolidate terms related to the theoretical aspects of intelligence, intelligence operations, intelligence strategies, security classification of information, obscure names of intelligence boards and organizations, and homeland security that remain scattered throughout professional, academic, and government agency sources, both in print, and on the Web. The novelty of this book lies in the scope of coverage and in supporting documentation. Mini–case studies, which add dimension to terms, make this book as much a guide to military history, intelligence strategy, and intelligence failure, as it is a map to the specialized, and often technical language of intelligence and homeland security.

In a reorganization of federal agency departments that the Office of the Inspector General (OIG) of the Department of Homeland Security (DHS)[3] called the "most significant transformation of the U.S. government since 1947, when President Truman merged the various branches of the armed forces into the Department of Defense to better coordinate the national defense against military threats," the physical and ideological structure of "homeland security" was created.[4] Generally speaking, "homeland security" has become a catchall phrase that describes a set of interlocking policies and practices that reflect domestic disaster preparedness, intelligence analysis, intelligence collection, intelligence sharing, surveillance, and counterintelligence activities.

On a federal level, the Department of Homeland Security's Information

Analysis and Infrastructure Protection Directorate (IAIP), alongside inter-agency bodies such as the Terrorist Threat Integration Center, longstanding members of the IC (FBI, CIA, NSA, for example), and the Northern Com-mand, or NORTHCOM, created in 2002 to provide intelligence analysis to military forces throughout the United States, come to homeland security with a unique statutory mandate, history, culture, technological capability, and set of policies and procedures related to the collection, analysis, and use of intel-ligence; but most significantly, these agencies bring to the table a vocabulary rich with the properties of stealth, surprise, threat, vulnerability, and warning. Language often reveals a great deal about the cognition and culture of a com-munity of interest.[5] This idea is especially true in relation to the language of the intelligence and homeland security communities. By way of language, *Words of Intelligence* offers researchers insight into the elusive practices of a closed and focused culture.

Many terms listed in *Words of Intelligence* represent the standard operating language of the IC; terms related to security classification of information and warning have been circulating in the public sphere and mass media since the inception of the cold war. By way of the national news and popular television shows such as *Alias* and *E-Ring*, the language of intelligence and homeland security frequently inform plots of television dramas and news shows.[6] How-ever, *Words of Intelligence* also includes more recent terms associated with homeland security and the post-9/11 regulatory arena.

The 2002 creation of the Department of Homeland Security, for example, gave rise to new terms such as *critical infrastructure protection, homeland security information*, and *homeland security advisory system*. While these terms reflect new ways of thinking about national security and terrorism, these terms also bear witness to the tension that exists between national se-curity concerns, privacy, terrorism, and citizen right to information.

What can be distilled from the specialized languages of the overlapping worlds of intelligence and homeland security—which one might say has been blurred into a post-9/11 apocalyptic landscape—is encapsulated in the words of General Carl von Clausewitz in 1831:

> The commander of an immense whole finds himself in a constant whirlpool of false and true information, of mistakes committed through fear, through negligence, through precipitation, of contraventions of his authority, either from mistaken or cor-rect motives, from ill will, true or false sense of duty, indolence or exhaustion, of accidents which no mortal could have foreseen.[7]

It is my great pleasure to be a part of this work. I hope *Words of Intelligence* will be a reference aid helpful to law enforcement officials, members of the homeland security and intelligence communities, researchers, policymakers, citizens, and students alike in decoding what is in many ways a foreign language.

> —Susan Maret, University of Denver's Library and Information Science Program and author of *On Their Own Terms: A Lexicon with an Emphasis on Information-Related Terms Produced by the U.S. Federal Government* (January 2006, Federation of American Scientists, http://www.fas.org/sgp/library/maret.pdf)

NOTES

1. *National security* is defined as "national defense or foreign relations of the United States." Executive Order 13292 "Further Amendment to Executive Order 12958, as Amended, Classified National Security Information." March 2003. http://www.archives.gov/federal-register/executive-orders/2003.html.

2. Office of Homeland Security. "National Strategy for Homeland Security." July 2002. http://www.whitehouse.gov/homeland/book/.

3. Office of the Inspector General. Department of Homeland Security. Semiannual Report to the Congress. October 1, 2002, to March 31, 2003. http://www.dhs.gov/interweb/assetlibrary/OIG_Spring_2003_SAR.pdf.

4. The two major pieces of legislation provide homeland security with its authority: "The Uniting and Strengthening America by Providing Appropriate Tools Required to Intercept and Obstruct Terrorism (USA PATRIOT ACT) Act of 2000," http://purl.access.gpo.gov/GPO/LPS17579, and the "Homeland Security Act of 2002," http://thomas.loc.gov/cgi-bin/query/z?c107:h.r.5005.enr. For background on the early (dis)organization of DHS, see Arthur S. Hulnick's *Keeping Us Safe: Secret Intelligence and Homeland Security*. Westport, Conn.: Praeger, 2004.

5. Rob Johnston. *Analytic Culture in the U.S. Intelligence Community: An Ethnographic Study.* Washington, D.C.: Center for the Study of Intelligence, Central Intelligence Agency: U.S. Supt. of Docs. 2005.

6. *Frontline.* "The Torture Question." October 18, 2005. http://www.pbs.org/wgbh/pages/frontline/. Frontline used *actionable intelligence* as if it were a public, widely understood term. It is defined in this work is "information that will force the consumer of the intelligence product to initiate action in mitigating an impending threat."

7. Carl von Clausewitz. *On War.* Chapter 7, "Perseverance." Trans. Col. J. J. Graham. London: Routledge & Kegan Paul, 1968, http://www.clausewitz.com/CWZHOME/On_War/BK3ch07.html.

Preface

Words are both extremely powerful and useless. They can communicate ideas, plans, hopes, and aspirations as well as being inadequate in transferring emotions, feelings, thoughts, and insight. It is not uncommon to hear someone say "I'm just looking for the right word" to display their thoughts. Additionally, the spoken language is fueled by sounds that comprise words, which in turn can both cause and prevent action to occur. For those individuals responsible for national security, however, words are also an important tool in fighting the enemy.

Over the years, people who work in the intelligence community have developed their own language. The reason for this, as in other professions, is typically to provide clarity of thought, a communal sense of understanding, and the rapid transmission of knowledge.

In the intelligence business, this is especially important as this country seeks to respond quickly in the "global war on terrorism." Collecting information and transforming it into intelligence for dissemination to prevent future attacks has always been the raison d'etre for the intelligence community, as well as providing an advantage in diplomatic affairs. After World War II, the main focus of the intelligence community was to understand the threat posed by the Soviet Union and its allies; but since the attacks on the World Trade Center and the Pentagon on September 11, 2001, that focus has shifted to understanding the threat posed by transnational terrorist groups.

To meet the challenges of this new century, the intelligence community has undergone its first massive reform since the 1947 National Security Act, when the Central Intelligence Agency, the National Security Agency, and the Department of Defense were created. Recently, with the establishment of the Department of Homeland Security and a Director of National Intelligence, the intelligence community has taken on new duties and responsibilities. The wall between foreign intelligence and domestic law enforcement has been crumbling. Additionally, intelligence must be transmitted to state and local public administrators, health officials, transportation planners, and industry (to name but a few) in times of a possible domestic attack. As it has been explicitly written in the National Intelligence Reform Act of 2004, a "trusted information network" is needed to promote "sharing of intelligence and homeland security information among all relevant federal departments, state and local authorities, and relevant private-sector entities." However, if these officials are going to work together, they need to speak the same language.

Finding an intelligence lexicon is not difficult. There are many intelligence lexicons published by federal, state, and local governments, agencies, and departments in addition to commercial publications that focus on terrorism, intelligence, or homeland security. However, *Words of Intelligence* is different for several reasons. First, this book seeks in plain language to define terms that anyone can understand. Typically, it is not uncommon to get *analysis* confused with *assessment*, or *clandestine operations* confused with *covert operations*. However, as you will learn from this book, there is a major difference between these words and terms that are sometimes used interchangeably and incorrectly. It is my hope that in simple nontechnical terms, this book can be used as a primer for those interested in intelligence and homeland security, and a clarifying agent to those who thought they knew after working in the field for many years. Second, this book is to be used as a guide in how to develop and use intelligence by offering a topic index. This can help the analyst sharpen or develop knowledge that will make her or him a better analyst or consumer of intelligence. For example, I have listed different forms of intelligence analysis mythologies or deception techniques, which I hope will be the starting point for further investigation. Third, this book has over 400 footnotes. Although I have combed through many intelligence publications to provide a common listing of terms, some terms are based on my own inventiveness. In some instances, there are several meanings for one word and I took it upon myself to boil it down to a common definition. Fourth, this book has lots of examples. As does any author, I hope that the reader will eagerly read *Words of Intelligence* from cover to cover as a reward for all the time and effort that was put into it. However, I have no doubt that should you pick up this book and read it randomly, you will gain some insight, if not a few enjoyable tidbits of information. Finally, the goal of this book is to develop the first all-source intelligence and homeland security lexicon for those who collect, produce, and disseminate intelligence and those who will need to use it.

Acknowledgments

I would like to thank Professor Frank Hughes at the Joint Military Intelligence College and Professor David Schum at George Mason University for their assistance in understanding evidence-based methodology, and Kenneth Gerhart for his input and review of the manuscript.

Abbreviations and Acronyms

Some abbreviations have multiple meanings; those meanings unrelated to intelligence, homeland security, or warning are not included in this list.

AAR	After Action Report
ACCIS	Association of County/City Information Services
ACINT	Acoustical Intelligence
ACOE	Army Corps of Engineers
ACOM	U.S. Atlantic Command
ACOUSTINT	Acoustical Intelligence
ACS	Automated Case System (FBI)
ACS/C4I	Assistant Chief of Staff for Command, Control, Communications, Computers, and Intelligence
ACSI	Assistant Chief of Staff for Intelligence
ADIS	Arrival Departure Information System
ADNET	Anti-Drug Network
AGILE	Advanced Generation of Interoperability for Law Enforcement
AIA	USAF Air Intelligence Agency
AIG	Address Indicator Group
AIS	Automated Information System; Automatic Identification System (Maritime)
AMC	Army Material Command
AMI	Air and Marine Interdiction Program
ANALIT	Analyst-to-Analyst informal message
AO	Area of Operations
AOI	Area of Interest
AOR	Area of Responsibility
APCO	Association of Public Safety Communications Officials

APHIS	Animal and Plant Health Inspection Service (DHS)
APHL	Agency for Public Health Laboratories
AR	Administrative Report
ARAC	Atmospheric Release Advisory Capability (DOE)
ARC	American Red Cross
ARES	Amateur Radio Emergency Services
ARG	Accident Response Group (DOE)
ASD	Assistant Secretary of Defense
ASD/C3I	Assistant Secretary of Defense for Command, Control, Communications, and Intelligence
ASD-HD	Assistant Secretary of Defense for Homeland Defense
ASTHO	Association of State and Territorial Health Officials
ATAC	Anti-Terrorism Advisory Council
ATIX	Anti-Terrorism Information Exchange
ATS	Automated Targeting System
ATSA	Aviation and Transportation Security Act
ATSDR	Agency for Toxic Substances and Disease Registry
ATTF	Anti-Terrorism Task Force
AVIC	Area Veterinary in Charge
BATFE	Bureau of Alcohol, Tobacco, Firearms and Explosives
BATS	Bombing and Arson Tracking System (ATF)
BCBP	Bureau of Customs and Border Security
BCIS	Bureau of Citizenship and Immigration Services
BCRT	Regional Drug Task Force Biological/Chemical Response Team
BCS	Border Cargo Selectivity
BDA	Battle Damage Assessment
BDRP	Biological Defense Research Program (U.S. Navy)
BERT	Public Health Bioterrorism Emergency Response Team
BICE	Bureau of Immigration and Customs Enforcement
BOLO	Be on the Lookout
BRAC	Bioterrorism Response Advisory Committee
BT	Bioterrorism
BTS	Border and Transportation Security Directorate
BW	Biological Warfare
C2	Command and Control
C2W	Command and Control Warfare
C3	Command, Communications, and Control

C3I	Command, Communications, Control, and Intelligence
C/B-RRT	Chemical Biological Rapid Response Team
C-RATING	Condition Rating System (for military readiness)
C-TPAT	Customs-Trade Partnership against Terrorism
CA	Civil Affairs
CAC	Crisis Action Center
CAIRA	Chemical Accident/Incident Response and Assistance
CAP	Civil Air Patrol; Corrective Action Plan
CARI	Contractor Access Restricted Information
CARVER	Criticality, Accessibility, Recoverability, Vulnerability, Effect, Recognizability
CAT	Crisis Action Team
CAW	Center for Asymmetric Warfare
CBDCOM	Chemical Biological, Defense Command
CBIRF	Chemical and Biological Incident Response Force
CBO	Community-Based Organizations
CBP	Customs Border Protection
CBPMO	Customs and Border Patrol Modernization Office
CBR	Chemical, Biological, Radiological
CBRED	Chemical, Biological, Radiological, Environmental Defense Response
CBRNE	Chemical, Biological, Radiological, Nuclear, Explosive
CBS	Customer and Border Protection (part of DHS)
CBW	Chemical and Biological Warfare
CCD	Camouflage, Cover, and Deception
CCP	Consolidated Cryptologic Program; Citizen Corps Program
CCRF	Commissioned Corps Readiness Force (PHS)
CD	Communicable Disease
CDC	Centers for Disease Control and Prevention
CDP	Center for Domestic Preparedness
CDRG	Catastrophic Disaster Response Group
CDTAC	Counter-Drug Technology Assessment Center
CEMNET	Comprehensive Emergency Management Network
CEMP	Comprehensive Emergency Management Plan
CENTCOM	Central Command
CEP	Circular Error Probable

CERCLA	Comprehensive Environmental Response, Compensation, and Liability Act
CERT	Community Emergency Response Teams
CFA	Category Functional Area
CFDA	Catalog of Federal Domestic Assistance
CFR	Code of Federal Regulation
CHER-CAP	Comprehensive HAZMAT Emergency Response, Capability Assessment Program
CHIP	Computer Hacking and Intelligence Property
CI	Counterintelligence
CIA	Central Intelligence Agency
CIAO	Critical Infrastructure Assurance Office
CIC	Combined Intelligence Center
CII	Critical Infrastructure Information
CINC	Commander-in-Chief
CIO	Central Imagery Office
CIP	Critical Infrastructure Protection
CIRC	Computer Incident Response Center
CIRG	Critical Incident Response Group
CIS	Citizenship and Immigration Services
CISM	Critical Incident Stress Management
CIVA	Critical Infrastructure Vulnerability Assessment
CIWC	Combined Intelligence Watch Center
CJCS	Chairman of the Joint Chiefs of Staff
CJCSI	Chairman of the Joint Chiefs of Staff Instruction
CMT	Crisis Management Team
CNO	Chief of Naval Operations
CNSS	Committee for National Security Systems
CNTK	Controlled Need-to-Know
CNWDI	Critical Nuclear Weapons Design Information
COA	Course of Action
COG	Continuity of Government
COMINT	Communications Intelligence
COMPUSEC	Computer Security
COMSEC	Communications Security
CONPLAN	Concept of Operations Plan; Concept Plan
COOP	Continuity of Operations
COP	Common Operating Picture
COPS	Community Oriented Policing Services
COTS	Commercial-Off-the-Shelf
CPR	Command Position Report

CPTED	Crime Prevention through Environmental Design
CPX	Command Post Exercise
CRITIC	Critical Intelligence Message
CRRA	Capabilities Review and Risk Assessment
CS	Civil Support
CSA	Customs Self-Assessment
CSEPP	Chemical Stockpile Emergency Preparedness Program
CSG	Council of State Governments
CSIL	Critical and Sensitive Information List
CSP	Contingency Support Package
CSS	Central Security Service
CST	Civil Support Team
CSTARC	Cyber Security Tracking Analysis and Response Center
CSTE	Council of State and Territorial Epidemiologists
CT	Counter-Terrorism
CTC	Counter-Terrorism Center
D&D	Denial and Deception
DA	Delegated Authority
DAE	Disaster Assistance Employee (also SAE, for Stafford Act Employee)
DAG	DSSCS Address Group
DAO	Defense Attache Office
DAWS	Defense Automated Warning System
DCCC	Defense Collection Coordination Center
DCD	Disease Conditions Database
DCE	Defense Coordinating Element
DCI	Director of Central Intelligence
DCID	Director of Central Intelligence Directive
DCO	Defense Coordinating Officer
DCSINT	Deputy Chief of Staff for Intelligence
DDCI	Deputy Director of Central Intelligence
DDI	Deputy Director for Intelligence; Duty Director for Intelligence
DDO	Deputy Director for Operations
DEA	Drug Enforcement Administration
DEFCON	Defense Readiness Condition
DEFSMAC	Defense Special Missile and Aerospace Center
DEST	Domestic Emergency Support Team
DEW	Distant Early Warning

DF	Direction Finding
DFO	Disaster Field Office
DGWS	Defense Global Warning System
DHHS	Department of Health and Human Services
DHS	Department of Homeland Security
DHSHQ	Department of Homeland Security Headquarters; Defense HUMINT Headquarters
DI	Directorate of Intelligence (CIA and DIA)
DIA	Defense Intelligence Agency
DIAC	Defense Intelligence Analysis Center
DII	Defense Information Infrastucture
DINSUM	Daily Intelligence Summary
DIO	Defense Intelligence Officer (DIA); Defense Intelligence Organization (Australia)
DIRNSA	Director of the National Security Agency
DISN	Defense Information System Network
DIST	Disaster Information Systems Clearinghouse
DIWS	Defense Intelligence Warning System
DMAT	Disaster Medical Assistance Team (FEMA)
DMORT	Disaster Mortuary Operational Response Team (FEMA)
DNI	Director of National Intelligence; Director of Naval Intelligence
DO	Directorate of Operations (CIA)
DOC	Department of Commerce
DOCEX	Document Exploitation
DoD	Department of Defense
DoDD	Department of Defense Directive
DODIIS	Department of Defense Intelligence Information System
DOE	Department of Energy
DOI	Department of the Interior
DOJ	Department of Justice
DOS	Department of State
DOSTN	Department of State Telecommunications Network
DOT	Department of Transportation
DPETAP	Domestic Preparedness Equipment, Technical Assistance Program
DR/DIA	Director of the Defense Intelligence Agency
DRC	Disaster Recovery Center
DRM	Disaster Recovery Manager

DSN	Defense Switched Network
DSSCS	Defense Special Security Communications System
DT	Domestic Terrorism
DWI	Disaster Welfare Inquiry
E&E	Evasion and Escape
EAO	Energy Assurance Office
EAS	Emergency Alert System
EC	Emergency Coordinator
ECM	Electronic Countermeasures
ECCM	Electronic Counter-Countermeasures
EDI	Electronic Data Interchange
EEFI	Essential Elements of Friendly Information
EEI	Essential Elements of Information
EFR	Emergency Responder
EFSEC	Energy Facility Site Evaluation Council
EICC	Emergency Information and Coordination Center (FEMA)
EIS	Epidemic Intelligence Service
ELECTRO-OPTINT	Electro-Optical Intelligence
ELINT	Electronic Intelligence
ELSEC	Electronics Security
EMA	Emergency Management Agency
EMAC	Emergency Management Assistance Compact
EMRT	Emergency Medical Response Team
EMSEC	Emissions Security
EMS	Emergency Medical Services
EO	Executive Order
EOC	Emergency Operations Center
EOD	Explosive Ordnance Disposal
EOF	Emergency Operations Facility
EOP	Emergency Operations Plan or Procedures
EP&R	Emergency Preparedness and Response (DHS)
EPA	Environmental Protection Agency
EPCRA	Emergency Planning Community Right-to-Know Act
EPLO	Emergency Preparedness Liaison Officer
EPZ	Emergency Planning Zone
ERAMS	Environmental Radiation Ambient Monitoring System (EPA)
ERC	Emergency Response Coordinator
ERDO	Emergency Response Duty Officer

ERT	Emergency Response Team; Environmental Response Team (EPA); Evidence Response Team (FBI)
ERT-A	Emergency Response Team, Advanced Element
ERT-N	Emergency Response Team, National
ESA	Energy Security and Assurance; Environmentally Sensitive Area
ESF	Emergency Support Function
ESSENCE	Electronic Surveillance System for the Early Notification of Community-Based Epidemics
EST	Emergency Support Team (FEMA)
ETC	Emergency Telecommunications
EUCOM	European Command
EW	Electronic Warfare
FAA	Federal Aviation Administration
FAMS	Federal Air Marshall Service
FAR	Federal Acquisition Regulations
FAS	Federation of American Scientists
FBI	Federal Bureau of Investigation
FCI	Foreign Counterintelligence
FCO	Federal Coordinating Officer
FDA	Food and Drug Administration
Fed CIRC	Federal Computer Incident Response Center
FEMA	Federal Emergency Management Agency
FERC	FEMA Emergency Response Capability
FESC	Federal Emergency Support Coordinator
FGI	Foreign Government Information
FHWA	Federal Highway Administration
FI	Finished Intelligence; Foreign Intelligence
FID	Flame Ionization Detector
FINCEN	Financial Crimes Enforcement Network
FIRECOM	Fire Communications
FISINT	Foreign Instrumental Signals Intelligence
FLETC	Federal Law Enforcement Training Center
FMAC	Freight Mobility Advisory Committee
FMSIB	Freight Mobility Strategic Investment Board
FOA	Field Operating Agency
FOC	FEMA Operations Center
FOG	Field Operations Guide
FOIA	Freedom of Information Act
FORMAT	Foreign Materiel Intelligence

FOUO	For Official Use Only
FPF	Fallout Protective Factor
FPS	Federal Protective Service
FRA	Federal Railroad Association
FRD	Formerly Restricted Data
FRERP	Federal Radiological Emergency Response Plan
FRMAC	Federal Radiological Monitoring and Assessment Center
FRP	Federal Response Plan
FS	Fire Service
FSS	Federal Supply Service
FTA	Federal Transit Administration
FTS	Federal Telecommunications System
FTTTF	Foreign Terrorist Tracking Task Force
G	Gamma
GA	Governmental Administrative
GCJIN	Global Criminal Justice Information Network
GDIP	General Defense Intelligence Program
GENSER	General Service Communications System
GETS	Government Emergency Telecommunications Service
GID	Generic Indicator Directory
GIEWS	Global Information and Early Warning System on Food and Agriculture
GIG	Global Information Grid Defense Sector
GIGO	Garbage In, Garbage Out
GII	Global Information Infrastructure
GIS	Geographic Information Systems
GMDSS	Global Maritime Defense and Safety System
GOTS	Government-Off-the-Shelf
GPS	Global Positioning System
GTIN	Global Trade Identification Number
HACCP	Hazard Analysis and Critical Control Point
HAN	Health Alert Network
HAN LAP	Health Alert Network Local Health Assistance Project
HAZCAT	Hazard Categorizing
HAZMAT	Hazardous Material
HD	Homeland Defense
HDER	Homeland Defense Equipment Reuse Program
HEAR	Hospital Emergency Administrative Radio

HEICS	Hospital Emergency Incident Command System
HEWS	Humanitarian Early Warning System
HHS	Health and Human Services
HIDTA	High Intensity Drug Trafficking Area
HIFCA	High Intensity Financial Crime Area
HIVA	Hazard Identification and Vulnerability Assessment
HLS	Homeland Security
HLT	Hurricane Liaison Team (FEMA)
HLW	High Level Waste
HMRU	Hazardous Materials Response Unit (FBI)
HPSCI	House Permanent Select Committee on Intelligence
HRSA	Health Resources and Services Administration
HSARPA	Homeland Security Advanced Research Projects Agency
HSAS	Homeland Security Advisory System
HSC	Homeland Security Council
HSEEP	Homeland Security Exercise and Evaluation Program
HSOC	Homeland Security Operations Center
HSPD	Homeland Security Presidential Directive
HUMIN	THuman Intelligence
HZ	Hazardous Materials Personnel
I^2	Instability Indicator
I-DAY	Intelligence Day
I&W	Indications and Warning
IA	Information Analysis; Information Assurance
IACP	International Association of Chiefs of Police
IAD	Information Assurance Directorate
IAEA	International Atomic Energy Agency
IAFC	International Association of Fire Chiefs
IAFIS	Integrated Automated Fingerprint Identification System
IAIP	Information Analysis and Infrastructure Protection Directorate (DHS)
IALEIA	International Association of Law Enforcement Intelligence Analysts
IAP	Incident Action Plan
IC	Intelligence Community; Incident Command
ICAP	Incident Communications Action Plan
ICBM	Inter-Continental Ballistic Missile
ICC	Intelligence Coordination Center

ICDDC	Interstate Civil Defense and Disaster Compact
ICE	Immigration and Customs Enforcement
ICP	Incident Command Post
ICS	Incident Command System; Intelligence Community Staff
IED	Improvised Explosive Device
IFF	Identification Friend or Foe
IGA	Intergovernmental Agreement
IGN	Intergovernmental Network
II	Imagery Interpretation
IIEA	International Intelligence Ethics Association
IIMG	Interagency Incident Management Group
IIPO	Information Integration Program Office
IIT	Nuclear Regulatory Commission's Incident Investigation Team
IITF	Information Infrastructure Task Force
IL	Indicator List
IMINT	Imagery Intelligence
IMS	Incident Management System
IMT	Incident Management Team
IND	Improvised Nuclear Device
INFOSEC	Information Systems Security
INFOSYS	Information System
INFOWAR	Information Warfare
INR	Bureau of Intelligence and Research (State Department)
INTSUM	Intelligence Summary
INRP	Initial National Response Plan
INS	Immigration and Naturalization Service
INTREP	Intelligence Report
IO	Information Operations
IOB	Intelligence Oversight Board
IOF	Interim Operating Facility
IOSS	Interagency OPSEC Support Staff
IP	Infrastructure Protection
IPFO	Interim Principle Federal Official
IR	Incident Response, Information Requirements
IRIS	Incident Response Information System
IRM	Information Resources Management
IS	Information Superiority
ISAO	Information Sharing Analysis Organization

ISR	Intelligence, Surveillance, and Reconnaissance
IST	Incident Support Team
IT	International Terrorism
ITF	Intelligence Task Force
IW	Information Warfare
IWG	Infrastructure Working Group
IXO	Information Exploitation Office
J-2	Director of Intelligence for Joint Chiefs of Staff
J-3	Director for Operations for Joint Chiefs of Staff
JAC	Joint Analysis Center
JCMEC	Joint Captured Materiel Exploitation Center
JCS	Joint Chiefs of Staff
JDEC	Joint Document Exploitation Center
JDISS	Joint Deployable Intelligence Support System
JDCC	Joint Data Coordination Center
JFO	Joint Field Office
JHOC	Joint Harbor Operations Center
JIB	Joint Information Bureau
JIC	Joint Intelligence (or Information) Center
JIDC	Joint Interrogation and Debriefing Center
JIOC	Joint Intelligence Operations Center or Command
JIS	Joint Information System
JOC	Joint Operations Center
JP	Joint Publication
JPA	Joint Powers Authority
JRAC	Joint Rear Area Coordinators
JRIES	Joint Regional Information Exchange System
JSCP	Joint Strategic Capabilities Plan
JSCR	Joint Security Commission Report
JSOC	Joint Special Operations Command
JTF	Joint Task Force
JTTF	Joint Terrorism Task Force
JTWG	Joint Terrorism Working Group
JWICS	Joint Worldwide Intelligence Communication System
LASINT	Laser Intelligence
LCAT	Logistics Closeout Assistance Teams
LEA	Law Enforcement Agency
LEIU	Law Enforcement Intelligence Unite
LEOC	Local Emergency Operations Center
LEPC	Local Emergency Planning Committee

LERC	Local Emergency Response Coordinator
LERN	Law Enforcement Radio Network
LETPP	Law Enforcement Terrorism Prevention Program
LIC	Low Intensity Conflict
LIMDIS	Limited Dissemination
LNO	Liaison Officer
LOU	Limited Official Use Information
LPD	Low Probability of Detection
LPI	Low Probability of Intercept
MAC Group	Multi-Agency Coordinating Group
MACA	Military Assistance to Civil Authorities
MACS	Multi-Agency Coordination Systems
MASINT	Measurement and Signature Intelligence
MATRIX	Multistate Anti-Terrorism Information Exchange
MCBAT	Medical Chemical and Biological Advisory Teams
MCTFER	Military–Civilian Task Force for Emergency Response
MDITDS	Defense Intelligence Threat Data Migration System
MEDINT	Medical Intelligence
MEDNET	Medical Emergency Delivery Network
MI	Military Intelligence
MIB	Military Intelligence Board
MIP	Military Intelligence Program
MLAT	Mutual Legal Assistance Treaty
MLS	Multilevel Security
MMRS	Metropolitan Medical Response System
MOA	Memorandum of Agreement
MOU	Memorandum of Understanding
MRC	Medical Reserve Corps
MRTE	Medical Readiness, Training, and Education Committee
MSCA	Military Support to Civil Authorities
NABC	National Agricultural Biosecurity Center
NATO	North Atlantic Treaty Organization
NAWAS	National Warning System
NBDAC	National Bio-Weapons Defense Analysis Center
NCA	National Command Authority
NCAP	National Customs Automation Program
NCC	National Coordinating Center
NCHRP	National Cooperative Highway Research Program
NCIC	National Crime Information Center

NCID	National Center for Infectious Disease
NCP	National Contingency Plan
NCS	Noncritical-Sensitive
NCSC	National Computer Security Center
NCTC	National Counterterrorism Center
NDA	Nondisclosure Agreements
NDIC	National Defense Intelligence Centre (Canada)
NDMOC	National Disaster Medical Operations Center
NDMS	National Disaster Medical System
NEDSS	National Electronic Disease Surveillance System
NEIS	National Earthquake Information Service
NEMA	National Emergency Managers Association
NENA	National Emergency Number Association
NEOC	National Emergency Operations Center (FEMA)
NERP	National Emergency Repatriation Plan
NERRTC	National Emergency Response and Rescue Training Center
NEST	National Emergency Search Team (DOE)
NFIB	National Foreign Intelligence Board
NFIC	National Foreign Intelligence Community
NFIP	National Foreign Intelligence Program
NGA	National Geospatial-Intelligence Agency
NGB	National Guard Bureau
NGO	Non-Governmental Organization
NIAID	National Institute of Allergy and Infectious Disease
NIBRS	National Incident-Based Reporting System
NIC	National Intelligence Council; National Incident Commander
NICC	National Interagency Coordination Center
NICS	National Instant Criminal Background Check System
NID	National Intelligence Daily
NIE	National Intelligence Estimate
NIFCC	National Interagency Fire Coordination Center
NIH	National Institute of Health
NII	National Information Infrastructure
NIIMS	National Interagency Incident Management System
NIJ	National Institute of Justice
NIMD	Novel Intelligence from Massive Data
NIMS	National Incident Management System
NIO	National Intelligence Officer

NIO/W	National Intelligence Officer for Warning
NIOSH	National Institute for Occupational Safety and Health
NIPC	National Infrastructure Protection Center; National Imagery and Photo Center
NIRT	Nuclear Incident Response Team
NISA	National Infrastructure Simulation and Analysis
NIST	National Intelligence Support Team
NJTTF	National Joint Terrorism Task Force
NLETS	National Law Enforcement Telecommunications System
NMCC	National Military Command Center (J3/JCS)
NIMD	Novel Intelligence From Massive Data
NMJIC	National Military Joint Intelligence Center (DIA)
NMRT	National NBC Medical Response Team (HHS)
NOAA	National Oceanic and Atmospheric Administration
NOCONTRACT	Not Releasable to Contractors/Consultants
NODP	National Office of Domestic Preparedness
NOFORN	Not Releasable to Foreign Nationals
NOIWON	National Operations and Intelligence Watch Officers Network
NORAD	North American Aerospace Defense Command
NORTHCOM	Northern Command
NOSIC	Naval Ocean Surveillance Information Center
NRC	Nuclear Regulatory Commission
NRCC	National Resource Coordination Center
NRDA	National Resource Damage Assessment
NRP	National Response Plan
NRS	National Response System
NSA	National Security Agency; National Security Area
NSC	National Security Council
NSDD	National Security Decision Directive
NSDI	National Spatial Data Infrastructure
NSEERS	National Security Entry-Exit Registration System
NSEP	National Security Emergency Preparedness
NSF	National Strike Force
NSFCC	National Strike Force Coordination Center
NSI	National Security Information
NSOC	National Signals Intelligence Operations Center; National Security Operations Center (NSA)
NSRP	National Search and Rescue Plan
NSSE	National Security Special Event

NSTS	National Secure Telecommunications System
NSTISSI	National Security Telecommunications and Information Systems Security Instruction
NTAC	United States Secret Service National Threat Assessment Center
NUCINT	Nuclear Intelligence
NVOAD	National Voluntary Organizations Active in Disasters
NVRD	Non-Proliferation and Verification R&D
NWS	National Warning Staff
OB	Order of Battle
ODP	Office of Domestic Preparedness
OEP	Office of Emergency Preparedness
OER	Office of Emergency Response (DHHS)
OES	Office of Emergency Services
OHS	Office of Homeland Security
OICC	Operational Intelligence Coordination Center
ONE	Office of National Estimates
ONI	Office of Naval Intelligence
OOTW	Operations Other Than War
OPCON	Operational Control
OPG	Operations Planners Group
OPHP	Office of Public Health Preparedness (DHHS)
OPS	Operations
OPSC	Office of Private Sector Coordination
OPSEC	Operational Security
OPSMAN	Operations Manual
OPTINT	Optical Intelligence
ORCON	Originator Controlled
OSC	On-Scene Coordinator/Commander
OSD	Office of the Secretary of Defense
OSINT	Open Source Intelligence
OSP	Operational Support Package
PACOM	Pacific Command
PAG	Protective Action Guide; Public Affairs Guidance
PCII	Protected Critical Infrastructure Information
PDB	President's Daily Brief
PDD	Presidential Decision Directive
PHEPR	Public Health Emergency Preparedness and Response
PHIMS	Public Health Issues Management System
PHIN	Public Health Information Network

PHOTINT	Photo Intelligence
PI	Photographic Interpretation or Photographic Interpreter
PIO	Public Information Officer
PIP	Partners in Protection
PIR	Priority Intelligence Requirements
POC	Point of Contact
PPAG	Proposed Public Affairs Guidance
PROPIN	Proprietary Information Involved
PSYOP	Psychological Operations
PTE	Potential Threat Elements
RACES	Radio Amateur Civil Emergency Services
RAD	Risk Assessment Division
RADINT	Radar Intelligence
RAPTR	Radio Analysis Prediction Tool Repository
RCECC	Regional Communications and Emergency Coordination Center
RCP	Regional Contingency Plan
RD	Restricted Data
RDD	Radiological Dispersal Devices
RDI	Remodeling Defense Intelligence
REAC/TS	Radiation Emergency Assistance Center/Training Site (DOE)
REOC	Regional Emergency Operations Center
RERT	Radiological Emergency Response Team (EPA)
RFI	Request for Information
RII	Request for Intelligence Information
RINT	Radiation Intelligence, Unintentional
RISS	Regional Information Sharing System
ROC	Regional Operations Center (FEMA)
RQ	Reportable Quantity
RRIS	Rapid Response Information System (FEMA)
RRT	Regional Response Team
RS	Risk Sensitive
RTF	Response Task Force (DOD)
S&T	Science and Technology
SAC	Special Agent in Charge (FBI); Strategic Air Command
SAMI	Sources and Methods Information
SAP	Special Access Program
SAR	Search and Rescue

SARDA	State and Regional Disaster Airlift Plans
SBU	Sensitive But Unclassified
SCBA	Self-Contained Breathing Apparatus
SCCI	Senate Select Committee on Intelligence
SCI	Sensitive Compartmented Intelligence; State Critical Infrastructure
SCIF	Sensitive Compartmented Information Facility
SCM	Survivable Crisis Management
SCR	Status Change Report
SECDEF	Secretary of Defense
SEL	Standardized Equipment List
SENTRI	Secure Electronic Network for Traveler Rapid Inspection
SI	Special Intelligence
SIGINT	Signals Intelligence
SIGSEC	Signals Security
SIO	Special Information Operations
SIOC	Strategic Interagency Operations Center; Strategic Information and Operations Center
SIOP	Single Integrated Operational Plan
SIPRNET	Secret Internet Protocol Router Network
SITREP	Situation Report
SNIE	Special National Intelligence Estimate
SNTK	Special Need-to-Know
SOP	Standard Operating Procedures
SPINTCOMM	Special Intelligence Communication
SSO	Special Security Officer
START	Scientific and Technical Analysis and Response Team
STATE/INR	State Department Bureau of Intelligence and Research
STISAC	Surface Transportation Information Sharing and Analysis Center
STRACNET	Strategic Rail Corridor Network
SWAT	Special Weapons and Tactics
SWO	Senior Watch Officer
SWOT	Strengths, Weaknesses, Opportunities, and Threats
TACINTEL	Tactical Intelligence
TAISS	Telecommunications and Automate Information Systems Security
TARU	Technical Advisory Response Unit

TAT	Technical Assistance Team
TEA	Threat Environment Assessment
TECHINT	Technical Intelligence
TELINT	Telemetry Intelligence
TEMPEST	Transient Electromagnetic Pulse Surveillance Technology
THREATCON	Threat Condition
TI	Technical Intelligence
TIA	Terrorist Incident Annex
TIARA	Tactical Intelligence and Related Activities
TIIAP	Telecommunications and Information Infrastructure Assistance Program
TIP	Terrorist Interdiction Program
TIPS	Terrorism Information and Preventive Systems
TMSARM	Transportation Security Administration Maritime Self-Assessment Risk Model
TRANSEC	Transmission Security
TSA	Transportation Security Administration
TSC	Terrorist Screening Center
TSOB	Transportation Security Oversight Board
TSWG	Technical Support Working Group
TTIC	Terrorist Threat Integration Center
UC	Unified Command
UC/IC	Unified Command/Incident Command
UCNI	Unclassified Controlled Nuclear Information
UCR	Uniform Crime Reports
UCS	Unified Command System
USAF	United States Air Force
USAR	Urban Search and Rescue
USCG	United States Coast Guard
USDI	Under Secretary of Defense for Intelligence
USFA	United States Fire Administration (FEMA)
USFS	United States Forest Service
USRT	Urban Search and Rescue Team (FEMA)
USSS	United States Secret Service
W-Day	Warning Day
WATCHCON	Watch Condition
WCR	WATCHCON Change Report
WHSR	White House Situation Room
WLT	Warning Lead Time
WMD	Weapons of Mass Destruction

WMD-CST	Weapons of Mass Destruction Civil Support Teams
WME	Weapons of Mass Effect
WNINTEL	Warning Notice: Intelligence Sources or Methods Involved
WWMCCS	Worldwide Military Command and Control System

The Dictionary

– A –

A-TEAM/B-TEAM CONCEPT (ALSO KNOWN AS BLUE TEAM/ RED TEAM CONCEPT). An experimental method developed within the Intelligence Community in the mid-1970s to improve the quality of estimates, specifically the National Intelligence Estimate (NIE) on important warning problems through competitive and alternative analysis. The "A-team" usually included U.S. intelligence analysts, while the "B-team" consisted of members outside of the Intelligence Community. Both teams would look at the identical warning problem and take different sides of an issue.[1]

A-TYPE DECEPTION. Purposeful intent to increase ambiguity by surrounding a target with irrelevant information; confusion based on a lack of certainty. Its aim is to keep the adversary unsure of one's true intentions, especially an adversary who has initially guessed right. A number of alternatives are developed for the target's consumption, built on misinformation that is both plausible and sufficiently significant to cause the target to expend resources to cover it.[2] According to one observer, it may be that Saddam Hussein felt that the U.S. was conducting *A-type deception* on him as he prepared Iraq to invade Kuwait.

> The problem of deterring Saddam, even assuming that Western intelligence assessed an attack on Kuwait as a distinct probability, subsequently became mired in diplomatic ambiguity, with the U.S. trying to stand firm and yet at the same time weakening its tough stance by issuing curiously contradictory "clarifications." For example, when the U.S. moved KC-135 tanker aircraft and ships to the Gulf on 21 July "to lay down a marker for Saddam Hussein," in the words of the Pentagon, an aide to the Secretary of the Navy rushed to "clarify the situation" by telling the press that the ships were not on alert. On 24 July, when the Pentagon stated that the "U.S. was committed to . . . supporting the self-defense of our friends in the Gulf," officials specifically refused to confirm whether the U.S. would go to Kuwait's aid if Kuwait were attacked.[3]

See also M-TYPE DECEPTION; ACTIVE DECEPTION; DENIAL AND DECEPTION; PASSIVE DECEPTION.

AARDWOLF. A nickname for a report written by an in-country agent that provides a formal assessment of the conditions in their country.

ABSOLUTE SURPRISE. A conjectural notion that an event or act can occur without any indications. Mostly relegated to science-fiction novels and movies when men and machines suddenly appear "out of nowhere" which is impossible since all attacks have indications, although they were likely ignored or failed to be collected by the victim. For example, "The U.S. and Canadian response to the Bears [Russian aircraft] comes in the wake of Russian boasts earlier this month that its warplanes buzzed the aircraft carrier USS Kitty Hawk in the Sea of Japan on October 17 and November 9. The Russian SU-24 reconnaissance planes and SU-27 interceptors flew close enough to the USS Kitty Hawk in the Sea of Japan to take photographs of the carrier." Russian air force chief General Anatoly Kornukov told the Interfax news agency that the aircraft's approach came as an *absolute surprise* to the Kitty Hawk, "which didn't raise their fighters into the air until the second flight."[4]

ACCELERATOR. Any event, action, or decision by an influential person that becomes a catalyst to an impending threat scenario. For example, as cited in one intelligence report, "Any new discriminatory laws or restrictive actions imposed by the dictatorial government are *accelerators* that will ultimately bring down the government."[5]

ACCEPTABLE RISK. The level of loss a society or community considers acceptable given existing social, economic, political, cultural, technical, and environmental conditions as defined by the United Nations.[6]

ACCESS (SOMETIMES FOLLOWING THE WORD *AUTHORIZED*). Ability or opportunity to gain knowledge of classified information; commonly confused with the term, **need-to-know**. It should be understood that having the ability to receive classified information (i.e., *access*), does not entitle the holder to receive any or all classified information (i.e., need-to-know). According to the 1947 National Security Act,

> The term "authorized," when used with respect to *access* to classified information, means having authority, right, or permission pursuant to the provisions of a statute, Executive order, directive of the head of any department or agency engaged in foreign intelligence or counterintelligence activities, order of any United States court, or provisions of any Rule of the House of Representatives or resolution of the Senate which assigns responsibility within the respective House of Congress for the oversight of intelligence activities.[7]

See also ACCOUNTABILITY; CLASSIFIED INFORMATION; NEED-TO-KNOW.

ACCOUNTABILITY. Principle that an individual is entrusted to safeguard and control equipment, keying material, and information and is answerable to proper authority for the loss or misuse of that equipment or information.[8]

ACCOUNTABILITY INFORMATION. A set of records, often referred to as an audit trail, that collectively provides documentary evidence of the processing or other actions related to the information's security.

ACCURACY. The extent to which an evaluation of an intelligence source or an intelligence assessment is truthful or valid; an important attribute of the credibility of a source of evidence.

ACOUSTICAL INTELLIGENCE (ACINT OR ACOUSTINT). Intelligence derived from the collection and processing of acoustical phenomena (i.e., sources that generate waves). *See also* SOURCES OF INTELLIGENCE.

ACTIONABLE INTELLIGENCE. Information that will force the consumer of the intelligence product to initiate action in mitigating an impending threat. For example, in a newspaper article it was reported,

> President Bush said that an intelligence memo he read shortly before September 11, 2001, contained no *actionable intelligence* that would have helped him to try to prevent the 9/11 attacks. The [August 6, 2001, memo "Bin Laden Determined to Strike in US"] was no indication of a terrorist threat. According to the President, there was not a time and place of an attack. "It said Osama bin Laden had designs on America. Well, I knew that. What I wanted to know was, is there anything specifically going to take place in America that we needed to react to."[9]

In another example,

> [National Security Adviser Condoleezza] Rice was wrong when she said it wouldn't have done any good to have the FBI director, CIA director and other top law enforcement and anti-terrorism officials meet regularly in the summer of 2001 to sift through the warnings that preceded the 9/11 attacks. Rice, the president's national security adviser, said there weren't enough specifics or actionable intelligence to justify such meetings. Lower-level officials, led by [National Terrorism Chief Richard] Clarke, met regularly instead. According to Clark, "When you're told there's going to be a major terrorist attack, but 'oh, by the way, we don't know where or when,' that's all the more reason to put down whatever else

it is you're doing . . . roll up your sleeves and get involved in trying to find that actionable intelligence."[10]

See also MURKY INTELLIGENCE.

ACTIVE DECEPTION. Measures designed to mislead by causing an object or situation to seem threatening when a threat does not exist. *Active deception* normally involves a calculated policy of disclosing half-truths supported by appropriate "proof" signals or other material evidence. The intelligence network of the deceived must pick up this information. The deceived must "discover" the evidence himself; he must work hard for it to be more convinced of its authenticity and importance. (Frequently, information that is easily obtained appears to be less credible and of doubtful value.)[11] For example, during World War I Great Britain used *active deception* in the form of dummy airfields and flare paths. These phony installations had a dual purpose of attracting German strafing and bombing raids and consequently diverting the enemy airplanes away from the real Allied airfields. Additionally, these bogus installations exaggerated the number of operational airfields, which deceived the enemy about Allied military strength in the sector. *See also* A-TYPE DECEPTION; DENIAL AND DECEPTION; PASSIVE DECEPTION.

ADVERSARIAL APPROACH. The view that the other side or party in a conflict is an enemy that must be defeated and destroyed without compromise.

ADVISORY SENSITIVITY ATTRIBUTES. User-supplied indicators of file sensitivity that alert other users to the sensitivity of a file so that they may handle it appropriate to its defined sensitivity.[12]

AGENCY, INTELLIGENCE. A type of organization or individual engaged in collecting and/or processing information.[13]

AGENDA-SETTING THEORY. When news or other information made available to the public by the media ultimately defines what is considered significant. This theory (and the use of this term) was developed in a study by Maxwell E. McCombs and Donald L. Shaw published in 1972. The researchers interviewed 100 undecided voters in Chapel Hill, North Carolina, and asked them what issues they were most concerned about in the coming 1968 U.S. election. Both men found an almost perfect correlation between the types of media stories covered and how often, and the voters' concern for the same issues. Additional studies have confirmed that agenda-setting does in fact take place, and that media attention is the most important factor involved in shaping the public's view as to what is important in the world and at home. *See also* CNN EFFECT.

AGENT. A person who is authorized by an intelligence agency or security service to obtain, or assist in obtaining, information for intelligence or counterintelligence purposes.

AGENT OF INFLUENCE. An individual who can be used to influence covertly foreign officials, opinion molders, organizations, or pressure groups in a way which will generally advance a country's objective, or to undertake specific action in support of a country's objectives.[14]

ALERT CENTER. A site for the review of all incoming current intelligence information that possesses, or has **access** to, extensive communications for alerting local personnel. An additional responsibility may include the ability to task appropriate external collection assets within the system. *See also* INDICATIONS CENTER; WARNING CENTER; WATCH CENTER.

ALERT FATIGUE. A condition that exists when a constant state of alert is enacted, resulting in the deterioration of readiness for action. For example,

> When the Israelis launched their sudden attack into Lebanon in 1982, Palestinian surprise was due in part to *alert fatigue* or the *cry-wolf syndrome*. This phenomenon results from the desensitization of an entity's warning capability because the threatened attack or event did not occur. On possibly as many as four occasions prior to the June attack, Palestinian forces predicted and prepared for the expected Israeli attack. Each time the attack never came. It is not surprising, therefore, that the PLO saw the events in early June as a repeat of previous Israeli saber rattling. Arafat's presence outside of Lebanon on the day before the attack dramatized this point.[15]

See also CRY-WOLF SYNDROME.

ALERT MEMORANDUM. Correspondence issued by high-level intelligence officials to policymakers to warn them about developments abroad that may be of major concern to the country's national security; a memorandum coordinated within the Intelligence Community if time permits.

ALL-SOURCE INTELLIGENCE. Products and/or organizations and activities that incorporate all sources of information, most frequently including human resources intelligence, imagery intelligence, measurement and signature intelligence, signals intelligence, and open-source data in the production of finished intelligence. In intelligence collection, a phrase that indicates that in the satisfaction of intelligence requirements, all collection, processing, exploitation, and reporting systems and resources are identified for possible use and those most capable are tasked. *See also* SOURCES OF INTELLIGENCE.

ANALYSIS. A systematic approach to problem solving; the process of separating intelligence data into distinct, related parts or elements and examining those elements to determine essential parameters or related properties. Often the word *analysis* is incorrectly interchanged with **assessment**. To understand the difference, it is usually said, "*analysis* is what you know and an *assessment* is what you believe." *See also* ASSESSMENT.

ANALYSIS AND PRODUCTION. The conversion of processed information into intelligence through the integration, evaluation, analysis, and interpretation of all-source data and the preparation of intelligence products in support of known or anticipated user requirements.[16]

ANALYSIS OF COMPETING HYPOTHESES. Identification of alternative explanations (considered hypotheses) and the evaluation of all evidence that will disconfirm rather than confirm the hypotheses. This method involves 8 steps, according to Richard J. Heuer, of the Center for Strategic Initiatives:[17]

1. Identify the possible hypotheses to be considered. Use a group of analysts with different perspectives to brainstorm the possibilities.
2. Make a list of significant evidence and arguments for and against each hypothesis.
3. Prepare a matrix with hypotheses across the top and evidence down the side. Analyze the "diagnosticity" of the evidence and arguments—that is, identify which items are most helpful in judging the relative likelihood of the hypotheses.
4. Refine the matrix. Reconsider the hypotheses and delete evidence and arguments that have no diagnostic value.
5. Draw tentative conclusions about the relative likelihood of each hypothesis. Proceed by trying to disprove the hypotheses rather than prove them.
6. Analyze how sensitive your conclusion is to a few critical items of evidence. Consider the consequences for your analysis if that evidence were wrong, misleading, or subject to a different interpretation.
7. Report conclusions. Discuss the relative likelihood of all the hypotheses, not just the most likely one.
8. Identify milestones for future observation that may indicate events are taking a different course than expected.

ANOMALY. An indication that an organization or person is conducting activity or has obtained knowledge that is inconsistent with known or expected knowledge already held by the analyst. Specifically, according to the Department of Justice, information that relates to U.S. national security information, processes, capabilities, or activities.[18]

AREAS OF CONCERN. Specific issues or incidents within a warning problem that require identifiable attention by the analyst, commander, or policymaker.

ARGUMENT. A type of discourse or text (a product)—the distillate of the practice of argumentation (the process)—in which the arguer seeks to persuade the other(s) of the truth of a proposition (hypothesis) by advancing the reasons, grounds, and evidence that support it.

ASSESSMENT. The process of combining all intelligence data into a unified, specific judgment; the result of analysis formed within the context of the intelligence environment. In some intelligence products, to include estimates, are found under the "Key Judgement(s)" section of the document. *See also* ANALYSIS.

ASSET. Any resource—a person, group, relationship, instrument, installation, or supply—at the disposition of an intelligence agency for use in an operational or support role. The term is normally applied to a person who is contributing to a clandestine mission, but is not a fully controlled agent by the government agency.[19]

ATTRIBUTES OF INTELLIGENCE QUALITY. Seven qualitative objectives used to support joint operations and standards against which intelligence activities and products are evaluated. A failure to achieve any one of these may contribute to a failure of operations. These seven objectives include timeliness (available and accessible in time to effectively be of use), objectivity (unbiased and free from any influence or constraint), usability (suitable for application upon receipt with additional analysis), readiness (must anticipate and be ready to respond to the existing and contingent intelligence requirements), completeness (meets responsibilities to accomplish a mission), accuracy (factually correct), and relevance (contributes to an understanding of the situation).[20]

AUTHENTICATION. Security measure designed to establish the validity of a transmission, message, or originator, or a means of verifying an individual's authorization to receive specific categories of information.[21]

AUTHENTICITY. An attribute of the credibility of tangible evidence, such as a document, message, or object, that indicates whether the tangible item is actually what it is represented to be.

AUTHORIZED FOR RELEASE TO [NAME OF COUNTRY OR INTERNATIONAL ORGANIZATION]. This marking is used to identify intelligence information that an originator has predetermined to be releasable or has released, through established foreign disclosure procedures and channels, to the foreign/international organization indicated. This marking may be abbreviated "REL [abbreviated name of foreign organization]."[22]

AWARENESS OF NATIONAL SECURITY ISSUES AND RESPONSE (ANSIR) PROGRAM. An FBI program that "disseminates unclassified national security threat [potential targets of intelligence and terrorist activities] and warning information to U.S. Corporations, law enforcement and other government agencies" through free e-mail notices. Information on this program can be found at http://www.fbi.gov/hq/ci/ansir/ansirhome.htm.

– B –

BACK-TELL. A DoD and NATO term for the transfer of information from a higher to a lower echelon of command.[23]

BASIC INTELLIGENCE. 1. The compilation of all available data and information on several subjects of broad interest to policymakers and other members of the Intelligence Community; fundamental, comprehensive, encyclopedic, and general reference-type material relating to political, economic, geographic, and military structure, resources, capabilities, and vulnerabilities of foreign nations. 2. Factual, fundamental, and relatively permanent information about all aspects of a nation—physical, social, economic, political, biographical, and cultural—which is used as a base for intelligence products in the support of planning, policymaking, and military operations.[24]

BASIC MEASURES OF MILITARY PREPAREDNESS. Minimal precautionary efforts, likely considered routine actions, against a potential future attack. *See also* EMERGENCY MEASURES OF MILITARY PREPAREDNESS.

BAYESIAN (DECISION) ANALYSIS. A technique developed by the Reverend Thomas Bayes in 1763, in which he advanced the proposition that subjective probabilities should be combined with frequency probabilities via what has come to be called Bayes' theorem, a very simple formula using conditional probabilities. According to the formula, the prior probability P (H) of proposition H is revised to posterior probability P (H/D) when the datum D is observed—and P (D/H) *and* P (D) are known as follows:

$$P\ (H/D)\ =\ \frac{P\ (H)\ \times\ P\ (D/H)}{P\ (D)}$$

In this formula, P (D/H) is the *likelihood* of the same information D given that proposition H is true. Even in this simple form, Bayes' theorem has apparent applications in international relations forecasting.[25]

BEAN-COUNTING ASSESSMENT. Mostly used as a pejorative term for estimates and forecasting based on quantitative or empirical analysis.[26] For example, General Wesley K. Clark, Supreme Allied Commander, Europe in a briefing to the press on NATO's ability to stop Serb aggression said:

> From the very beginning, we said we didn't believe in battle *bean-counting* as a way of measuring the effects of air power, although many continuously sought to go back to the old body count, bean-counting approach. Meanwhile, some accused of us of flying too high, of not wanting to risk our pilots while others chose to believe that we would strike only decoys or perhaps would hit nothing at all. The short answer of what we struck is clear. How much did we strike, and how much did we destroy? We destroyed and struck enough.[27]

See also ASSESSMENT.

BLACK. In the information-processing context, this denotes data, text, equipment, processes, systems, or installations associated with unencrypted information that requires no emanations security related protection. For example, electronic signals are "black" if bearing unclassified information.[28] *See also* RED.

BOOTLEGGING. Informal agreements by intelligence officers to share data outside established, formal channels; seen as a practice between analysts to share data by bypassing more formal channels of communication. *See also* STOVEPIPE WARNING.

BORN CLASSIFIED. The Atomic Energy Act has been with us since 1946. No law passed before or since gives the government such sweeping authority to keep information secret. Under the information control provisions of the Act, practically all information related to nuclear weapons and nuclear energy is "born classified": it is a government secret as soon as it comes into existence. No governmental act is necessary to classify information. Moreover, the information, defined as Restricted Data, remains secret until the government affirmatively determines that it may be published. A question latent in the language of the Act is whether privately developed or privately generated atomic energy information—information developed or generated without government funds and without **access** to classified government documents—is Restricted Data, and thus subject to the Act.[29]

BREVITY CODE. Provides no security but which has as its sole purpose the shortening of messages rather than the concealment of their content. Approved brevity codes may be used when preparing military records, publications, correspondence, messages, operation plans, orders, and reports.[30]

BRIEFING. Presentation, usually oral, of information. The preparation of an individual for a specific operation by describing the situation to be encountered, the methods to be employed, and the objective.[31]

BRITISH TEN-YEAR RULE. According to Richard Betts, a scholar on strategy,

> Those who see the whole interwar period [after World War I] as testimony to Britain's failure to get ready for World War II consider the *ten-year rule* the perfect symbol of the complacency that led to appeasement. . . . According to legend, the assumption that no war would occur for at least a decade guided British defense estimates and planning (the rule was renewed annually from 1919 to the early 1930s). In hindsight, the ten-year rule seems arbitrary, and, since it allegedly retarded defense expenditures, foolish.[32]

BYE. An unclassified term, no longer used, to describe sensitive programs and operational data.[33]

– C –

C-RATING SYSTEM. *See* CONDITION RATING SYSTEM.

CAMOUFLAGE. The act to employ or re-deploy material that seeks to confuse or mislead. "During the Indian nuclear tests in 1999 that took much of the world by surprise, the Indians knew exactly when the spy cameras would be passing over the testing facility near Pokharan in Rajasthan Desert and, in synchrony with the satellite orbits, scientists *camouflaged* their preparations."[34] *See also* DECEPTION.

CAPABILITY. The collective military, economic, political, scientific, and technical means, methods, and capacity of a nation. *See also* THREAT; INTENTION.

CASE OFFICER. A staff employee of a government intelligence agency who is responsible for handling agents.

CASSANDRA. One who prophesies disaster and whose warnings are unheeded. In Greek mythology. *Cassandra* had been granted the ability to see into the future but she was never believed. Among other things, *Cassandra* warned about the Trojan horse that the Greeks left, but her warning was ignored; term is usually capitalized. *See also* POLLYANNA.

CAUSAL ANALYSIS. *A method for analyzing* the possible causal associations among a set of variables. *See also* CAUSAL ASSOCIATION; CAUSAL RELATIONSHIP; CONGRUENCE ANALYSIS.

CAUSAL ASSOCIATION. *A relationship* between two variables in which a change in one brings about a change in the other. *See also* CAUSAL ANALYSIS; CAUSAL RELATIONSHIP; CONGRUENCE ANALYSIS.

CAUSAL RELATIONSHIP. The relationship of cause and effect; the cause is the necessary act or event that produces the effect. *See also* CAUSAL ANALYSIS; CAUSAL ASSOCIATION; CONGRUENCE ANALYSIS.

CAVEATED INFORMATION. A designator used with a classification to further limit the dissemination of restricted information. In addition to its classification, intelligence information and certain scientific or technical information may be subject to other controls on its distribution and handling. For example, Secret/ORCON would mean that the product is classified "Secret" with the caveat "Dissemination and Extraction of Information Controlled by Originator" (ORCON), which means that any additional distribution or inclusion in another document must be approved by the originator of the document. This particular caveat is usually used on intelligence information that could permit identification of a sensitive intelligence source or method. Other caveats are NOCONTRACT (not releasable to contractors or consultants), PROPIN (proprietary information is involved), NOFORN (not to be passed to foreign nationals), SCI (sensitive compartmented information), COMSEC (communications security), CRYPTO (cryptographic material), and WNINTEL (warning notice: intelligence sources or methods).

CHAOS THEORY. A means of explaining the dynamics of sensitive systems that seeks to find the underlying order in apparently random data or apparently random systems; used especially to understand the functioning of dysfunctional organizations.

CHECKLIST APPROACH. An instrument for practical evaluation by associating observation with a predetermined record or list; used by some intelligence analysts and collectors to identify gaps in knowledge by comparing what they see with what they want to know.

CIPHER. A cryptographic system in which arbitrary symbols or groups of symbols represent units of plain text.

CIRCULAR INTELLIGENCE. Information that is reported as an unconfirmed fact or assessment that is subsequently repeated in another agency's or analyst's assessment as a true report. The first agency or analyst sees it in someone else's report and seizes on it as independent proof that his or her own information has been confirmed by another source. For example, prior to the Yom Kippur War in 1973 between Israel and Egypt, *circular intelligence* was a contributing factor in lulling Israeli intelligence into a false sense of security:

> When the Israelis saw that the U.S. was not worried by the buildup, they confirmed their earlier judgments. If Washington was unruffled, concluded Mrs. Meir [the Prime Minister of Israel] and her inner policy group on 5 October, then why should they be? It was a classic and vicious example of "circular intelligence." (Washington was not worried about Egypt's military buildup because they received intelligence from the Israelis that there was nothing to worry about.) Everyone left the 5 October meetings uneasy and with a feeling that something was wrong. Egypt attacked the next day.[35]

See also HUGGER-MUGGER.

CLANDESTINE OPERATION. A secret intelligence collection activity or political, economic, propaganda, or paramilitary action conducted to ensure the secrecy of the operation. "In general, the secret missions carried out by the military have been defined as clandestine operations, which are not intended to be officially deniable and are subject to less rigorous rules for [Congressional] approval and oversight. . . . Senator Rockefeller expressed concern that the Pentagon's approach was too dismissive of the need for formal Congressional notification. 'I don't take lightly the distinction between clandestine and covert,' Senator Rockefeller said. 'It makes all the difference in the world.''[36] *See also* COVERT OPERATION.

CLASSIFICATION (OF INFORMATION OR INTELLIGENCE). 1. The act or process by which information is determined to be classified information; the process of determining and identifying the information we need to protect in the interests of national security—the information we need to conceal from the enemies and potential enemies of the United States.[37] 2. A category to which national security information and material is assigned to denote the degree of damage that unauthorized disclosure would cause to national defense or foreign relations of the United States and to denote the degree of protection required. There are three such categories.[38] *See also* CLASSIFICATION LEVELS.

CLASSIFICATION BY ASSOCIATION (ALSO KNOWN AS CLASSIFICATION BY COMPILATION). A situation where the mere fact that two or more items of information are related is in itself classified; can be associated with masking, which is the act of classifying one piece of information solely to protect a separate item of information.[39]

CLASSIFICATION CHALLENGE. Authorized holders of classified information who, in good faith, believe that specific information is improperly classified or unclassified "are encouraged and expected to challenge the classification status of the information. The challenge need not be more than a question as to why the information is or is not classified, or is classified at a certain level. No retribution or other negative action shall be taken for presenting a challenge."[40]

CLASSIFICATION LEVEL(S). 1. A classification level is assigned to information owned by, produced by or for, or controlled by the United States government. 2. A designation assigned to specific elements of information based on the potential damage to national security if disclosed to unauthorized persons. The three levels in descending order of potential damage are Top Secret, Secret, and Confidential:

Top Secret. The highest classification level applied to information, the unauthorized disclosure of which reasonably could be expected to cause exceptionally grave damage to the national security. Top-Secret Access Authorizations or Clearances are based on background investigations conducted by OPM or another government agency that conducts personnel security investigations. Top-Secret clearances permit an individual to have **access** on a **need-to-know** basis to Top Secret, Secret, and Confidential levels of National Security Information and Formerly Restricted Data as required in the performance of duties.

Secret. Information, the unauthorized disclosure of which reasonably could be expected to cause serious damage to the national security that the original classification authority is able to identify or describe; the classification level between Confidential and Top Secret applied to information whose unauthorized disclosure could reasonably be expected to cause serious damage to the national security.

Confidential. Information, the unauthorized disclosure of which reasonably could be expected to cause **damage to the national security** that the original classification authority is able to identify or describe; the lowest level of classification which consists of material which could be expected to cause some form of damage to national security.[41]

See also CAVEATED INFORMATION.

CLASSIFICATION MARKINGS (CONTROL MARKINGS, DISSEMINATION CONTROL MARKINGS).[42] The physical act of indicating on classified material the assigned classification or change therein, together with such additional information as may be required to show authority for the classification or change and any special limitation on such material. Identifies the expansion or limitation on the distribution of information to include restriction to use by certain agencies. Examples of control markings are:

- Authorized for Release To (REL)
- Confidential (Caution)—Proprietary Information Involved (PROPIN)
- Critical Nuclear Weapons Design Information (CNWDI)
- For Official Use Only (FOUO)
- Formerly Restricted Data (FRD)
- IMCON (Controlled Imagery)
- Not Releasable to Foreign Nationals (NOFORN)
- Originator Controlled (ORCON)
- Restricted Data (RD)
- Risk Sensitive (RSEN)
- SAMI (Sources and Methods Information)
- Unclassified Controlled Nuclear Information (UCNI)

CLASSIFIER. An individual who makes a classification determination and applies a security classification to information or material. A classifier may either be a classification authority or assign a security classification based on a properly classified source or a classification guide.[43]

CLIENTITIS. Overly sympathetic analysis of events in the target state; an unrealistic attempt to understand the motivations and values of the target country's leaders or major groupings from the perspective of the target. For example, Warren Christopher said at his Senate Confirmation Hearing to be Secretary of State, "More than ever before, the State Department cannot afford to have *clientitis*, a malady characterized by undue deference to the potential reactions of other countries. I have long thought the [U.S.] State Department needs an 'America Desk.' This Administration will have one—and I'll be sitting behind it."[44]

CLOSED INFORMATION. Information that either will never be made public or will become known decades after a particular action or event. Closed information is associated with "the right of an individual to see or use a particular type or level of classified information which is dependent on a need to see or know"; information that is compartmented, and there-fore not available to the public, and cannot be accessed except by those who hold special **access** clearances. Closed information is associated with a specific level of privilege.[45]

CNN EFFECT. The immediate rise of a real or perceived crisis that sustains public awareness and urges policymakers to take action. The acronym CNN stands for Cable News Network, which has come to symbolize all forms of mass media that focus on and magnify a single action, event, or decision by publicizing it worldwide. "Resisting the *CNN effect* may be one of the most important requirements of U.S. policymaking in the com-ing period."[46] The *CNN effect* of televised images of suffering has gener-ated public demands for action; it has been a key definer especially of humanitarian problems. (Television depicts only poorly the political com-plexities that produce such suffering, leading to inappropriately narrow or erroneous problem identification.)[47]

COALITION PRESS INFORMATION CENTER. *See* JOINT INFOR-MATION BUREAU.

CODEWORD. 1. Designed to provide special protection, beyond that pro-vided by the federal classification system, to a specific category of sensitive information. 2. A word that has been assigned a classification and a classified meaning to safeguard intentions and information regarding a classified plan or operation; a cryptonym used to identify sensitive intelligence data.[48]

CODEWORD COMPARTMENT. Security device designed to provide special protection, beyond that provided by the federal classification system, to a specific category of sensitive information.[49]

COGNITIVE DISSONANCE. The rejection of factual information or reality because it does not conform to previously held beliefs—mostly used by psychologists.

> A classic example is the case of "Yellow Rain" and discovery of lethal toxins in Southeast Asia and Afghanistan in the early 1980s. In spite of the overwhelming weight of confirmatory evidence accumulated over eight years, the findings continue to be challenged and contested, sometimes with offerings of bizarre scientific counter explanations that utterly defy common sense. The extreme reluctance to accept the evidence at face value cannot be attributed simply to the fact that intelligence could never meet the rigorous laboratory standards for evidence. Rather, it must surely lie in the unpleasantness of the implications insofar as they raise doubts about the viability of arms control agreements.[50]

COLLABORATIVE INTELLIGENCE. A working relationship between the consumer and the analyst in developing the requirements for collection and the development of the response to what has been collected.

COLLATERAL INTELLIGENCE. Information classified that does not contain sensitive compartmented information.

COLLECTING. An activity of information management: the continuous acquisition of relevant information by any means, including direct observation, other organic resources, or other official, unofficial, or public sources from the information environment.[51]

COLLECTION. The exploitation of sources by collection agencies, and the delivery of the information obtained to the appropriate processing unit for use in the production of intelligence. Also, obtaining information or intelligence information in any manner, including direct observations, liaison with official agencies, or solicitation from official, unofficial, or public sources, or quantitative data from the test or operation of foreign systems.[52]

COLLECTION PLAN. A plan for collecting information from all available sources to meet intelligence requirements and for transforming those requirements into orders and requests to appropriate agencies. [Note: The U.S. Army term is "intelligence, surveillance, and reconnaissance (ISR) plan."][53]

COMBAT INFORMATION. Unevaluated data gathered by or provided directly to a tactical unit, which, due to its highly perishable nature or the criticality of the situation, cannot be processed into tactical intelligence in time to satisfy the customer's tactical intelligence requirements.[54]

COMBAT INTELLIGENCE. Usually refers to the weather, enemy, and geographical features required by a military unit in the planning and conduct of combat operations. *See also* TACTICAL INTELLIGENCE.

COMBAT READINESS. Synonymous with **operational readiness,** usually relates to the missions or functions that will be required to perform in combat. *See also* OPERATIONAL READINESS.

COMBINED INTELLIGENCE WATCH CENTER (CIWC), ALSO KNOWN AS THE COMBINED INTELLIGENCE CENTER (CIC). The indications and warning center for worldwide threats from space, missile, and strategic air activity, as well as geopolitical unrest that could affect North America and U.S. forces/interests abroad. The center's personnel gather intelligence information to assist all the Cheyenne Mountain work centers in correlating and analyzing events to support North American Air Defense and U.S. Space Command decision makers.

COMMAND, CONTROL, COMMUNICATIONS, AND INTELLIGENCE (C3I). An integrated system of doctrine, procedures, organizational structure, personnel, equipment, facilities, communications, and supporting intelligence that provides authorities at all levels with timely and adequate data to plan, direct, and control their activities.

COMMUNICATIONS COVER. Concealing or altering of characteristic communications patterns to hide information that could be of value to an adversary.[55]

COMMUNICATIONS INTELLIGENCE (COMINT). Technical information and intelligence derived from foreign communications by other than the intended recipients; it does not include the monitoring of foreign public media or the intercept of communications obtained during the course of counterintelligence investigations within the United States. COMINT is produced by the collection and processing of foreign communications passed by electromagnetic means, with specific exceptions stated below, and by the processing of foreign encrypted communications, however transmitted. Collection comprises search, intercept, and direction finding. Processing comprises range estimation, transmitter/operator analysis, traffic analysis, cryptanalysts, decryption, study of plain text, the fusion of these processes, and the reporting of results. COMINT includes the fields of traffic analysis, cryptanalysis, and direction finding, and is a part of Signals Intelligence (SIGINT). *See also* SOURCES OF INTELLIGENCE.[56]

COMMUNITY OPEN-SOURCE PROGRAM OFFICE (COSPO). The COSPO develops, coordinates, and oversees the implementation of the Community Open-Source Program.

COMPARTMENTALIZATION. The practice of establishing special channels for handling sensitive intelligence information. The channels are limited to individuals with a specific need for such information and who are therefore given special security clearances in order to have access to it;[57] a nonhierarchical grouping of sensitive information used to control **access** to data more finely than with hierarchical security classification alone.[58] *See also* ACCESS; NEED-TO-KNOW.

COMPARTMENTATION OF INTELLIGENCE. Establishment and management of an organization so that information about the personnel, internal organization, or activities of one component is made available to any other component only to the extent required for the performance of assigned duties.

COMPETING HYPOTHESES. *See* ANALYSIS OF COMPETING HYPOTHESES.

COMPLEX EMERGENCY. A natural or manmade disaster with economic, social, and political dimensions. A humanitarian crisis in a country, region, or society where there is a total or considerable breakdown of authority resulting from internal or external conflict, and which requires an international response that goes beyond the mandate or capacity of any single agency and/or the ongoing United Nations country program.[59]

COMPROMISE. The disclosure of classified information to persons not authorized **access** thereto; the loss of control over, or known or suspected exposure of, classified information or material in whole or in part to unauthorized persons through loss, theft, capture, recovery by salvage, defection of individuals, unauthorized viewing, or any other means.

> Sen. Christopher "Kit" Bond argued Friday after returning from Iraq that recent disclosures about American intelligence gathering had blown the cover of key sources and made them targets for assassination. . . . He said defense and intelligence officials also had told him that potential sources of information were refusing to cooperate because they fear for their lives. "Sources that they've approached to work with them have said, 'I'm not going to work with you because you all can't keep a secret, and if it's known I'm working with you, it's a death warrant,'" Bond said. . . . He added, "There have been some serious impacts that make us much less safe because our intelligence has been **compromised** drastically."[60]

COMPUTER SECURITY ACT SENSITIVE INFORMATION. Any information of which the loss, misuse, unauthorized access to, or modification could adversely affect the national interest or the conduct of federal programs, or the privacy to which individuals are entitled under the Privacy Act, but which has not been specifically authorized under criteria established by an Executive Order or an Act of Congress to be kept secret in the interest of national defense or foreign policy.[61]

CONCEALMENT. The act of hiding or the purposeful intent of keeping from observation, discovery, or understanding.

CONCENTRATED WARNING. The responsibility of warning held by a singular body of analysts, focusing on **threat management,** whose sole duty and purpose is to communicate and forecast a possible threat. *See also* DISTRIBUTIVE WARNING.

CONCLUSION. A well-supported explanation of the final inference in the intelligence analysis thought process. *See also* ASSESSMENT; DEDUCTIVE LOGIC; HYPOTHESIS; INDUCTIVE LOGIC; INFERENCE.

CONDITION RATING SYSTEM (AKA, C-RATING). A measurement of a military unit's readiness in which standards have been established. For example, the U.S. Army's condition rating system for a unit includes the following five categories which are based on several variables such as personnel, equipment, and training. The five categories are C-1 (fully combat ready); C-2 (substantially ready with minor deficiencies); C-3 (marginally ready with major deficiencies); C-4 (not ready for combat, and would be unable to perform its warfare duties); and C-5 (not ready and scheduled for removal from service).[62]

CONDITIONING AND COVER. Routine or repetitive acts used to cloak intentions; for example, holding routine military maneuvers as cover for aggressive action.

CONFIDENCE LEVEL SCALE. A verbal and/or numerical value, used in a uniform and consistent manner, that indicates an assessment will be correct; usually based on the analyst's experience, judgment, and intuition. Typically, such a scale will include "confirmed" which would be a 95 percent or greater chance that the information and/or assessment is correct; "probable" which would be a 75 percent or greater chance that the information and/or assessment is correct; "likely" which would be a 50 percent or greater chance that the information and/or assessment is would be less than a 5 percent chance that the information and/or assessment is correct; "possible" which would be at least a 5 percent or greater chance that the information and/or assessment is correct; and "doubtful" which would be less than a 5 percent chance that the information and/or assessment is correct.

CONFIDENTIAL COMMERCIAL INFORMATION. Records provided by a submitter that may contain material exempt from release under the FOIA because disclosure could reasonably be expected to cause the submitter substantial competitive harm.

CONFIDENTIAL SOURCE. Any individual or organization that has provided, or that may reasonably be expected to provide, information to the United States on matters pertaining to the national security with the expectation that the information or relationship, or both, are to be held in confidence.[63]

CONFIDENTIALITY. Assurance that information is not disclosed to unauthorized individuals, processes, or devices.[64]

CONFIRMATION OF INFORMATION (INTELLIGENCE). An information item is said to be confirmed when it is reported for the second time, preferably by another independent source whose reliability is considered when confirming information.[65]

CONFLICT PREVENTION. Those measures that can be implemented before a difference or dispute escalates into violence, designed to counter the spread of conflict into other geographical areas, and finally those measures that prevent violence from flaring up again after the signing of a peace agreement or a cease-fire.[66]

CONGRUENCE ANALYSIS. The verification of data by using more than one instrument or source of data for assessing a threat on the same criterion. *See also* CAUSAL ANALYSIS; CAUSAL ASSOCIATION; CAUSAL RELATIONSHIP.

CONSEQUENCE ANALYSIS. Forecasting the *implications* of an event or *result* of an action rather than predicting *when* the event or action will occur. *See also* CONSEQUENCE MANAGEMENT.

CONSEQUENCE MANAGEMENT. Comprises those essential services and activities required to manage and mitigate problems resulting from disasters and catastrophes. Such services and activities may include transportation, communications, public works and engineering, fire fighting, information sharing, mass care, resources support, health and medical services, urban search and rescue, hazardous materials, food and energy;[67] sometimes confused with "crisis management." "Historical analysis of patterns of behavior of CBW terrorists, such as the choice of agent and delivery system, can also help improve the effectiveness of medical countermeasures and other *consequence management* [italics added] activities. Although some planning for worst-case scenarios is justified, the types of chemical and biological terrorism against which federal, state, and local planning should be primarily directed are small- to medium-scale attacks. Such a threat assessment is not the stuff of newspaper headlines, but the historical record surely justifies it."[68] *See also* CRISIS MANAGEMENT.

CONTINGENCY PLANNING PROCESS (ALSO REFERRED TO AS CRISIS ACTION PLANNING PROCESS). The development of a course of action to mitigate chance, uncertain, unforeseen, or accidental events. Typically, contingency planning involves six phases.[69] Refer to table 1.

CONTRACTOR ACCESS RESTRICTED INFORMATION (CARI). Unclassified information that involves functions reserved to the federal government as vested by the Constitution as inherent power or as implied power as necessary for the proper performance of its duties. In many instances, CARI prevents contractors from making decisions that would affect current or future contracts and procurement procedures, primarily during pre-award activities.[70]

Table 1.   Contingency planning process.

Phase 1: Situation Development	Phase 2: Crisis Assessment	Phase 3: Course of Action Development	Phase 4: Course of Action Selection	Phase 5: Execution Planning	Phase 6: Execution
Perception of event	Increased reporting	Issue warning order	Refine/ present course of action	Plan and/or alert order	Execute order
Problem recognition	Evaluation	Develop task force	Decide course of action	Develop operations	Give operations order
Assessment		Develop course of action		Force participation	
		Evaluate course of action			

CONTROL. 1. Authority of the agency that originates information, or its successor in function, to regulate access to the information. 2. The Department's legal authority over a record, taking into account the ability of the Department to use and dispose of the record as it sees fit, to legally determine the disposition of a record, the intent of the record's creator to retain or relinquish control over the record, the extent to which Department personnel have read or relied upon the record, and the degree to which the record has been integrated into the Department's record-keeping system or files.[71]

CONTROLLED ACCESS AREA. Specifically designated areas within a building where classified information may be handled, stored, discussed, or processed.[72]

CONTROLLED DOSSIER. Files of a particularly sensitive nature due to substantive content or method of collection, which are physically segregated from the body of ordinary materials.[73]

CONTROLLED INFORMATION. 1. Information conveyed to an adversary in a deception operation to evoke desired appreciations. 2. Information and indicators deliberately conveyed or denied to foreign targets to evoke invalid official estimates that result in foreign official actions advantageous to U.S. interests and objectives.[74]

CONTROLLED UNCLASSIFIED INFORMATION. Unclassified information to which access or distribution limitations have been applied according to national laws, policies, and regulations of the U.S. government. These types of information include, but are not limited to: patent secrecy data, confidential medical records, inter- and intra-agency memoranda which are deliberative in nature, data compiled for law enforcement purposes, data obtained from a company on a confidential basis, employee personal data, Privacy Act information, internal rules and practices of a government agency, which if released, would circumvent an agency policy and impede the agency in the conduct of its mission. *See also* INFORMATION.[75]

CONVERGENT EVIDENCE. The association of two or more items of evidence that favor the same conclusion. *See also* DIVERGENT EVIDENCE; REDUNDANT EVIDENCE.

CORRELATES OF WAR THEORY. According to this approach, national capabilities typically consist of demographic, industrial, and military characteristics, which are then measured by comparative percentages with other characteristics such as a nation's population, the number of cities with populations of 20,000 or more, energy consumption, iron and steel production, and military expenditures.[76]

CORRELATION ANALYSIS. Deciphering whether a relationship exists between two seemingly independent parameters or events. Time-based correlations are of fundamental importance when building a threat scenario.

COUNTERINFORMATION. Actions dedicated to controlling the information realm.[77]

COUNTERINTELLIGENCE (CI). 1. Intelligence activities conducted to protect, by identifying and counteracting the threat posed by hostile foreign governments, organizations or individuals engaged in espionage, sabotage, subversion, or terrorism. 2. Systematic acquisition of information concerning espionage, sabotage, terrorism, other intelligence activities, or assassinations conducted by or on behalf of terrorists, foreign powers, and other entities; divided between passive counterintelligence (personnel and property security activities) and active counterintelligence (counter subversion of counterespionage) defensive efforts against foreign intelligence activities or to neutralize hostile intelligence collection, and to deceive the enemy as to friendly capabilities and intentions.[78] *See also* SOURCES OF INTELLIGENCE.

COUNTERINTELLIGENCE FIELD ACTIVITY (CIFA). A transformation initiative created to lead the development of a "to-the-edge" counterintelligence system for the Department of Defense. Its mission is to produce a common Defense Department counterintelligence operational picture, and deliver unique and actionable information to key decision makers in federal, state, and local governments.[79]

COUNTER-TERRORISM CENTER (CTC). A Central Intelligence Agency 24-hour operation that has existed since 1986; various types of research and strategic documents are disseminated, and warning intelligence is primarily disseminated to other agencies working with the CTC; personnel size is classified. *See also* INFORMATION ANALYSIS AND INFRASTRUCTURE PROTECTION; JOINT TERRORISM TASK FORCE; TERRORIST THREAT INTEGRATION CENTER.

COURT RECORDS, TYPES. Refer to the following definitions:

Brief. A document used to submit a legal contention or argument to a court.

Discovery Documents. Used in pretrial information gathering; most federal and state courts are not requiring litigants to file copies of pretrial depositions, interrogatories, and other documents.

Juror Records. In some states, personal juror records are sealed by the court at the conclusion of a criminal trial.

Juvenile Records. In most states, juvenile court proceedings (individuals less than 21 years old) are closed to the press and public.

Memdispos (Memorandum Dispositions or Unpublished Opinions). Pursuant to Ninth Circuit Rule 36-3, not published in the Federal Reporter, nor do they have precedential value. Memdispos cannot be cited and are very controversial within the legal field. See Merritt and Brudney, "Stalking the Secret Law: What Predicts Publications in the United States Courts of Appeals," *Vanderbilt Law Review* 54 (2001): 71.

Official Reports. Court reports directed by statute.

Sealed. Records determined by either the court or parties to be too sensitive to be made public.

Unofficial Reports. Published without statutory direction.[80]

COVERT OPERATION. Military or political activities undertaken in a manner that disguises the identity of those taking the action; usually employed in situations where openly operating against a target would jeopardize the operation's success. An operation that is so planned and executed as to conceal the identity of or permit plausible denial by those conducting the operation. A *covert operation* differs from a *clandestine operation* in that emphasis is placed on concealment of identity of those conducting the operation (i.e., covert) rather than on concealment of the operation (i.e., clandestine). *See also* CLANDESTINE OPERATION.

CREDIBILITY. The extent to which something is believable; commonly used with reference to sources of evidence, to evidence itself, and to hypotheses based on evidence. Sometimes confused with "reliability" but there are differences: reliability is just one attribute of the credibility of certain forms of evidence, while credibility (of sources of evidence) is both context and time dependent. For example, a person or sensor may be more credible regarding certain events and at certain times but not so credible regarding other events or at other times. *See also* ACCURACY; AUTHENTICITY; EVIDENCE.

CREEPING NORMALCY. 1. The methodical increment of a country's military capability so that its more capable posture is unnoticeable and accepted over time by outside observers. For example, the North Korean Army has been accused of using a strategy of creeping normalcy to build up its forces near the Demilitarized zone next to South Korea.[81] 2. The way a major change can be accepted as normality if it happens slowly, in unnoticed increments, when it would be regarded as objectionable if it took place all at once or within a short time period. The "boiling frog" analogy is used to explain this concept: a frog can be boiled alive if the water is heated slowly enough but if a frog is placed in boiling water, it will jump out. The lesson to be learned is that people should make themselves aware of gradual change lest they suffer a catastrophic loss. [The biological basis for this story is uncertain.]

CRIMINAL INTELLIGENCE. Data which has been evaluated to determine that it is relevant to the identification of and the criminal activity engaged in by an individual who or organization which is reasonably suspected of involvement in criminal activity. [Certain criminal activities including but not limited to loan sharking, drug trafficking, trafficking in stolen property, gambling, extortion, smuggling, bribery, and corruption of public officials often involve some degree of regular coordination and permanent organization involving a large number of participants over a broad geographical area.][82]

CRIMINAL INTELLIGENCE SYSTEM. Arrangements, equipment, facilities, and procedures used for the receipt, storage, interagency exchange or dissemination, and analysis of criminal intelligence information.[83]

CRISIS. The convergence of rapidly unfolding events in an outcome that is detrimental to national security; the outcome is to some degree indeterminate, which could create elements of both threat and opportunity; critical timing and decision making under extreme personal and organizational stress. 2. An incident or situation involving a threat to the United States, its territories, citizens, military forces, possessions, or vital interests that develops rapidly and creates a condition of such diplomatic, economic, political, or military importance that commitment of U.S. military forces and resources is contemplated to achieve national objectives.[84]

CRISIS ACTION PLANNING PROCESS. *See* CONTINGENCY PLANNING PROCESS.

CRISIS MANAGEMENT. An organization's ability to prepare for perceived catastrophic events—such as terrorism—and its capacity to employ appropriate force and specialized capabilities to minimize damage to U.S. interests. Domestically, *crisis management* also employs every resource at the disposal of federal, state, and local governments. *See also* CONSEQUENCE MANAGEMENT; INDICATOR, CRITICAL.

CRITERIA FOR SUCCESS. Information requirements developed during the operations process that measure the degree of success in accomplishing the unit's mission. They are normally expressed as either an explicit evaluation of the present situation or forecast of the degree of mission accomplishment.[85]

CRITICAL AND SENSITIVE INFORMATION LIST. A list containing the most important aspects of a program or technology, whether classified or unclassified, requiring protection from adversary exploitation.[86]

CRITICAL INDICATOR. *See* INDICATOR, CRITICAL.

CRITICAL INFORMATION. Specific facts about friendly intentions, capabilities, and activities vitally needed by adversaries or competitors for them to plan and act effectively to guarantee failure or unacceptable consequences for mission accomplishment.[87]

CRITICAL INFRASTRUCTURE. According to section 2 of the Homeland Security Act of 2002, means, systems, and assets, whether physical or virtual, so vital to the United States that the incapacity or destruction of such systems and assets would have a debilitating impact on security, national economic security, national public health or safety, or any combination of those matters.

CRITICAL INFRASTRUCTURE INFORMATION. Information not customarily in the public domain and related to the security of critical infrastructure or protected systems:

(A) Actual, potential, or threatened interference with, attack on, compromise of, or incapacitation of critical infrastructure or protected systems by either physical or computer-based attack or other similar conduct (including the misuse of or unauthorized access to all types of communications and data transmission systems) that violates federal, state, or local law, harms interstate commerce of the United States, or threatens public health or safety.

(B) The ability of any critical infrastructure or protected system to resist such interference, compromise, or incapacitation, including any planned or past assessment, projection, or estimate of the vulnerability of critical infrastructure or a protected system, including security testing, risk evaluation thereto, risk management planning, or risk audit.

(C) Any planned or past operational problem or solution regarding critical infrastructure or protected systems, including repair, recovery, reconstruction, insurance, or continuity, to the extent it is related to such interference, compromise, or incapacitation.[88]

CRITICAL INTELLIGENCE. 1. Intelligence that requires immediate attention by a commander or policymaker and which may enhance or refute previously held beliefs about hostilities or actions, leading to a change of policy. 2. Information of such urgent importance to the security of the United States that it is directly transmitted at the highest priority to the President and other national decision-making officials before passing through regular evaluative channels. In the military it is intelligence that requires the immediate attention of the commander. It includes but is not limited to: (a) strong indications of the immediate outbreak of hostilities of any type (warning of attack); (b) aggression of any nature against a friendly country; (c) indications or use of nuclear/biological/chemical weapons (targets); and (d) significant events within potential enemy countries that may lead to modifications of nuclear strike plans.[89]

CRITICAL INTELLIGENCE MESSAGE (CRITIC). A message containing information indicating a situation or pertaining to a situation which affects the security or interest of the United States or its allies to such an extent that it may require the immediate attention of the President.[90]

CRITICAL OVERSIGHT INFORMATION. Information that speaks to the quality and integrity of their performance as policy makers, managers, or employees of our seaports, airports, and transit systems. It is budget information and details on revenue and spending. It is information about personnel and their qualifications, training, and performance. It is information about the construction and maintenance of new public assets, including the myriad change orders that seem an inevitable feature of the government contract process. It is information about deals with carriers and suppliers and vendors and tenants. It is also information about public convenience and use of the public areas—and about personal safety . . . critical oversight information has a connection with security.[91] *See also* SENSITIVE HOMELAND SECURITY INFORMATION.

CRYPTO. Marking or designator identifying COMSEC keying material used to secure or authenticate telecommunications carrying classified or sensitive U.S. government or U.S. government-derived information.[92]

CRYPTOGRAPHY. Art or science concerning the principles, means, and methods for rendering plain information unintelligible and for restoring encrypted information to intelligible form.[93]

CRY-WOLF SYNDROME (OR CRYING WOLF). The desensitization of observers after previous warnings have been issued without threatening consequences. For example, "In 1968, CIA analyst Hovey's bull's-eye analysis of North Vietnam's ability to strike at U.S. troops had made the rounds among the CIA's top brass and it was even dispatched to the White House, where President Johnson read it 15 days before the attack. However, a note from George Carver, a top CIA official, shot down Hovey's warning. Carver said Hovey was *crying wolf.*"[94] *See also* ALERT FATIGUE.

CUBAN MISSILE CRISIS. In October 1962, during a routine reconnaissance mission by a U.S. U-2 spy plane, it was an enormous surprise to

American policymakers that the Soviet Union was building a missile base in Cuba. The missile base would have reportedly been able to launch approximately 70 short- and intermediate-range ballistic missiles that could quickly carry nuclear warheads to American soil. Ultimately, the Soviets removed the bases from Cuba. For additional examples of surprise attacks, *see also* FALKLAND ISLANDS; IRAN, FALL OF THE SHAH; KHOBAR TOWERS; KOREAN WAR; MISSILE GAP; OPERATION BARBAROSSA; PEARL HARBOR; SINGAPORE; TET OFFENSIVE; YOM KIPPUR WAR.

CULTIVATION. A deliberate and calculated association with a person for the purpose of recruitment, obtaining information, or gaining control for these or other purposes.[95]

CURRENT INDICATIONS. Activities relating to information, in varying degrees of evaluation, which bear on the intention of a potentially hostile force to adopt or reject a course of action; or which bear on an impending crisis.

CURRENT INTELLIGENCE. Information gathered on a day-to-day basis; information of all types and forms concerning events of immediate interest characteristically focusing on descriptive snapshots of generally static conditions; highly perishable information covering events that is disseminated without delay and lacks complete evaluation, interpretation, analysis, or integration. The fall of the Shah in Iran (1978) is a classic case of intelligence warning with current intelligence. CIA and State Department daily reports, the primary vehicles for political intelligence, consistently failed to draw Washington's attention to Iran in the early spring and summer of 1978, following the worst rioting in a decade. Early identification of factors such as the Shah's vulnerability and mounting dissidence could have prevented the crisis that evolved between the two countries. *See also* COMBAT INTELLIGENCE; CURRENT OPERATIONAL INTELLIGENCE; ESTIMATIVE INTELLIGENCE; NEAR-REAL TIME; RESEARCH INTELLIGENCE; SCIENTIFIC AND TECHNICAL INTELLIGENCE; WARNING INTELLIGENCE.

CURRENT OPERATIONAL INTELLIGENCE. Intelligence required for final planning and execution of all operations; especially important to military commanders in executing a tactical operation.

CUSTODIAN. An individual who has possession of or is otherwise charged with the responsibility for safeguarding and accounting for classified information.[96]

CYCLE, INTELLIGENCE. A continuous process that includes five phases that encapsulate the work done within the intelligence community. The five phases include the planning and direction phase of what intelligence needs to be developed based on existing gaps of knowledge, the collection phase of obtaining the information, the processing phase of converting the raw information into finished products (to include transcription, translation, imagery interpretation, etc.), the analysis and assessment phase of turning this information into a "finished intelligence product" by evaluating and integrating the information, and the final phase of distributing the product to those that have a "need to know."

– D –

DAILY DIGEST. A 10- to 15-page report that provides a global perspective on a single issue and is sent by 1:00 p.m. Monday through Friday to more than 750 senior and mid-level foreign policy officials. The format is the same as the Early Report. It is also transmitted electronically via e-mail and the Internet where it reaches an expanding audience in the foreign policy community of the U.S. government, including the White House, the Departments of State, Defense, Justice, Treasury, and Commerce, the CIA, and both houses of Congress.[97]

DAILY INTELLIGENCE SUMMARY (DINSUM). A report that has daily analysis of possible crisis situations and a summary of relevant intelligence information that was disseminated within the past 24 hours.

DAMAGE ASSESSMENT. A determination of the effect of a compromise of classified information on national security.[98]

DAMAGE CAUSED BY UNAUTHORIZED DISCLOSURE. The decision to apply classification involves two subelements, both of which require the application of "reasoned judgment on the part of the classifier":

A determination that the unauthorized disclosure of the information could reasonably be expected to cause damage to the national security of the United States, and that the damage can be identified or described. It is not necessary for the original classifier to produce a written description of the damage at the time of the classification, but the classifier must be prepared to do so if the information becomes the subject of a classification challenge, a request for mandatory review for declassification, or a request under the Freedom of Information Act. A determination of the probable operations, technological and resource impact of classification.[99]

DAMAGE TO THE NATIONAL SECURITY. Harm to the national defense or foreign relations of the United States from the unauthorized disclosure of information, taking into consideration such aspects of the information as the sensitivity, value, utility, and provenance of that information.[100]

DANGEROUS ASSUMPTION. A conceptual framework that makes sense of complex and disparate data by providing intellectual shortcuts and an anchor for interpretation, to the detriment of security considerations. For example, "This reality adds to the risks associated with President Clinton's nuclear testing bridge-leap insofar as he makes the *dangerous assumption* that he will be able to 'direct the Department of Energy to prepare to conduct additional tests while seeking approval to do so from Congress' in the event another nation conducts a nuclear test before the end of September 1994. The human talents and diagnostic skills necessary to prepare and conduct such tests are no more immutable [*sic*] to change over time than are the weapons themselves."[101]

DATA. The lowest class of information on the cognitive hierarchy. Data consist of raw signals communicated by any nodes in an information system, or sensing from the environment detected by a collector of any kind (human, mechanical, or electronic).[102]

DATA AGGREGATION. Compilation of unclassified individual data systems and data elements that could result in the totality of the information being classified or of beneficial use to an adversary.[103]

DATABASE. That information that forms the basis for further inquiry; a set of data, consisting of at least one data file, that is sufficient for a given purpose.[104]

DATA MINING. 1. "The science of extracting useful information from large data sets or databases." 2. Application of database technology and techniques (such as statistical analysis and modeling) to uncover hidden patterns and subtle relationships in data and to infer rules that allow for the prediction of future results.[105]

DECAPITATION STRIKE. A planned attack on key government buildings and installations with the purpose of rendering useless the command and control functions of enemy forces. It is this type of strike that intensifies the element of a surprise attack by enhancing the notion of a "leaderless victim." The concept of "decapitation" refers to the metaphor of separating the "head from the body" and is similar to the "removal of the Intelligence Community and senior leadership from the warfighter."

> A clandestine nuclear detonation in the city [Washington, DC] would likely doom the U.S. president, the vice president, Cabinet members, the Joint Chiefs of Staff, and members of Congress who were there at the time. The chaos that such an attack would cause would be difficult to overstate. One of the more difficult questions to answer in the hours after such a [nuclear, biological and chemical terrorist] *decapitation attack* would be "who is in charge here?" This chaos would be compounded if the headquarters housing the U.S. regional CINC [Commander-in-Chief] and his staff also were to suffer a similar *decapitation strike* at the same time. It is possible that the national leadership and the regional military forces of the United States would be plunged into chaos for some time.[106]

DECEPTION. 1. Those measures designed to mislead a foreign power, organization, or person by manipulation, distortion, or falsification of evidence to induce a reaction prejudicial to his, her, or its interests. 2. The practice of employing various ruses to disguise real intentions and true capabilities. Commonly known as having the ability to provide misleading or false information in order to achieve the element of surprise; however, there is more to deception than that which meets the eye. There are three main reasons to conduct deception. One type of *deception* attempts to misdirect the enemy's attention, causing him to concentrate his forces in the wrong place. By doing this, the deceiver tries to make his adversary violate the principle of concentration of forces. An example would be the Allied deception plans that diverted German attention from the beaches of Normandy to Norway and Pas de Calais as possible landing sites for an Allied invasion. A second type of *deception* makes the adversary violate the so-called principle of economy of force, which causes the opponent to waste resources. An example of this would be any artificial radar signal that draws enemy firepower and attention such as when during World War II the British led the Germans to attack non-existent airfields and factories by setting up phony targets and interfering with German electronic navigation aids. Finally, a third type of deception is designed to surprise an opponent by creating a situation that will later catch him off-guard and unprepared for action when it occurs. Hitler's policy toward Russia until the eve of his attack on the country (Operation Barbarossa) in June 1941 would be a perfect example. It should also be noted that this third type of deception is related to the two mentioned earlier.[107] *See also* A-TYPE DECEPTION; ACTIVE DECEPTION; DENIAL AND DECEPTION; PASSIVE DECEPTION.

DECEPTION MEANS. Methods, resources, and techniques that can be used to convey information to the deception target. There are three categories of deception means: a. physical means—activities and resources used to convey or deny selected information to a foreign power (examples include military operations, including exercises, reconnaissance, training activities, and movement of forces; the use of dummy equipment and devices; tactics; bases, logistic actions, stockpiles, and repair activity; and test and evaluation activities); b. technical means—military materiel resources and their associated operating techniques used to convey or deny selected information to a foreign power through the deliberate radiation, re-radiation, alteration, absorption, or reflection of energy; the emission or suppression of chemical or biological odors; and the emission or suppression of nuclear particles; c. administrative means—resources, methods, and techniques to convey or deny oral, pictorial, documentary, or other physical evidence to a foreign power.[108]

DECLASSIFICATION. 1. The determination that classified information no longer requires, in the interests of national security, any degree of protection against unauthorized disclosure, coupled with a removal or cancellation of the classification designation. 2. The process of reviewing and disclosing previously designated (classified) national security and nuclear related information classified by U.S. government branches, departments, and agencies. Executive Order 12356 [Reagan; 1982], Executive Order 12958 [Clinton; 1995], and Executive Order 13292 [Bush; 2003] set the stage for declassification.

EO12356 set up a framework for affected agencies to review sensitive documents, specifically allowing declassification to take place within the originating agency.

EO12958 established a schedule beginning on October 17, 2001, for automatic declassification of historically valuable 25-year-old records that are not otherwise exempt. These records were to be automatically declassified after five years—the deadline came and went.

EO13292 moved the October 17, 2001, schedule to December 31, 2006, and has proven to be an exceptionally powerful tool for correcting classification abuses by subjecting them to the scrutiny of an interagency review panel; the Director of Central Intelligence may reject the panel's rulings unless overridden by the President.[109]

DEDUCTIVE LOGIC. 1. Reasoning from the general to the specific. 2. A conclusion is inferred by applying the rules of a logical system to manipulate statements of belief (premises) to form new, logically consistent statements of belief (conclusions). If the premises are true, the conclusion must necessarily be true. 3. Inferences are made in which the conclusion about particulars follows necessarily from general or universal premises (key facts). The key facts are included in the premises. There is no risk in drawing the conclusion. For example, if premise 1 is that all men are strong and premise 2 is that Socrates is a man, the inference is that Socrates is strong. *See also* CONCLUSION; HYPOTHESIS; INDUCTIVE LOGIC; INFERENCE.

DEFECTOR. A person who, for political or other reasons, has repudiated his or her country and may be in possession of information of interest to another government. *See also* DOUBLE AGENT.

DEFENSE AUTOMATED WARNING SYSTEM (DAWS). The only automated software package used within the U.S. Department of Defense Indications and Warning System to monitor, produce, and record I&W database message traffic. It automatically updates I&W matrix/status boards and historically files electronic messages by I&W report type, permitting rapid recovery of I&W data. Additionally, DAWS has an integrated message handling capability and a message generation template package.

DEFENSE CONDITION (DEFCON). Progressive alert postures primarily for use between the Joint Chiefs of Staff and the commanders of unified commands. DEFCON levels progress to match situations of varying military severity; DEFCONs are phased increases in combat readiness. In general terms:

DEFCON 5 translates to normal peacetime readiness.

DEFCON 4 translates to normal, increased intelligence and strengthened security measures.

DEFCON 3 translates to an increase in force readiness above normal readiness.

DEFCON 2 translates to a further increase in force readiness, but less than maximum readiness.

DEFCON 1 translates to maximum force readiness.

Examples of when DEFCONs were changed include the Cuban Missile

Crisis in 1962, when the U.S. Strategic Air Command (SAC) was placed on DEFCON 2 for the first time in history, while the rest of U.S. military commands (with the exception of the U.S. Air Forces in Europe) went on DEFCON 3. On October 22, 1962, SAC responded by establishing DEF-CON 3, and ordered B-52s on airborne alert. Tension grew and the next day SAC declared DEFCON 2, a heightened state of alert, ready to strike targets within the Soviet Union. On October 6, 1973, Egyptian and Syrian forces launched a surprise attack on Israel. On October 25, U.S. forces went on DEFCON 3 alert status, as possible intervention by the Soviet Union was feared. On October 26, SAC and Continental Air Defense Command reverted to normal DEFCON status. On October 31, U.S. European Command (less the Sixth Fleet) went off DEFCON 3 status. The Sixth Fleet resumed its normal DEFCON status on November 17, 1973. *See also* THREAT CONDITION; WATCH CONDITION.

DEFENSE INTELLIGENCE AGENCY (DIA). This agency issues a number of periodic and special warning reports designed to give guidance on threats to the U.S. commands around the world. The *Weekly Intelligence Forecast* and the *Weekly Warning Forecast Report* include assessments from the various commands. The *Quarterly Warning Forecast* reviews a broad range of potential developments that could have an impact on U.S. security interests. In addition, DIA and the Unified Commands, as members of the Defense I&W system, publish two ad hoc products as issues arise: the *Warning Report* is an assessment of a specific warning issue; the *Watch Condition Change* is a notification of a change—either up or down—in the threat level presented by a specific warning problem. The *Warning Report* is the vehicle by which the Department of Defense's indications and warning system communicates warning intelligence that is worthy of the immediate, specific attention of senior U.S. officials within the Washington area.[110]

DEFENSE INTELLIGENCE PRODUCTION. The integration, evaluation, analysis, and interpretation of information from single or multiple sources into finished intelligence for known or anticipated military and related national security consumer requirements.

DEGRADE. In information operations, it is the use of nonlethal or temporary means to reduce the effectiveness or efficiency of an adversary's command and control systems and its information collection efforts or means.[111]

DELIBERATE COMPROMISE OF CLASSIFIED INFORMATION.
The act, attempt, or reported contemplation of intentionally conveying classified documents, information, or material to any unauthorized person, including unauthorized public disclosure.[112] The U.S. Code § 798 is actually titled "Disclosure of Classified Information." The word "deliberate" is not mentioned. Meets the following qualifications:[113] Whoever knowingly and willfully communicates, furnishes, transmits, or otherwise makes available to an unauthorized person, or publishes, or uses in any manner prejudicial to the safety or interest of the United States or for the benefit of any foreign government to the detriment of the United States any classified information:

- concerning the nature, preparation, or use of any code, cipher, or cryptographic system of the United States or any foreign government
- concerning the design, construction, use, maintenance, or repair of any device, apparatus, or appliance used or prepared or planned for use by the United States or any foreign government for cryptographic or communication intelligence purposes
- concerning the communication intelligence activities of the United States or any foreign government
- obtained by the processes of communication intelligence from the communications of any foreign government, knowing the same to have been obtained by such processes.

DELPHI METHOD. "[A method] designed to deal with cases where several experts are available to contribute and pool their opinions on some particular issue. First used in the early 1950's by the RAND Corporation for military estimation problems. Depending on the complexity of the subject matter, ten to fifty experts/specialists are required. A questionnaire (or interview) is prepared asking for the probability of occurrences of certain events (such as technological breakthroughs by a certain date—or alternatively, for the date by which the occurrence is judged to have a given probability, or even for an entire probability distribution over time).

Round 1. A first set of estimated answers is solicited. Sometimes the respondents are asked to select only the questions about which they consider themselves especially competent. Alternatively, answers to all questions may be requested, accompanied by a self rating of relative competence for each question.

Round 2. The participants are then provided with the Round I response distribution which is usually presented in terms of the median and the first and third quartiles. And new, possibly revised, responses are solicited.

Round 3. The resulting response distribution is fed back, together with a summary of the argument, defending relatively deviant responses. Again, the participants are asked for re-estimates.

Round 4. Again, the new response distribution and a summary of the counter arguments are fed back, and a final set of answers is issued based on due considerations of all arguments and counter-arguments that were presented.

The medians of the responses of this final round are then accepted as the group's position, representing the nearest thing to a consensus that is attainable. A report on the outcome usually also includes an indication of the residual spread of opinions, as well as of minority arguments in defense of deviant opinions, particularly in cases where sizeable dissent remains."[114]

DEMONSTRATION. Activity to divert a victim's strength and attention from the real or primary operation; to fix the enemy's local forces by actual combat, hopefully drawing forces into irrelevant battle. *See also* DIVERSION; FABRICATION; FEINT.

DENIAL AND DECEPTION (ALSO KNOWN AS D&D). *Denial* is the ability to prevent or impair the collection of intelligence by the enemy, and *deception* is the ability to mislead intelligence gathering by providing a distortion of reality. "Precise forecasts of the growth in ballistic missile capabilities over the next two decades—tests by year, production rates, weapons deployed by year, weapon characteristics by system type and circular error probable (CEP)—cannot be provided with confidence. *Deception and denial* efforts are intense and often successful, and U.S. collection and analysis assets are limited. Together they create a high risk of continued surprise. The question is not simply whether we will have warning of an emerging capability, but whether the nature and magnitude of a particular threat will be perceived with sufficient clarity in time to take appropriate action. Concealment *denial and deception* efforts by key target countries are intended to delay the discovery of strategically significant activities until well after they had [*sic*] been carried out successfully. The fact that some of these secret activities are discovered over time is to the credit of the U.S. Intelligence Community. However, the fact that there are delays in discovery of those activities provides a sharp warning that a great deal of activity goes undetected."[115]

DEPARTMENT OF DEFENSE DIRECTIVE. Broad policy document containing what is required by legislation, the President, or the Secretary of Defense to initiate, govern, or regulate actions or conduct by the DoD Components within their specific areas of responsibilities; used to establish or describe policy, programs, and organizations; define missions; provide authority; and assign responsibilities. One-time tasking and assignments are not appropriate in DoD Directives.[116]

DEPARTMENT OF DEFENSE INTELLIGENCE INFORMATION SYSTEM (DODIIS). The combination of Department of Defense personnel, procedures, equipment, computer programs, and supporting communications that support the timely and comprehensive preparation and presentation of intelligence and information to military commanders and national-level decision makers.

DEPARTMENT OF STATE SENSITIVE BUT UNCLASSIFIED. Information that originated within the Department of State which warrants a degree of protection or administrative control and meets the criteria for exemption from mandatory public disclosure under FOIA. Prior to 26 January 1995, this information was designated and marked LOU [Limited Use Only]. The LOU designation is no longer used.[117]

DERIVATIVE CLASSIFICATION. 1. Derivative classification is a determination that a document or material contains or reveals information already classified. 2. A determination that information is in substance the same as information currently classified, and the application of classification markings.[118]

DEROGATORY INFORMATION. 1. Unfavorable information regarding an individual which brings into question the individual's eligibility or continued eligibility for **access** authorization or suitability for federal employment. *Derogatory information* shall include, but is not limited to, information that the individual has:

a. Committed, prepared or attempted to commit, or aided, abetted, or conspired with another to commit or attempt to commit any act of sabotage, espionage, treason, terrorism, or sedition.

b. Knowingly established or continued a sympathetic association with a saboteur, spy, terrorist, traitor, seditionist, anarchist or revolutionist, espionage agent, or representative of a foreign nation whose interests are inimical to the interests of the United States, its territories or possessions, or with any person advocating the use of force or violence to overthrow the government of the United States or any state or subdivision thereof by unconstitutional means.

c. Knowingly held membership in or had a knowing affiliation with, or has knowingly taken action which evidences a sympathetic association with the intent of furthering the aims of, or adhering to, and actively participating in, any foreign or domestic organization, association, movement, group, or combination of persons which advocates or practices the commission of acts of force or violence to prevent others from exercising their rights under the Constitution or laws of the United States or any state or subdivision thereof by unlawful means.

d. Publicly or privately advocated, or participated in the activities of a group or organization, which has as its goal, revolution by force or violence to overthrow the government of the United States or the alteration of the form of government of the United States by unconstitutional means with the knowledge that it will further those goals.

e. Parent(s), brother(s), sister(s), spouse, or offspring residing in a nation whose interests may be inimical to the interests of the United States.

f. Deliberately misrepresented, falsified, or omitted significant information from a Personnel Security Questionnaire, a Questionnaire for Sensitive (or National Security) Positions, a personnel qualifications statement, a personnel security interview, written or oral statements made in response to official inquiry on a matter that is relevant to a determination regarding eligibility for DOE **access** authorization, or proceedings conducted pursuant to Sec. 710.20 through Sec. 710.31.

g. Failed to protect classified matter, or safeguard special nuclear material; or violated or disregarded security or safeguards regulations to a degree which would be inconsistent with the national security; or disclosed classified information to a person unauthorized to receive such information; or violated or disregarded regulations, procedures, or guidelines pertaining to classified or sensitive information technology systems.

h. An illness or mental condition of a nature which, in the opinion of a psychiatrist or licensed clinical psychologist, causes or may cause a significant defect in judgment or reliability.

i. Refused to testify before a congressional committee, federal or state court, or federal administrative body, regarding charges relevant to eligibility for DOE, or another federal agency's **access** authorization.

j. Been, or is, a user of alcohol habitually to excess, or has been diagnosed by a psychiatrist or a licensed clinical psychologist as alcohol dependent or as suffering from alcohol abuse.

k. Trafficked in, sold, transferred, possessed, used, or experimented with a drug or other substance listed in the Schedule of Controlled Substances established pursuant to section 202 of the Controlled Substances Act of 1970 (such as marijuana, cocaine, amphetamines, barbiturates, narcotics, etc.) except as prescribed or administered by a physician licensed to dispense drugs in the practice of medicine, or as otherwise authorized by federal law.

l. Engaged in any unusual conduct or is subject to any circumstances which tend to show that the individual is not honest, reliable, or trustworthy; or which furnishes reason to believe that the individual may be subject to pressure, coercion, exploitation, or duress which may cause the individual to act contrary to the best interests of the national security. Such conduct or circumstances include, but are not limited to, criminal behavior, a pattern of financial irresponsibility, conflicting allegiances, or violation of any commitment or promise upon which DOE previously relied to favorably resolve an issue of **access** authorization eligibility.[119]

DESCRIPTIVE ANALYSIS. Provides no evaluation or interpretation of collected data, but instead organizes and structures the data so that they can subsequently be used for interpretation. Typical tasks associated with this type of analysis are compiling, organizing, structuring, indexing and cross-checking; examples of descriptive analytic tasks would include maps and public records (e.g., phone books, birth records, etc.). *See also* INFERENTIAL ANALYSIS.

DETECTABLE ACTIONS. Physical actions or whatever can be heard, observed, imaged, or detected by human senses or by active/passive technical sensors, including emissions that can be intercepted.

DEVIL'S ADVOCATE OR DEVIL'S ADVOCACY. An official appointed to argue a point of view, with which he or she may or may not personally agree, for the purpose of ensuring that all aspects of a matter are fully considered; challenging strongly held view(s) or consensus by developing the possible case for an alternative explanation. This is considered most effective when challenging key assumptions that are critically important to the analytic process of developing an assessment. *See also* A-TEAM/B-TEAM CONCEPT.

DIRECT INFORMATION WARFARE. Changing the adversary's information without involving the intervening perceptive and analytical functions.[120]

DIRECTION FINDING. A procedure for obtaining bearings or radio frequency emitters by using a highly directional antenna and a display unit on an intercept receiver or ancillary equipment.

DIRECTOR OF NATIONAL INTELLIGENCE (DNI). One of the recommendations of the National Commission on the Terrorist Attacks Upon the United States ("9/11 Commission") was to replace the position of the Director of Central Intelligence (DCI) with a National Intelligence Director (NID) who would oversee and coordinate national intelligence agencies and programs. The DNI coordinates the 15 agencies that comprise the Intelligence Community (IC), and is the principal intelligence advisor to the president and the statutory intelligence advisor to the National Security Council.

DISASTER (HUMANITARIAN). A serious disruption of the functioning of a community or a society causing widespread human, material, economic, or environmental losses that exceed the ability of the affected community or society to cope using its own resources. A *disaster* is a function of the risk process. It results from the combination of hazards, conditions of vulnerability, and insufficient capacity or measures to reduce the potential negative consequences of risk.[121]

DISASTER ALERT. The period from the issuing of a public warning of an imminent disaster to its actual impact. The period during which pre-impact precautionary or disaster containment measures are conducted.[122]

DISASTER PREPAREDNESS. Measures that ensure the readiness and ability of a society to forecast and take precautionary measures in advance of an imminent threat and respond to and cope with the effects of a disaster by organizing and delivering timely and effective rescue, relief, and other appropriate post-disaster assistance.[123]

DISASTER PREVENTION. Originally defined as "measures designed to prevent natural phenomena from causing or resulting in disaster or other emergency situations." The term has now been largely replaced by "mitigation" in the recognition that few disasters can be prevented definitively.[124]

DISASTER RELIEF. Those external relief supplies and services which assist in meeting the immediate needs of those affected by a disaster.[125]

DISASTER RESPONSE. Sum total of all the decisions and actions taken during and after a disaster, to include those actions related to immediate relief, rehabilitation, and reconstruction.[126]

DISASTER RISK MANAGEMENT, HUMANITARIAN. The systematic process of using administrative decisions, organization, operational skills, and capacities to implement policies, strategies, and coping capacities of the society and communities to lessen the impacts of natural hazards and related environmental and technological disasters. This comprises all forms of activities, including structural and nonstructural measures to avoid (prevention) or to limit (mitigation and preparedness) adverse effects of hazards.[127]

DISASTER TEAM. A multidisciplinary, multisectarian group of persons qualified to evaluate a disaster so as to bring the necessary relief.[128]

DISCLOSURE. A transfer by any means of a record, a copy of a record, or the information contained in a record to a recipient other than the subject individual, or the review of a record by someone other than the subject individual.

DISCOVERY. The process where evidence is collected and hypotheses are generated and linked through arguments. The process iterates between search and inquiry and involves asking questions about evidence in order to establish its relevance, credibility, and inferential force on the postulated conclusions. The process may be marked by hypotheses in search of evidence at the same time evidence is in search of hypotheses (inductive and deductive reasoning). Discovery is aided by imaginative reasoning—e.g., methods of marshaling existing thought and evidence that act to stimulate new insights of existing evidence (abductive reasoning).[129]

DISCOVERY PROCESS. A process controlled by a court, designed to compel the exchange of information before a trial. Discovery allows one party to question other parties, and sometimes witnesses; discovery also allows one party to force the others to produce requested documents or other physical evidence. One major purpose of discovery is to assess the strength or weakness of an opponent's case, with the idea of opening settlement talks. The most common types of discovery are interrogatories, which consist of written questions the other party must answer under penalty of perjury, and depositions, which involve an in-person session at which one party to a lawsuit has the opportunity to ask oral questions of the other party or her witnesses under oath while a written transcript is made by a court reporter. Other types of pretrial discovery consist of written requests to produce documents and requests for admissions, by which one party asks the other to admit or deny key facts in the case.[130]

DISCRETIONARY ACCESS CONTROL. Restricting access to files based on the identity and need-to-know of users and/or groups to which the files belong. *See also* ACCESS; NEED-TO-KNOW.

DISINFORMATION. 1. Carefully contrived misinformation prepared by an intelligence service for the purpose of misleading, deluding, disrupting, or undermining confidence in individuals, organizations, or governments. 2. Information disseminated primarily by intelligence organizations or other covert agencies designed to distort information or deceive or influence U.S. decision makers, U.S. forces, coalition allies, key actors, or individuals via indirect or unconventional means.[131] 3. False and irrelevant information made available to deceive. For example, according to one report,

> Iraq's *disinformation* charges usually originate in their media and have been widely and often uncritically repeated by sympathetic media in Yemen, Algeria, Tunisia, Jordan, and, to a lesser extent, media in Pakistan, Morocco, Mauritania, Bangladesh, and other countries. Iraqi *disinformation* is often picked up and disseminated by otherwise responsible news media that fail to verify a story's source or facts. Iraqi ambassadors and embassy spokesmen have also made blatant *disinformation* claims in media appearances worldwide. *Disinformation* is a cheap, crude, and often very effective way to inflame public opinion and affect attitudes. It involves the deliberate production and dissemination of falsehoods by a government for a political purpose. *Disinformation* differs fundamentally from misinformation—unintentional errors which occur when facts are unclear and deadline pressures are urgent—in its clearly misleading and propagandistic purposes. Iraq's *disinformation* strategy is predictable. Its leaders have tried to make it appear that: Iraq is strong and the multinational coalition is weak; Israel is part of the multinational coalition; Allied Forces are committing crimes against Islam and atrocities in general; the United States is at odds with various countries in the coalition.[132]

DISSEMINATE. An information management activity: to communicate relevant information of any kind from one person or place to another in a usable form by any means to improve understanding or to initiate or govern action.[133]

DISSEMINATION AND EXTRACTION OF INFORMATION CONTROLLED BY ORIGINATOR (ORCON). 1. This marking is used with a security classification to enable the originator to supervise the use of information. 2. This marking may be used only on Intelligence Information that clearly identifies or would reasonably permit ready identification of an intelligence source or method that is particularly susceptible to countermeasures that would nullify or measurably reduce its effectiveness.[134]

DISSENT CHANNEL. Reserved for consideration of dissenting or alternative views on substantive foreign policy matters but it may not be used to address any nonpolicy issue.[135]

DISTANT EARLY WARNING (ALSO KNOWN AS THE "DEW LINE"). A radar network constructed by the United States and Canada to ensure a four-hour warning of a Soviet air attack. Specifically, it was a passive detection system intended to give advance notice to both the military and civil defense authorities regarding the deployment of Russian air bombers. The DEW line's radar stations could chart aircraft heading toward the North American continent. Of primary concern was the first-strike capability of the Soviet Union. This project, a joint effort undertaken by the governments of Canada and the United States of America, was a massive undertaking. First considered as far back as 1946, it went through several abortive attempts to bring it to fruition before its completion in 1957. At its completion, the 22 radar stations spanned 5944 kilometers. It took over 25,000 people to build it. After it was completed, the usefulness of the system suffered an almost immediate decline for several reasons, including the system's inability to detect the deployment of either nuclear-armed submarines or intercontinental ballistic missiles (ICBMs), the rapid growth and superior results that can be obtained from the use of satellites, and more advanced warning stations that were constructed in Alaska and the country of Greenland. It was the development of the cruise missile that finally sounded the death knell for the DEW line. Today most of the stations are abandoned ruins, victims of both technology and diplomacy.[136]

DISTRIBUTIVE WARNING. The process of warning, emanating from several analysts or agencies, whose focus may overlap, and whose duties may have purposes other than to communicate and forecast a possible threat. *See also* CONCENTRATED WARNING.

DIVERGENT EVIDENCE. Two or more items of evidence that support different conclusions. *See also* CONVERGENT EVIDENCE; REDUNDANT EVIDENCE.

DIVERSION. An act perpetrated for the purpose of turning attention or interest from a given area. Two modes of diversion are feints and demonstrations. *See also* DEMONSTRATION; FABRICATION; FEINT.

DOCUMENT EXPLOITATION (DOCEX). The systematic extraction of information from documents either produced by the threat, having been in the possession of the threat, or that are directly related to the current or future threat situation for the purpose of producing intelligence or answering information requirements. This may be conducted in conjunction with **human intelligence (HUMINT)** collection activities or may be conducted as a separate activity.[137]

DOSSIER. An official file of investigative, intelligence, or CI materials collected on behalf of the U.S. Army. May consist of documents, film, magnetic tape, photographs, or a combination thereof. May be "personal," referring to an individual, or "impersonal," referring to a thing, event, or organization.[138]

DOUBLE AGENT. Agent in contact with two opposing intelligence services, only one of which is aware of the double agent contact; a person who pretends to spy on a target organization on behalf of an organization, but in fact is loyal to that target organization. A "triple agent" pretends to be a double agent for the target organization, but in fact is working for the controlling organization all along. Usually, he or she keeps the trust of the target organization by feeding information to them which is apparently very important, but is in fact misleading or useless. *See also* DEFECTOR.

DOUBLE BLIND. Slang term that usually refers to a condition describing an analyst who purposely skews information or intelligence to support an already-held contention or perspective, to further advance a theory or scenario. *See also* CLIENTITIS.

DOWNGRADING. 1. Changing a security classification from a higher to a lower level. 2. A determination made by a declassification authority that information classified and safeguarded at a specified level shall be classified and safeguarded at a lower level.[139]

DRIVERS (ALSO KNOWN AS KEY VARIABLES). Uncertain factors that analysts judge most likely to determine the outcome of a complex situation. "Late last year the NIC published a report called Global Trends 2015 which presented the results of close collaboration between U.S. government specialists and a wide range of experts outside the government, on our best judgments of major *drivers* and trends that will shape the world of 2015."[140]

DRUG ENFORCEMENT ADMINISTRATION SENSITIVE INFOR-MATION. Unclassified information originated by the Drug Enforcement

Administration that requires protection against unauthorized disclosure to protect sources and methods of investigative activity, evidence, and the integrity of pretrial investigative reports. The Department of Defense has agreed to implement protective measures for DEA-sensitive information in its possession. Types of information to be protected include:

a. Information and material that are investigative in nature.

b. Information and material to which access is restricted by law.

c. Information and material that are critical to the operation and mission of the DEA.

d. Information and material the disclosure of which would violate a privileged relationship.

Access to DEA-sensitive information is given only to people with a valid need to know the information. A security clearance is not required. DEA-sensitive information in the possession of the Department of Defense may not be released outside the Department without authorization by the DEA.[141]

DUAL-USE. Knowledge or technology that can have both commercial and military application. For example, there is concern among U.S. policymakers that many *dual-use* technologies that can be used by terrorist groups in conducting effective attacks (such as the Global Positioning System tracking system, commercial imagery from space, or cryptography) cannot be denied to U.S. overseas customers without undermining the country's economic growth.

– E –

EARLY REPORT. Seven- to nine-page document based on reporting of editorial commentary from major posts commenting on the issues of the day. It is electronically transmitted to high-level officials at the White House, State Department, and Pentagon and other senior affairs decision makers by 8:00 a.m. Monday through Friday.[142]

EARLY WARNING, HUMANITARIAN. The provision of timely and effective information, through identified institutions, that allows individuals exposed to a hazard to take action to avoid or reduce their risk and prepare for effective response. According to the United Nations, early warning systems include a chain of concerns, namely: understanding and mapping the hazard; monitoring and forecasting impending events; processing and disseminating understandable warnings to political authorities and the population, and undertaking appropriate and timely actions in response to the warnings.[143]

ECONOMIC INTELLIGENCE. The collection and production of foreign intelligence pertaining to the development, production, labor, finance, and taxation of a nation's economic system as well as the distribution and consumption of goods and services.

ELICITATION. Acquisition of information from a person or group in a manner that does not disclose the intent of the interview or conversation. A technique of human source intelligence collection, generally overt, unless the collector is other than he or she purports to be.[144] *See also* HUMAN INTELLIGENCE; SOURCES OF INTELLIGENCE.

ELECTRO-OPTICAL INTELLIGENCE (ELECTRO-OPTINT). *See* SOURCES OF INTELLIGENCE.

ELECTRONIC COUNTERMEASURES (ECM). The division of electronic warfare involving actions taken to prevent or reduce an enemy's effective use of the electromagnetic spectrum. Electronic countermeasures include electronic jamming, which is the deliberate radiation, reradiation, or reflection of electromagnetic energy with the goal of impairing the electronic equipment used by an enemy, and electronic deception, which is intended to mislead the enemy in the interpretation of information received by his electronic system.

ELECTRONIC COUNTER-COUNTERMEASURES (ECCM). Electronic warfare that involves actions taken to ensure the effective use of the electromagnetic spectrum despite an enemy's use of electronic countermeasures.

ELECTRONIC INTELLIGENCE (ELINT). Technical and intelligence information derived from foreign, non-communications, electromagnetic radiations emanating from other than atomic detonation or radioactive sources; produced by the collection (observation and recording), and the processing for subsequent intelligence purposes of that information. *See also* SOURCES OF INTELLIGENCE.

ELECTRONIC SURVEILLANCE. Surveillance conducted on a person, group, or other entity by electronic equipment which is often highly sophisticated and extremely sensitive.[145]

ELECTRONIC WARFARE. Any military action involving the use of electromagnetic and directed energy to control the electromagnetic spectrum or to attack the enemy. The three major subdivisions within electronic warfare are electronic attack, electronic protection, and electronic warfare support.

ELEMENTS OF NATIONAL POWER. All the means available for employment in the pursuit of national objectives as determined by available indicators. *See also* NATIONAL POWER.

EMERGENCY. An extraordinary situation in which people are unable to meet their basic survival needs, or there are serious and immediate threats to human life and well-being. An *emergency* situation may arise as a result of a disaster, a cumulative process of neglect or environmental degradation, or when a disaster threatens and emergency measures have to be taken to prevent or at least limit the effects of the eventual impact.[146]

EMERGENCY MEASURES OF MILITARY PREPAREDNESS. Additional efforts undertaken to buttress the basic measures of readiness, usually in response to strategic warning, to counter a massive attack. *See also* BASIC MEASURES OF MILITARY PREPAREDNESS.

EMERGENCY MEDICAL SYSTEM. The aggregate of material resources and personnel needed to deliver medical care to those with an unpredicted, immediate health need outside established medical facilities.[147]

EMERGENCY MEDICINE. The specialized institutional system and resources required to meet immediate and unexpected medical needs.[148]

EMERGENCY OPERATIONS CENTER. Officially designated facility for the direction and coordination of all activities during the response phase of a disaster.[149]

EMERGENCY RESPONSE. The action taken immediately following a disaster warning or alert to minimize or contain the eventual negative effects, and those actions taken to save and preserve lives and provide basic services in the immediate aftermath of a **disaster**, and for as long as an emergency situation prevails.

ENEMY. An individual, group, organization, or government that must be denied critical information. The term is synonymous with *competitor* or *adversary*.

EPIDEMIC INTELLIGENCE SERVICE (EIS). A part of the Centers for Disease Control and Prevention, which comes under the U.S. Department of Health and Human Services; it "was established in 1951 following the start of the Korean War as an early warning system against biological warfare and man-made epidemics. The program, composed of medical doctors, researchers, and scientists who serve in two-year assignments, today has expanded into a surveillance and response unit for all types of epidemics, including chronic disease and injuries."[150]

ESPIONAGE. The act of obtaining, delivering, transmitting, communicating, or receiving information in respect to the national defense with an intent or reason to believe that the information may be used to the injury of the United States or to the advantage of any foreign nation.[151]

ESSENTIAL ELEMENTS OF FRIENDLY INFORMATION (EEFI). Key questions likely to be asked by adversary officials and intelligence systems about specific friendly intentions, capabilities, and activities, so they can obtain answers critical to their operational effectiveness.

ESSENTIAL ELEMENTS OF INFORMATION (EEI). Critical items of information regarding the enemy and the environment needed by the commander by a particular time to relate with other available information and intelligence in order to assist in reaching a logical decision.[152]

ESTIMATE. Analysis of a situation, development, or trend that identifies its major elements, interprets its significance, and appraises the possibilities and the potential results of the various actions that might be taken; an appraisal of a nation's capabilities, vulnerabilities, and potential courses of action. *See also* FORECAST; PREDICTION.

ESTIMATIVE INTELLIGENCE. 1. Category of intelligence analysis in which judgments are made despite incomplete information. There are two basic types: What is going on? and what will happen?[153] 2. A type of intelligence that projects or forecasts potential foreign courses of action and developments; implications or predictive judgment on a possible course of action by a potential enemy; an appraisal of the capabilities, vulnerabilities, and potential courses of action of a foreign nation or combination of nations. *See also* CURRENT INTELLIGENCE; CURRENT OPERATIONAL INTELLIGENCE; COMBAT INTELLIGENCE; RESEARCH INTELLIGENCE; SCIENTIFIC AND TECHNICAL INTELLIGENCE; WARNING INTELLIGENCE.

ESTIMATIVE PROBABILITY. Used in **assessments**, it is an assigned qualitative or quantitative value that an action, event, or decision will occur. Sherman Kent, considered the "father of intelligence analysis" at the Central Intelligence Agency, sought consistency in interpretation in the following terms:

Near certainty (and equivalent terms such as *highly likely*)	90–99%
Probable (and equivalent terms such as *most likely*)	60–90%
Even chance	40–60%
Improbable (and equivalent terms such as *not likely*)	10–40%
Near impossibility (and equivalent terms such as *highly unlikely*)	1–10%[154]

EVALUATION OF INTELLIGENCE. Appraisal of an item of information or intelligence collected in terms of credibility, reliability, pertinency, and accuracy. This appraisal is accomplished at each stage of the **intelligence cycle**, which can be changed based on the different contexts of that stage. Specifically, the reliability of a source is based on a standard letter system, while the accuracy of the information is based on a standard number system. It is this letter-number combination that is part of the evaluation and appraisal of the information or intelligence. For example, intelligence rated B4 means that although this source is "usually reliable," the accuracy of the information is "doubtful."

The evaluation is based on the following scales: A. completely reliable, B. usually reliable, C. fairly reliable, D. not usually reliable, E. unreliable, F. reliability cannot be judged, 1. confirmed by other source, 2. probably true, 3. possibly true, 4. doubtful, 5. improbable, and 6. truth cannot be judged.

EVIDENCE. 1. The many types of information presented to a judge or jury designed to convince them of the truth or falsity of key facts; typically includes testimony of witnesses, documents, photographs, items of damaged property, government records, videos, and laboratory reports.[155] 2. Incoming datum, of whatever kind, becomes evidence when its relevance to hypotheses of interest is established. 3. A datum becomes evidence in some analytic problem when its relevance to conjectures (hypotheses) being considered is established; always a relative term—it signifies a relation between two facts; evidence about an event and the event itself are not the same.[156] *See also* PROOF.

EVIDENTIAL VALUE. Usefulness of records in documenting the organization, functions, and activities of the agency creating or receiving them; considered in appraising records for permanent retention.[157]

EXCEPTIONAL THEORY. Projecting an adversary's behavior based heavily on explanations of the past in specific incidents, where unusual possibilities may turn out to be relevant; assuming deviance of behavior rather than continuity.[158] *See also* NORMAL THEORY.

EXECUTION INFORMATION. Information that communicates a decision and directs, initiates, or governs action, conduct, or procedure.[159]

EXECUTIVE ORDER (EO). 1. Executive orders are official documents, numbered consecutively, through which the President of the United States manages the operations of the federal government. The text of executive orders appears in the daily *Federal Register* as each executive order is signed by the President, and received by the Office of the Federal Register. The text of executive orders beginning with Executive Order 7316 of March 13, 1936, also appears in the sequential editions of Title 3 of the *Code of Federal Regulations* (CFR). 2. The presidential system of information restriction that grew out of World War Two became an "extravagant and indefensible system of denial" exercised by the executive branch that had no "standing in law." Historian Arthur Schlesinger says, "Secrecy by definition meant that policies were undertaken without consent. It would therefore be in the interest of Presidents to reopen the Presidency. But recent Presidents either have become so enamored of the short-run conveniences of secrecy, or else had enough to conceal, they forgot the long-run necessity, above all for the Presidency itself, of open government."[160] 3. The President's authority to issue executive orders derives from powers enumerated, implied, and inferred by the Constitution, as well as from authority delegated to the President by federal statute. 4. "Stroke of the pen. Law of the Land. Kinda cool."[161] In the overwhelming majority of cases, executive orders and proclamations are an appropriate public way of guiding the actions of numerous federal agencies and other components of the executive branch. While thousands of executive orders have been issued over the last two centuries, federal courts have been extremely reluctant to challenge executive authority. When executive orders are issued without a constitutional or legal basis, they imply the Separation of Powers Doctrine that underpins divided government.

EXFORMATION. Explicitly discarded information that is in our heads when or before we say anything at all. In everyday language if something contains information, it is a result of the production of *exformation* (which is really a summary or abbreviation suitable for guiding a transaction). *Exformation* is "perpendicular" to information. What is rejected before expression; it is about the mental work we do to probe what we want to say.[162] In a very loose sense, it is that information that pertains to the context of what we know and why we know it.

EXPLICIT KNOWLEDGE. Tangible, external, documented knowledge that has been captured and codified into abstract human symbols (such as logical propositions, and structured and natural language) that can be stored, repeated, and passed along to other humans because it is impersonal and universal. Examples are newspapers, reports, and data of any kind. *See also* TACIT KNOWLEDGE.

EXPLOIT. In information operations, to gain access to adversary command and control systems to collect information or to plant false or misleading information.[163]

EXPLOITABLE RESOURCES. Formulae, designs, drawings, research data, computer programs, technical data packages, and the like, which are not considered records within the congressional intent of reference because of development costs, utilization, or value. These items are considered exploitable resources to be utilized in the best interest of all the public and are not preserved for informational value nor as evidence of agency functions. Requests for copies of such material shall be evaluated in accordance with policies expressly directed to the appropriate dissemination or use of these resources. Requests to inspect this material to determine its content for informational purposes shall normally be granted, unless inspection is inconsistent with the obligation to protect the property value of the material, as, for example, may be true for patent information and certain formulae, or is inconsistent with another significant and legitimate governmental purpose.[164]

EXPLOITATION. 1. Taking full advantage of success in military operations, following up initial gains, and making permanent the temporary effects already achieved. 2. Taking full advantage of any information that has come to hand for tactical, operational, or strategic purposes. 3. An offensive operation that usually follows a successful attack and is designed to disorganize the enemy in depth.

EXPORT-CONTROLLED INFORMATION. Information and technology that may be released only to foreign nationals or foreign persons in accordance with the Export Administration Regulations (15 CFR parts 730– 774) and the International Traffic in Arms Regulations (22 CFR parts 120–130), respectively. Export controls regulate the transfer of certain information and potential equipment to foreign nationals, and "therefore constrain who can participate in associated research and educational activities."[165]

EXTREMELY SENSITIVE INFORMATION. Information and material related to the Single Integrated Operational Plan (SIOP) for the conduct of nuclear war fighting operations.[166]

– F –

FABRICATION. A deceptive practice of creating a totally unreal event or situation. *See also* DEMONSTRATION; DIVERSION; FEINT.

FABRICATOR. Individuals or groups who, without genuine resources, invent information or inflate or embroider over news for personal gain or for political purposes.

FACT. An event or action that has occurred and has been verified by two independent sources.

FALKLAND ISLANDS. A surprise occupation by Argentina on a British colony even though there was abundant evidence of Argentine intent to invade. British estimates on March 30, 1982, stated that an invasion was not imminent but three days later Argentine marines landed and began occupying the islands. See also OPERATION BARBAROSSA, PEARL HARBOR; SINGAPORE; TET OFFENSIVE; YOM KIPPUR WAR.

FATIDIC. (Pronounced fay-TID-ik.) Adjective; of or relating to predicting fates; prophetic. From Latin *fatidicus*, from *fatum* (fate) and *dicere* (to say). *See also* ONEIROMANCY.

FEEDBACK. In information operations, information that reveals how the deception target is responding to the deception story and if the military deception plan is working.[167]

FEINT. An act intended to divert a victim's attention from the main target of an attack by contriving a mock attack where actual combat is not intended; in other words, simulating a buildup for an imminent attack. During World War II, General Eisenhower's headquarters developed a feint, codenamed FORTITUDE, to distract German attention from the real landing area in Normandy. Allied radio messages were broadcast in such a way as to divert attention from the south of England to a spoof headquarters in Scotland. "A very busy signals staff contrived, by sending out the right sort of dummy wireless traffic, to assemble a fictitious 4th Army in Scotland. The 'wireless training' of this army contained some purposeful indiscretions. By these furtive, impressionistic and devious indiscretions, FORTITUDE sought to let the Germans convince themselves of what they had always wanted to believe anyway—that the invaders would pour across the Channel at the narrowest point, from Dover to the Pas de Calais; the build-up in Scotland itself suggested a preliminary feint-like assault on southern Norway. In fact, so conclusive did the evidence seem to be that more than a month after the invasion in Normandy, Hitler declared that 'the enemy will probably attempt a second landing in the 15th Army sector'—the zone of the Pas de Calais."[168] *See also* DECEPTION; DEMONSTRATION; DIVERSION; FABRICATION.

FIG LEAF. An event or activity of seemingly minor consequence used for the justification of a larger or more important and significant action; often used as an excuse. "He [Secretary of State Dean Rusk] said he felt we might be confronted by serious uprisings all over Latin America if U.S. forces were to go in, not to mention the temptation that the commitment of such forces in Cuba would provide elsewhere in the world. In this connection he again mentioned the possibility of a physical base on the Isle of Pines for a provisional government that we could recognize. This he thought would be a powerful step forward. What we needed was a *fig leaf*. A Cuban provisional government on the Isle of Pines, for example, could sink Soviet ships carrying supplies to Castro with less danger than would be the case with direct involvement of U.S. forces."[169]

FILE SERIES. File units or documents arranged according to a filing system or kept together because they relate to a particular subject or function, result from the same activity, document a specific kind of transaction, take a particular physical form, or have some other relationship arising out of their creation, receipt, or use, such as restrictions on access or use.[170]

FILES. An arrangement of records. The term is used to denote papers, photographs, photographic copies, maps, machine-readable information, or other recorded information regardless of physical form or characteristics, accumulated or maintained in filing equipment, boxes, or machine-readable media, or on shelves, and occupying office or storage space.[171]

FINISHED INTELLIGENCE (FI). Raw information analyzed and corroborated. It should be produced in a consistent format to enhance utility and regularly **disseminated** to a defined audience.[172]

FORECAST. This term should not be confused with **prediction**. Whereas predictions assert the occurrence of some event with certainty ("insurgents will capture the city next year"), a forecast is a probabilistic statement ("there is a 3–1 chance that the insurgents will capture the city next year"). A prediction may be viewed as a limiting case of a *forecast*, where the assigned probability reaches the level of certainty; however, forecasts very rarely take the form of predictions. Also, forecasts may refer either to events or to trends, and these changes must be verifiable if forecasts are to be operationally meaningful. "This puts a special strain on forecasts in social science areas as opposed to, say, technological forecasts, because the terminology we tend to use ('risking dissatisfaction,' 'détente,' 'nationalism') does not always have the crispness necessary to allow unambiguously verifiable assertions. As a consequence, forecasts, in order to be meaningful, sometimes have to be formulated in terms of certain indicators. If possible, these are social or political indicators whose values are objectively measurable."[173] "[South Korean] Seoul-based banks demand that the government honor the payment guarantee at the earliest date possible, as they have failed to receive the loans from Russia. But analysts *forecast* that the government payment is unlikely within the year. And the banks may even fail to get the payment by next year, given the protracted negotiations regarding the state budget toward that end."[174] *See also* ESTIMATE; PREDICTION.

FOREIGN CIVIL INTELLIGENCE. Intelligence derived from all sources regarding the social, political, and economic aspects of governments and civil populations, their demographics, structures, capabilities, organizations, people, and events. (This definition has been based on consideration of several alternatives to describe civilian social, political, and economic information: 1. Civil Considerations—the political, social, economic, and cultural factors of an AOR (area of responsibility; Army FM 3-07 paragraph 2.7); 2. Civil Considerations—the influence of manmade infrastructure, civilian institutions, and attitudes and activities of the civilian leaders, populations, and organizations within an AOR on the conduct of military operations (Army FM-06); and 3. "Cultural Intelligence" defined in USMC Urban GIRH and often cited by Retired General Anthony Zinni).[175]

FOREIGN GOVERNMENT INFORMATION (FGI). Defined in Executive Order 12958 (Clinton April 1995):

(1) information provided to the U.S. Government by a foreign government or governments, an international organization of governments, or any element thereof, with the expectation that the information, the source of the information, or both, are to be held in confidence.

(2) information produced by the U.S. pursuant to or as a result of a joint arrangement with a foreign government or governments, or an international organization of governments, or any element thereof, requiring that the information is to be held in confidence. Bush Executive Order 13292 makes FGI classified information.[176]

FOREIGN INSTRUMENTAL SIGNALS INTELLIGENCE (FISINT). *See* SOURCES OF INTELLIGENCE.

FOREIGN INTELLIGENCE INFORMATION. Relating to the capabilities, intentions, or activities of foreign governments or elements thereof, foreign organizations, or foreign persons (Section 218 of the Patriot Act amends the Foreign Intelligence Surveillance Act of 1978); allows the sharing of foreign intelligence information between agencies, and gives license to intelligence officers who conduct electronic surveillance to "coordinate efforts" with law enforcement to coordinate investigations.[177]

FOREIGN INTELLIGENCE SURVEILLANCE COURT. This organization implements the Foreign Intelligence Surveillance Act of 1978 (FISA), which authorizes electronic surveillance and unconsented physical searches to occur inside the Unites States for the purpose of collecting "foreign intelligence." The Court is composed of seven U.S. District Court judges who are appointed to the FISA Court by the chief justice of the

Supreme Court and who serve for seven years. The Court of Review consists of three U.S. District of Appeals Court judges.

FOREIGN TERRORIST TRACKING TASK FORCE (FTTTF). According to Attorney General Ashcroft, the FTTTF's mission includes "barring terrorists from entering the United States, and tracking down and deporting those who do enter the United States—to the maximum extent permitted by law." Created October 29, 2001, by President George W. Bush by way of Homeland Security Presidential Directive-2. This Task Force is responsible for 1. denying entry into the United States of aliens associated with, suspected of being engaged in, or supporting terrorist activity; and 2. locating, detaining, prosecuting, or deporting any such aliens already present in the United States. The Task Force is staffed by personnel from the Department of State, the INS, the FBI, the Secret Service, the Customs Service, the Intelligence Community, military support components, and other federal agencies.[178]

FORMAL ACCESS APPROVAL. Process for authorizing access to classified or sensitive information with specified access requirements, such as Sensitive Compartmented Information (SCI), or Privacy Data, based on the specified access requirements and a determination of the individual's security eligibility and **need-to-know.**[179]

FORMERLY RESTRICTED DATA (FRD). 1. Classified information jointly determined by the DOE and the DoD to be related to the military utilization of atomic weapons and be adequately safeguarded as National Security Information (NSI); sometimes referred to as "classified atomic energy information." There is little difference between National Security Information and Formerly Restricted Data except for the cumbersome requirement for joint DOE-DoD determinations on declassification and the process for sharing the information with other nations—a process largely redundant with other mechanisms for achieving similar objectives.[180]

FOR OFFICIAL USE ONLY (FOUO). 1. Unclassified information that may only be shared with individuals who are determined to have a "need to know" it. In the DHS, employees and contractors are required to sign a special Non-Disclosure Agreement before receiving access to this information. According to the DHS, "to identify unclassified information of a sensitive nature, not otherwise categorized by statute or regulation, the unauthorized disclosure of which could adversely impact a person's privacy and welfare, the conduct of a federal program, or other programs or operations essential to the national interest." Within DHS, the caveat "For Official Use Only" will be used to identify SBU information within the DHS community that is not otherwise governed by statute or regulation. At this point the designation applies only to DHS advisories and bulletins. 2. This designation is used by the Department of Defense and a number of other federal agencies to identify information or material which, although unclassified, may not be appropriate for public release.[181]

FREEDOM OF INFORMATION ACT (FOIA). In 1953, Congressman John Moss, considered the father of the Freedom of Information Act, requested information from the Eisenhower Civil Service Commission to verify its claim that 2,800 federal employees had been fired due to "security reasons." Moss required the information to discern whether these terminations entailed allegations of disloyalty, espionage, or other conditions (Moynihan 173). The Civil Service Commission refused to supply the information to Moss, who learned that as a member of Congress, he had no legal recourse to force the Commission to disclose the information. In response, Moss convened the Special Government Information Subcommittee in 1955, "tasked with monitoring executive secrecy." Moss and his committee determined "the right to know has suffered." The Committee's investigations led to greater understanding of security classification in the executive branch, how secrecy not only impairs the political participation of Congress but also damages citizen participation. It would be a long, tortuous 11 years before FOIA was realized. In seeking a model for FOIA, Moss looked for guidance on information rights from the U.S. Constitution, English common law, statutory law, and federal case law.[182]

FREEDOM OF INFORMATION EXEMPTIONS. 1. The Freedom of Information Act outlines nine categories of information that is exempt from disclosure: documents classified for national security reasons, internal personnel rules and practices, documents exempted by statute, trade secrets, inter/interagency materials (executive privilege), personnel and medical records, records "compiled for law enforcement purposes," information used in regulating financial institutions (bank examination reports), geological information about oil wells and water resources. Additionally, the post-9/11 "Critical Infrastructure Information" (CII), which "relates to the production, generation, transportation, transmission, or distribution of energy; could be useful to a person in planning an attack on critical infrastructure," is exempt from mandatory disclosure under the Freedom of Information Act (5 U.S.C. 552). Critical infrastructure information as defined in the Patriot Act is exempt from FOIA (see Exemption 2). Moreover, on October 12, 2001, Attorney General John Ashcroft issued a memorandum to the heads of all departments and agencies that supersedes the Department of Justice FOIA policy memorandum that had been in effect since October 1993. The Ashcroft memo "establishes a new 'sound legal basis' standard governing the Department of Justice's decisions on whether to defend agency actions under the FOIA when they are challenged in court. This differs from the 'foreseeable harm' standard that was employed under the predecessor memorandum. Under the new standard, agencies should reach the judgment that their use of an FOIA exemption is on sound footing, both factually and legally, whenever they withhold requested information."[183]

FREE FLOW OF INFORMATION. A means by which open government allows the press, interested individuals, and others to see and hear what is going on in government, and take the initiative to publicize, comment upon, and influence governmental activities.[184]

FUGITIVE DOCUMENTS. Federal agency publications that are not sent to the Government Printing Office for inclusion in the Federal Depository Library Program (FLDP) which supplies libraries with public (not classified or potentially sensitive) information.[185]

– G –

GAMMA (G). Unclassified term used to describe a type of sensitive compartmented information (SCI).[186]

GAP ANALYSIS. An evaluation of differences between an organization's situation or position, and its desired future using specific strategies and allocation of capabilities to close the gap.

GENERIC INDICATOR DIRECTORY (GID). Any source document that contains a listing of a general set of indicators from which to choose in developing a specific indicator list for a given warning problem or concern.

GEOINT. The exploitation and analysis of imagery and geospatial information to describe, assess, and visually depict physical features and geographically referenced activities on the surface of the planet.

GEOSPATIAL INFORMATION. Foundation information upon which all other battlespace information is referenced to form the common operational picture.[187]

GLOBAL INFORMATION AND EARLY WARNING SYSTEM ON FOOD AND AGRICULTURE (GIEWS). Located under the Food and Agriculture Organization of the United Nations, the system provides annual reports with a global perspective on the production, stocks, and trade of cereals and other basic food commodities. Publications contain analyses of trends and prospects of hunger worldwide and statistical information on developments in the world cereal markets, export prices, and ocean freight rates. GIEWS also produces "special reports and alerts" that describe the food supply and agricultural situation in countries or subregions experiencing particular food supply difficulties. They also alert the international community on measures to be taken. *See also* HUMANITARIAN EARLY WARNING SYSTEM.

GLOBAL INFORMATION ENVIRONMENT. All individuals, organizations, or systems, most of which are outside the control of the military or National Command Authorities, that collect, process, and **disseminate** information to national and international audiences.[188]

GLOBAL INFORMATION GRID DEFENSE SECTOR (GIG). The globally interconnected, end-to-end set of information capabilities, associated processes, and personnel for collecting, processing, storing, disseminating, and managing information on demand to warfighters, policymakers, and support personnel including all owned and leased communications and computing systems and services, software (including applications), data, security services, and other associated services necessary to achieve information superiority. It also includes National Security Systems as defined in Section 5142 of the Clinger-Cohen Act of 1996.[189]

GLOBAL INFORMATION INFRASTRUCTURE (GII). Worldwide interconnections of the information systems of all countries, international and multinational organizations, and international commercial communications.[190]

GOVERNMENT INFORMATION. Information that is owned by, produced by or for, or is under the control of the U.S. government.

GOVERNMENT-OFF-THE-SHELF (GOTS). An item that has been developed by the government and produced to military or commercial standards and specifications, is readily available for delivery from an industrial source, and can be procured without change to satisfy a military requirement.

GRAY LITERATURE. Material not well covered by conventional book trade channels. Information contained within this category is often not available in any other kind of source. Gray literature is intrinsically more difficult to identify, acquire, process, access, and otherwise handle than conventional literature. Examples include, but are not limited to, conference papers, trade literature, electronic bulletin boards, and foreign government reports. The most significant point to make about the value of gray literature is that the information it contains often is not available in any other kind of source.[191]

GRAYMAIL. The threat by defendants and their counsel to press for the release or disclosure of sensitive (national security) information, classified information, or state secrets during a trial.

GREY LITERATURE. Not declassified; downgraded from secret to confidential; that which is produced on all levels of government, academics, business, and industry in print and electronic formats, but which is not controlled by commercial publishers.

GROUPTHINK. A concept that faulty decision making occurs when a group does not consider alternatives and desires unanimity at the expense of quality decisions. Groupthink can lead to seeking out few alternative solutions because there is an illusion of invulnerability (i.e., "we all can't be wrong"). Some symptoms of groupthink are when there is no critical discussion of information, a sharing of stereotypes to guide decisions, a strong moral climate and the suppression of true feelings among the participants in the group.[192]

GSA SENSITIVE BUT UNCLASSIFIED BUILDING INFORMATION (GSA-SBU-BI). Information concerning General Services Administration (GSA) Public Building Services controlled space, including owned, leased, or delegated federal facilities. GSA-SBU-BI includes building designs such as floor plans, construction plans and specifications, renovation/alteration plans, equipment plans and locations, building operating plans, information used for building services contracts and/or contract guard services, or any other information considered a security risk.[193]

– H –

HEALTH ALERT NETWORK (HAN). Provides rapid and timely access to emergent health information and evidence-based practices and procedures for effective public health preparedness, response, and service on a 24/7 basis; provides health information and the infrastructure to support the dissemination of that information at the state and local levels covering 90 percent of the population. The HAN Messaging System currently directly and indirectly transmits health alerts, advisories, and updates to over one million recipients.

HIGH 2 INFORMATION. Substantial internal matters, the disclosure of which would risk circumvention of a legal requirement; records that "are related solely to the internal personnel rules and practices of an agency."[194]

HIGH-IMPACT/LOW-PROBABILITY ANALYSIS. Focus is on a seemingly unlikely event that would have major policy consequences if it happened; seeks to sensitize analysts to the potential impact of seemingly low-probability events that would have major repercussions.

HOLY GRAIL. A specific indication considered notional because of its rarity, that clearly delineates the exact time, location, or intention of a future course of action (such as an attack); a singular piece of data that fully validates all previous existing intelligence **analysis** or **assessments**. For example, although the U.S. had intercepted Japanese message traffic prior to the attack on Pearl Harbor, not one of the messages was the *holy grail* that stated the day, time, and avenues of approach of the attack. According to some cynics in the warning community, decision makers will not act unless their warning message contains information from this source. *See also* ACTIONABLE INTELLIGENCE.

HOMELAND SECURITY ADVISORY COUNCIL (HSAC). Homeland Security Advisory Council (HSAC) provides advice and recommendations to the Secretary on matters related to homeland security. The Council is comprised of leaders from state and local government, first responder communities, the private sector, and academia. Provides organizationally independent advice and recommendations to the Secretary of Department aiding in the creation and implementation of critical and actionable policy relating to the security of the American homeland. The HSAC shall provide the Secretary advisory services on policy development and advisory recommendations developing the implementation of comprehensive strategies to secure the United States from terrorists threats, attacks, and/or national emergencies.[195]

HOMELAND SECURITY ADVISORY SYSTEM (HSAS), DEPARTMENT OF HOMELAND SECURITY (DHS). Established by Homeland Security Presidential Directive-03 in March 2002, it is a system designed to provide information regarding the risk of terrorist acts to federal, state, and local authorities and to the American people by providing a set of graduated "threat conditions" that would increase as the risk of the threat increases. "This system is intended to create a common vocabulary, context, and structure for an ongoing national discussion about the nature of the threats that confront the homeland and the appropriate measures that should be taken in response. It seeks to inform and facilitate decisions appropriate to different levels of government and to private citizens at home and at work." The higher the **threat condition**, the greater the risk of a terrorist attack. Risk includes both the probability of an attack occurring and its potential gravity. Threat conditions shall be assigned by the attorney general in consultation with the assistant to the president for Homeland Security. The decision whether to publicly announce threat conditions shall be made on a case-by-case basis by the attorney general in consultation with the assistant to the president for Homeland Security. . . . A decision on which threat condition to assign shall integrate a variety of considerations. This integration will rely on qualitative assessment, not quantitative calculation. Higher threat conditions indicate greater risk of a terrorist act, with risk including both probability and gravity. Despite best efforts, there can be no guarantee that, at any given threat condition, a terrorist attack will not occur. An initial and important factor is the quality of the threat information itself. The *evaluation of this threat information shall include, but not be limited to, the following factors*: To what degree is the threat information credible? To what degree is the threat information corroborated? To what degree is the threat specific and/or imminent? How grave are the potential consequences of the threat?

Low Condition (Green). This represents a low risk of terrorist attacks. Federal departments and agencies should consider the following general measures in addition to the agency-specific Protective Measures they develop and implement: refining and exercising as appropriate preplanned Protective Measures; ensuring personnel receive proper training on the Homeland Security Advisory System and specific preplanned department or agency Protective Measures; and institutionalizing a process to assure that all facilities and regulated sectors are regularly assessed for vulnerabilities to terrorist attacks, and all reasonable measures are taken to mitigate these vulnerabilities.

Guarded Condition (Blue). This indicates a general risk of terrorist attacks. In addition to the Protective Measures taken in the previous Threat Condition, Federal departments and agencies should consider the following general measures in addition to the agency-specific Protective Measures that they will develop and implement: checking communications with designated emergency response or command locations; reviewing and updating emergency response procedures; and providing the public with any information that would strengthen its ability to act appropriately.

Elevated Condition (Yellow). Condition Yellow is a significant risk of terrorist attacks. In addition to the Protective Measures taken in the previous Threat Conditions, Federal departments and agencies should consider the following general measures in addition to the Protective Measures that they will develop and implement: increasing surveillance of critical locations; coordinating emergency plans as appropriate with nearby jurisdictions; assessing whether the precise characteristics of the threat require the further refinement of preplanned Protective Measures; and implementing, as appropriate, contingency and emergency response plans.

High Condition (Orange). This represents a high risk of terrorist attacks. In addition to the Protective Measures taken in the previous Threat Conditions, Federal departments and agencies should consider the following general measures in addition to the agency-specific Protective Measures that they will develop and implement: coordinating necessary security efforts with Federal, state, and local law enforcement agencies or any National Guard or other appropriate armed forces organizations; taking additional precautions at public events and possibly considering alternative venues or even cancellation; preparing to execute contingency procedures, such as moving to an alternate site or dispersing their workforce; and restricting threatened facility access to essential personnel only.

Severe Condition (Red). Red is a severe risk of terrorist attacks. Under most circumstances, the Protective Measures for a Severe Condition are not intended to be sustained for substantial periods of time. In addition to the Protective Measures in the previous Threat Conditions, Federal departments and agencies also should consider the following general measures in addition to the agency-specific Protective Measures that they will develop and implement: increasing or redirecting personnel to address critical emergency needs; assigning emergency response personnel and pre-positioning and mobilizing specially trained teams or resources; monitoring, redirecting, or constraining transportation systems; and closing public and government facilities.[196]

HOMELAND SECURITY INFORMATION. Any information possessed by a federal, state, or local agency that relates to the threat of terrorist activity; relates to the ability to prevent, interdict, or disrupt terrorist activity; would improve the identification or investigation of a suspected terrorist or terrorist organization; or would improve the response to a terrorist act.[197]

HOMELAND SECURITY OPERATIONS MORNING BRIEF. Comprised of mostly suspicious activity reports minus any information on U.S. persons contained within criminal intelligence protected by privacy laws; is shared on a Sensitive But Unclassified (SBU) level with about 1,500 federal, state, and local intelligence and law enforcement agencies and subscribers.[198]

HORIZONTAL INTEGRATION. Refers to the desired end-state where intelligence of all kinds flows rapidly and seamlessly to the warfighter, and enables **information dominance** warfare.

HUGGER-MUGGER. (Term of unknown origin.) 1. The manipulation of information that produces false signals which are believed to be true indications. For example, *hugger-mugger* occurred among **watch officers** in the 1970s when the CIA generated stories detrimental to Chilean President Salvador Allende, creating so much activity that U.S. **watch centers** began picking up false information that the CIA itself had planted, and reported it back to Washington. 2. Secret, stealthy, confused, or disorderly in reference to intelligence operations. For example, as written by Shakespeare: "Thick and unwholesome in their thoughts and whispets// For good Polonius' death, and we have done but greenly// In hugger-mugger to intet him: poor Ophelia// Divided from herself and her fair judgment// Without the which we are pictures, or mere beasts."[199] In another example, "Most reporting from Kosovo still tilts toward the Albanians and against the Serbs even though, for many months, the real story has been about NATO's failure to prevent the ethnic cleansing of Serbs. Why should this be? One reason is that many of the reporters in Kosovo are old Balkan hands that first reported Serbian atrocities in Bosnia and then Serbian excesses in Kosovo. They are *hugger-mugger* with Albanian intellectuals such as the journalist Veton Surroi. Their mindset is such that they find it very difficult to see the Serbs as victims. In a sense they are reporting the last war rather than what is going on now."[200]

HUMAN INTELLIGENCE (HUMINT). (DoD, NATO.) A category of intelligence derived from information collected and provided by human sources. In the U.S. Army and Marine Corps usage, human intelligence operations cover a wide range of activities encompassing reconnaissance patrols, aircrew reports and debriefs, debriefing of refugees, interrogations of prisoners of war, and the conduct of counterintelligence force protection source operations.[201] *See also* ELICITATION; NATIONAL CLANDESTINE SERVICE; SOURCES OF INTELLIGENCE.

HUMANITARIAN EARLY WARNING SYSTEM (HEWS). Developed in 1994 in the United Nations' Department of Humanitarian Affairs. HEWS was the first database program designed primarily to collect quantitative information on a number of countries highly susceptible to complex emergencies. However, due to a shortage of personnel to update and maintain the database this system became a major disappointment and it was unable to provide sufficient early warning.[202] *See also* GLOBAL INFORMATION AND EARLY WARNING SYSTEM ON FOOD AND AGRICULTURE; WEB SITES, ACTIVE EARLY WARNING SYSTEMS: HUMANITARIAN EARLY WARNING SYSTEM.

HYPOTHESIS. 1. Something assumed for the purpose of argument; a theory to be later proven or disproven. 2. A general proposition put forward as a possible explanation for known facts from which additional investigations can be planned to generate evidential data that will tend to strengthen or weaken the basis for accepting the proposition as the best or strongest explanation of the available information. *See also* ASSESSMENT; CONCLUSION; DEDUCTIVE LOGIC; HYPOTHESIS TESTING; INDUCTIVE LOGIC; INFERENCE.

HYPOTHESIS TESTING. The selection of evidence and the asking of questions which will search for evidence that can strengthen or weaken various propositions. *See also* CONCLUSION; DEDUCTIVE LOGIC; HYPOTHESIS; INDUCTIVE LOGIC; INFERENCE.

– I –

IMAGERY INTELLIGENCE (IMINT). Representations of objects reproduced electronically or by optical means on film, electronic display devices, or other media; usually derived from visual photography, radar sensors, infrared sensors, lasers, and electro-optics. The National Geospatinal-Intelligence Agency manages all imagery intelligence activities in the U.S. Intelligence Community, to include collection, processing, exploitation, dissemination, archiving, and retrieval. *See also* SOURCES OF INTELLIGENCE.

IMMEDIATE MESSAGE. A precedence category reserved for messages relating to situations that gravely affect the security of national or allied forces or people and requires immediate delivery to the addressees.

INCIDENT. An event directly affecting a country's personnel or interests that may have broader repercussions and lead to a crisis.

INCIDENT MANAGEMENT SYSTEM (IMS). Integrates practices in emergency preparedness and response into a comprehensive national framework to enable responders at the local, state, and federal levels to effectively manage domestic incidents regardless of the cause, size, or complexity. The goals of the NIMS are to:

- Standardize organizational structures, processes, and procedures
- Standardize training, exercising, and personnel qualifications
- Standardize equipment acquisition and certification
- Create interoperable communications processes, procedures, and systems
- Support technologies—voice and data communications systems, information systems, data display systems, and specialized technologies

INDICATION. A specific act or decision an enemy has taken as part of an aggressive action. An expected action or decision that if, or when, it occurs, signifies the unfolding of a threatening scenario. *See also* INDICATOR; INTENTION; SIGNPOSTS.

INDICATIONS ANALYSIS. A deductive process for evaluating the significance of observed intelligence against an established list of indicators to signify an increase in the hostile policy/attitudes of an aggressor. These factors are logical or plausible moves or acts, based on Western reasoning or observed during past conflicts or crises, or based on the results of intelligence assessments of enemy strategic offensive military doctrine and strategic standard operating procedures.

INDICATIONS AND WARNING (I&W). A generic term usually associated with intelligence activities needed to detect and report time-sensitive knowledge of foreign events that could threaten a country's allies, its citizens abroad, or the country's military, economic, or political interests.[203]

INDICATIONS AND WARNING INTELLIGENCE. Information that alerts or warns of an impending course of action by a foreign power that is detrimental to the interests of a country. This information is the product of recognition and correlation of threat indications and the synthesis of a threat posture.[204]

INDICATIONS AND WARNING SYSTEMS. A network of intelligence production facilities with analytical resources capable of contributing to or developing **indications and warning intelligence,** and disseminating this product within their own command and to other facilities, organizations, or commands.

INDICATIONS CENTER. An intelligence situation room distinguished by around-the-clock operations, comprehensive communications, concentration on all aspects of possible enemy attack or other situations which might require action by the military, and adherence to procedures established for operation within an **indications and warning system**. Sometimes it may be the focal point for performing the operational intelligence functions for a command. *See also* ALERT CENTER; WARNING CENTER; WATCH CENTER.

INDICATIONS WATCH OFFICER. An intelligence **watch officer** or duty officer who serves in an **indications center**; trained to identify indications of hostilities and cope with other intelligence matters requiring immediate action.[205]

INDICATOR. A generalized, theoretical statement of a course of action or decision that is expected to be taken in preparation for an aggressive act and that can be used to guide intelligence collection resources. Commonly, *indicators* are developed from enemy doctrine, or from previous military operations or exercises, and an analyst's ability to apply logic and common sense. "The progress that the Government of Lebanon is making in counternarcotics through the steps being taken toward acceding to the 1988 Convention on Narcotics and the drafting of laws addressing money laundering schemes, constitute grounds for cautious optimism. The willingness of the Government of Lebanon to pursue the prosecution of a member of Parliament is another indicator of its increased seriousness in its counternarcotics efforts."[206]

INDICATOR, CRITICAL (ALSO KNOWN AS KEY INDICATORS). Those actions or decisions that will immediately and directly affect a threat scenario; constitute a small portion of the overall number of **indicators** which can easily be monitored. "Detection of excessive ammunition production and export would be a *critical indicator* of impending armed conflict, since no military operation can succeed without adequate ammunition supplies, despite adequate numbers of weapons."[207]

INDICATOR, FINAL. That event, action, or decision prior to the anticipated deed or battle; used in economics, it measures the effect of an intervention on an individual's well-being, and can sometimes be divided into outcome and impact indicators.[208] *See also* INDICATOR, IMPACT; INDICATOR, OUTCOME.

INDICATOR, HARD. Any generalized, theoretical action, usually focusing on capabilities that can be linked without a doubt to intentions of an aggressor. For example, the forward deployment of tanks, armored personnel carriers, or the sudden expansion of medical facilities or beds in a hospital would be *hard indicators* that a target country is planning, without a doubt, aggressive action. *See also* INDICATOR, SOFT.

INDICATOR, IMPACT. Used in economics, this measures key dimensions of well-being such as freedom from hunger, literacy, good health, empowerment, and security.[209]

INDICATOR, INPUT. Used in economics, it measures the financial and physical resources dedicated to a goal.[210]

INDICATOR, INTERMEDIATE. An event, action, or decision that contributes to the process of achieving a chosen final path or goal; used in economics, these are divided into "input" or "output" indicators, depending on the process. *See also* INDICATOR, INPUT; INDICATOR, OUTPUT.

INDICATOR, OUTCOME. Used in economics; capture access to, use of, and satisfaction with public services; access to credit; representation in political institutions; and so on. These are not dimensions of well-being themselves, but are key elements that contribute toward well-being.[211]

INDICATOR, OUTPUT. Used in economics, measures the goods and services that are produced by the inputs.

INDICATOR, SOFT. A generalized, theoretical action that focuses on capabilities and may be linked to possible intentions of an aggressor. For example, an increase in the number of military personnel for a scheduled training exercise would be a *soft indicator* that the country may be planning to go to war. *See also* INDICATOR, HARD.

INDICATOR ELEMENT. A term used mostly in communications and signals intelligence analysis to distinguish message traffic; not considered a strategic indications and warning term.

INDICATOR LIST (IL). A list of the factors or acts (military, political, economic, diplomatic, and internal actions) an enemy might be expected to take if it intended to initiate hostilities; these factors are logical/plausible moves or acts based on ostensible evidence, that have been observed during past conflicts and crises, and that result from intelligence assessments of enemy strategic offensive military doctrine and strategic-level standard operating procedures.

INDICATOR ORGANIZATION. A counterintelligence term for a model group or organization that represents several other groups or organizations seeking the same political or ideological goals. In instances where counterintelligence and security assets are limited, the prototype would be targeted for extensive surveillance, and the results would be considered applicable to the other organizations in the set.

INDUCTIVE LOGIC. 1. Reasoning from the specific to the general. 2. A method of inference by which a more general belief is developed by observing a limited set of observations or instances. 3. Inferences are made in generalized conclusions from particular instances. They go beyond what is known in the key facts or premises. For example, if premise 1 is that Socrates is a man and premise 2 is that Socrates is strong, the inference is that all men are strong. *See also* CONCLUSION; DEDUCTIVE LOGIC; HYPOTHESIS; INFERENCE.

INFERENCE. 1. Conclusions derived from facts or from other inferences such as forecasts, predictions, extrapolations, and estimates; a conclusion that is logically drawn after reviewing certain facts or premises; a deduction. 2. The reasoning process that creates, modifies, and maintains belief and in which we reason from evidence toward conclusions. *See also* ARGUMENT; CONCLUSION; DEDUCTIVE LOGIC; HYPOTHESIS; INDUCTIVE LOGIC; INFERENCE NETWORK.

INFERENCE NETWORK. Directed acyclic graphs whose nodes indicate propositions and whose arcs represent probabilistic linkages among those nodes. *See also* ARGUMENT; CONCLUSION; DEDUCTIVE LOGIC; HYPOTHESIS; INDUCTIVE LOGIC; INFERENCE.

INFERENTIAL ANALYSIS. The use of collected relevant data sets (evidence) to infer and synthesize explanations that describe the *meaning* of the underlying data.[212] *See also* DESCRIPTIVE ANALYSIS.

INFORMATION. 1. Unevaluated material, at all levels of reliability and from any source, which may contain intelligence information. To distinguish between information and intelligence, information is data that have been collected but not further developed through analysis, interpretation, or correlation with other data and intelligence. The application of analysis transforms information into intelligence; both information and intelligence are important, and both may exist together in some form. They are not, however, the same thing, and thus they have different connotations, applicability, and credibility.[213] 2. Any communication or representation of knowledge such as facts, data, or opinions in any medium or form, including textual, numerical, graphic, cartographic, narrative, or audiovisual. 3. Any knowledge that can be communicated or documentary material, regardless of its physical form or characteristics, which is owned by, produced by or for, or is under the control of the United States government. 4. Knowledge that can be communicated by any means.[214]

INFORMATION ANALYSIS AND INFRASTRUCTURE PROTECTION (IAIP). Consists of all Department of Homeland Security capabilities to identify and assess current and future threats, mapped to vulnerabilities, with the purpose of producing timely, actionable warning, prevention, and protective action. The directorate represents the DHS part in the IC (Intelligence Community) of agencies, and will primarily be a consumer of CIA, NSA, and FBI intelligence products, but will also issue sector-specific advisories, warnings, guidelines, and best practices. Personnel size is approximately 200 analysts. *See also* COUNTERTERRORISM CENTER; JOINT TERRORISM TASK FORCE; TERRORIST THREAT INTEGRATION CENTER.

INFORMATION ASSURANCE. Information operations that protect and defend information and information systems by ensuring their availability, integrity, authentication, confidentiality, and non-repudiation.

INFORMATION ATTACK. Directly corrupting information without visibly changing the physical entity within which it resides.[215]

INFORMATION DOMINANCE. The degree of information superiority that allows the possessor to use information systems and capabilities to achieve an operational advantage in a conflict or to control the situation in operations other than war while denying those capabilities to the adversary.[216]

INFORMATION ENVIRONMENT. 1. Aggregate of individuals, organizations, or systems that collect, process, or **disseminate** information; also included is the information itself. 2. (DoD) The aggregate of individuals, organizations, or systems that collect, process, or disseminate information; also included is the information itself.[217]

INFORMATION EXPLOITATION OFFICE (IXO). Responsible for developing technologies for sensing, exploitation, command/control, and information integration.

INFORMATION FRATRICIDE. The results of employing information operations elements in a way that causes effects in the information environment that impede the conduct of friendly operations or cause adverse effects on friendly forces.[218]

INFORMATION FUNCTION. Any activity involving the acquisition, transmission, storage, or transformation of information.

INFORMATION GATHERING AND ANALYSIS. 1. The specific actions taken to gain information about a system element or critical acquisition process for which the level of knowledge is insufficient to permit an informed decision to be made with respect to other risk-handling options.[219]

INFORMATION LIFE CYCLE. Thirteen stages through which information passes, typically characterized as creation or collection, processing, dissemination, use, storage, and disposition:

1. Created and produced (by authors in all agencies, in all branches, at all levels, and in many different formats and mediums).
2. Cataloged and indexed (metadata tools applied).
3. Temporary and permanent availability and entitlement established (ownership and disclosure rights of creators, publishers, disseminators, licensees, franchisees).
4. Published in the public domain or withheld from disclosure pursuant to a wide variety of statutes, internal agency policies, foreign agreements, and so forth.

5. Put into files, databases, collections, holdings, and other storage repositories.
6. Communicated, disseminated, and distributed.
7. Searched for and retrieved (full text, abstracts, key words).
8. Used for decision making and problem solving.
9. Archived.
10. Re-used over and over again by government officials, journalists, archivists, researchers, citizens, and others (information recycled).
11. Disposed of (temporarily or permanently).
12. Expunged or destroyed if permanent retention period exceeded.
13. Need for new information to replace old information established.[220]

INFORMATION MANAGEMENT. Provision of relevant information to the right person at the right time in a usable form to facilitate situational understanding and decision making. It uses procedures and information systems to collect, process, store, display, and **disseminate** information.[221]

INFORMATION OPERATIONS (IO). 1. Actions taken to affect adversary information and information systems while defending one's own information and information systems. 2. Any action involving the acquisition, transmission, storage, or transformation of information that enhances the employment of military forces. 3. (DoD) Actions taken to affect adversary information and information systems while defending one's own information and information systems. (Army) The employment of the core capabilities of electronic warfare, computer network operations, psychological operations, military deception, and operations security, in concert with specified supporting and related capabilities, to affect and defend information and information systems and to influence decision making.[222]

INFORMATION OWNER. An official with statutory or operational authority for specified information and responsibility for establishing the controls for its generation, collection, processing, dissemination, and disposal.[223]

INFORMATION REQUIREMENTS (IR). Those items of information regarding the enemy and his or her environment which need to be collected and processed in order to meet the intelligence requirements of a commander. (Army) All information elements the commander and staff require to successfully conduct operations.[224]

INFORMATION RESOURCES MANAGEMENT (IRM). The planning, budgeting, organizing, directing, training, controlling, and management activities associated with the burden, collection, creation, use, and dissemination of information by agencies. The term includes the management of information and related resources, such as federal information processing resources. Information resources management planning is an integral part of overall mission planning. Agencies need to plan from the outset for the steps in the **information life cycle.** When creating or collecting information, agencies must plan how they will process and transmit the information, how they will use it, how they will protect its integrity, what provisions they will make for access to it, whether and how they will **disseminate** it, how they will store and retrieve it, and finally, how the information will ultimately be disposed of.[225]

INFORMATION SECURITY (INFOSEC). 1. Protection of unauthorized access to or modification of information, whether in storage, processing, or transit, and against the denial of service to authorized users or the provision of service to unauthorized users, including those measures necessary to detect, document, and counter such threats. 2. The protection and defense of information and information systems against unauthorized access or modification of information, whether in storage, processing, or transit, and against the denial of service to authorized users. Information security includes those measures necessary to detect, document, and counter such threats. Information security is composed of computer security and communications security. 3. Protecting information and information systems from unauthorized **access,** use, disclosure, disruption, modification, or destruction in order to provide:

(A) integrity, which means guarding against improper information modification or destruction, and includes ensuring information nonrepudiation and authenticity

(B) confidentiality, which means preserving authorized restrictions on access and disclosure, including means for protecting personal privacy and proprietary information

(C) availability, which means ensuring timely and reliable access to and use of information

(D) authentication, which means utilizing digital credentials to assure the identity of users and validate their access.[226]

INFORMATION SECURITY OVERSIGHT OFFICE (ISOO). An agency within the National Archives and Records Administration (NARA), the ISOO develops security classification policies (including classifying, declassifying, and safeguarding national security information or information generated within the federal government and industry, including the National Industrial Security Program (NISP); ISOO receives its policy and program guidance from the National Security Council. ISOO evaluates the effectiveness of the security classification programs established by government and industry to protect information vital to "national security interests." ISOO authority rests with Executive Order 12958.[227]

INFORMATION SHARING. The term "information sharing" suggests that the federal government entity that collects the information "owns" it and can decide whether or not to "share" it with others—a concept deeply embedded in the Intelligence Community's culture. This concept should be rejected. Information collected by the Intelligence Community—or for that matter, any government agency—belongs to the U.S. government. Officials are fiduciaries who hold the information in trust for the nation. They do not have authority to withhold or distribute it except as such authority is delegated by the President or provided by law. As noted elsewhere, the Director of National Intelligence should take an important, symbolic first step toward changing the Intelligence Community's culture by jettisoning this term—perhaps in favor of the term "information integration" or "information access."[228]

INFORMATION SHARING AND ANALYSIS ORGANIZATION (ISAO). Any formal or informal entity or collaboration created or employed by public or private sector organizations for purposes of:

1. Gathering and analyzing CII in order to better understand security problems and interdependencies related to critical infrastructure and protected systems in order to ensure the availability, integrity, and reliability thereof
2. Communicating or sharing CII to help prevent, detect, mitigate, or recover from the effects of an interference, compromise, or incapacitation problem related to critical infrastructure or protected systems
3. Voluntarily disseminating CII to its members, federal, state, and local governments, or to any other entities that may be of assistance in carrying out the purposes specified in this section.[229]

INFORMATION SUPERIORITY (IS). 1. Capability to collect, process, and **disseminate** an uninterrupted flow of information while exploiting or denying an adversary's ability to do the same. 2. That degree of dominance in the information domain which permits the conduct of operations without effective opposition. (Army) The operational advantage derived from the ability to collect, process, and disseminate an uninterrupted flow of information while exploiting or denying an adversary's ability to do the same.[230]

INFORMATION SYSTEM (IS, ALSO CALLED INFOSYS). 1. A discrete set of information resources (e.g., personnel, data, software, computers, and communications equipment) organized for the collection, processing, maintenance, use, sharing, dissemination, or disposition of information. 2. The entire infrastructure, organization, personnel, and components that collect, process, store, transmit, display, **disseminate**, and act on information. (Army) The equipment and facilities that collect, process, store, display, and disseminate information. This includes computers—hardware and software—and communications, as well as policies and procedures for their use.[231]

INFORMATION WARFARE (IW). 1. Actions taken to achieve information superiority by affecting adversary information, information-based processes, and information systems, while defending one's own information, information-based processes, and information systems and computer-based networks. 2. The use of information to achieve our national objectives. 3. Any action to deny, exploit, corrupt, or destroy the enemy's information and its functions; protecting ourselves against those actions; and exploiting our own military information functions.[232]

INFORMATION WARRIOR. A new breed of soldier to be created within the military. This soldier would be a part of an Information Corps that would "promote jointness where it is critically needed (information interoperability), elevate information as an element of war, develop an information warrior ethos and curriculum, and heighten DOD attention to the global civilian net." According to Martin C. Libicki, "this brave new soldier would not only be sent into the information battlefield, but would also be involved in intelligence-based warfare (which consists of the design, protection, and denial of systems that seek sufficient knowledge to dominate the battlespace."[233]

INFORMED COMPLIANCE. The concepts of "informed compliance" and "shared responsibility" were introduced into the Tariff Act of 1930 and Title VI of the North American Free Trade Agreement Implementation Act (NAFTA). Under Section 484 of the Tariff Act, as amended, 19 U.S.C. Section 1484, it is up to the importer of record to ensure "reasonable care to enter, classify and value imported merchandise, and provide any other information necessary to enable Customs to properly assess duties, collect accurate statistics and determine whether any other applicable legal requirement is met."[234]

INFORMED CONSENT. 1. Basic elements of *informed consent.* In seeking *informed consent,* the following information shall be provided to each subject:

(A) A statement that the study involves research, an explanation of the purposes of the research and the expected duration of the subject's participation, a description of the procedures to be followed, and identification of any procedures which are experimental.

(B) A description of any reasonably foreseeable risks or discomforts to the subject. Respect for persons requires that subjects, to the degree that they are capable, be given the opportunity to choose what shall or shall not happen to them. This opportunity is provided when adequate standards for informed consent are satisfied. While the importance of informed consent is unquestioned, controversy prevails over the nature and possibility of an informed consent. Nonetheless, there is widespread agreement that the consent process can be analyzed as containing three elements: information, comprehension, and voluntariness.

Most codes of research establish specific items for disclosure intended to assure that subjects are given sufficient information. These items generally include: the research procedures, their purposes, risks, and anticipated benefits, alternative procedures (where therapy is involved), and a statement offering the subject the opportunity to ask questions and to withdraw at any time from the research. Additional items have been proposed, including how subjects are selected, the person responsible for the research, etc.[235]

INFOSPHERE. Cyberspace relating to internetted computers, communications infrastructure, online conferencing entities, databases and information utilities, and a "fifth dimension" of war which has been traditionally fought on land, air, and sea. Space control of the infosphere is defined as the ability to use the infosphere for the furtherance of strategic objectives and the ability of the enemy to do the same.[236]

INFRARED INTELLIGENCE (IRINT). *See* SOURCES OF INTELLIGENCE.

INFRASTRUCTURE ATTACK. An attack designed to significantly compromise the function of a whole infrastructure rather than individual components. "*Attacks against infrastructure* are relatively new and are of interest in the study of information warfare. In considering infrastructure vulnerabilities, threats to both individual systems and the infrastructure itself must be evaluated when considering criminal activity. Both share similar enablers as a pre-requisite to compromise; however, *infrastructure attacks* require a more concerted and coordinated effort and provide better data points for indicator and warning analysis."[237]

INSTABILITY INDICATOR (I².) At the strategic level it is a key action, decision, or event that can impact the stability of governance for a specific location at the local or national level, while at the tactical level it is a specific issue or factor that may represent a potential threat to a unit's operations and protection. *See also* INDICATOR.

INSTRUMENTS OF NATIONAL POWER. All of the means available to the government in its pursuit of national objectives. They are expressed as diplomatic, economic, informational, and military.[238]

INTEGRITY (OF INFORMATION). 1. Keeping information accurate, i.e., keeping it from being modified or corrupted. 2. The security of information—protection of the information from unauthorized access or revision, to ensure that the information is not compromised through corruption or falsification. 3. The state that exists when information is unchanged from its source and has not been accidentally or intentionally modified, altered, or destroyed.[239]

INTELINK. Began testbed operation in 1994; is both an architectural framework and an integrated intelligence dissemination and collaboration service providing uniform methods for exchanging intelligence among intelligence providers and users. The Intelink framework conforms to the future direction of the National Information Infrastructure (NII). The Intelink service was patterned after the Internet model in which a variety of institutions have come together in the context of a global network to share information. The Intelink intelligence network links information in the various classified databases of the U.S. intelligence agencies (e.g., FBI, CIA, DEA, NSA, USSS, NRO) to facilitate communication and the sharing of documents and other resources.[240]

INTELLIGENCE. A body of information and the conclusions drawn therefrom that is acquired and furnished in response to the known or perceived requirements of customers; it is often derived from information that may be concealed or not intended to be available for use by the acquirer; it is the product of a cyclical process. A term to refer collectively to the function, activities, or organizations that are involved in the process of planning, gathering, and analyzing information of potential value to decision makers and to the production of intelligence. The product resulting from the collection, collation, evaluation, analysis, integration, and interpretation of all collected information.[241]

INTELLIGENCE ACTIVITY. An activity that an agency within the Intelligence Community is authorized to conduct.[242]

INTELLIGENCE ANALYSIS. 1. A process by which intelligence is produced and which reflects allegiance to the methods of rigor and precision, science, and logical techniques in order to illuminate and interpret (value-adding) the nature and implication of concepts and information; 2. A process that reflects demonstrable reasoning and procedures. *See also* INFORMATION; INTELLIGENCE DATA; INTELLIGENCE (AS A) PRODUCT.

INTELLIGENCE ASSESSMENT. A phenomenon that encompasses most analytical studies dealing with subjects of policy significance; thorough in its treatment of subject matter but, unlike **estimative intelligence,** an assessment may not attempt to project future developments and their implications; usually coordinated within the producing organization but may not be coordinated with other intelligence agencies. *See also* ESTIMATIVE INTELLIGENCE.

INTELLIGENCE COLLECTION PLAN. A plan for gathering information from all available sources to meet an intelligence requirement. Specifically, a logical plan for transforming specific requests for information (possible indicators) into orders to collection sources within a required time limit. *See also* INDICATOR; SCENARIO.

INTELLIGENCE COMMUNITY. As identified in Executive Order 12333, the terms "intelligence community" and "agency, or agencies within the intelligence community" refer to the following organizations: the Central Intelligence Agency, the National Security Agency, the Defense Intelligence Agency, Offices within the Department of Defense for the collection of specialized national foreign intelligence through reconnaissance programs, the Bureau of Intelligence and Research of the Department of State, the intelligence elements of the military services (Army, Navy, Air Force, and Marine Corps), the Federal Bureau of Investigation, the Department of the Treasury, the Department of Energy, the Drug Enforcement Administration, and staff elements of the Central Intelligence Agency.[243] 2. The IC is a federation of 16 executive branch agencies and organizations that work separately and together to conduct intelligence activities necessary for the conduct of foreign relations and the protection of the national security of the United States. These activities include:

> Collection of information needed by the President, the National Security Council, the Secretaries of State and Defense, and other Executive Branch officials for the performance of their duties and responsibilities; production and dissemination of intelligence; collection of information concerning, and the conduct of activities to protect against, intelligence activities directed against the US, international terrorist and international narcotics activities, and other hostile activities directed against the US by foreign powers, organizations, persons, and their agents; special activities; administrative and support activities within the US and abroad necessary for the performance of authorized activities; and such other intelligence activities as the President may direct from time to time. Members of the IC are: Central Intelligence Agency (CIA); within the DoD, the National Security Agency (NSA), the National Reconnaissance Office (NRO), and the National Geospatial-Intelligence Agency (NGA), the Defense Intelligence Agency (DIA); State Department's Bureau of Intelligence and Research (INR); Federal Bureau of Investigation (FBI); intelligence organizations of the four military services (Air Force, Army, Navy, and Marines); Department of Homeland Security (DHS); Coast Guard, now part of DHS; Energy Department; Department of the Treasury; and Drug Enforcement Agency (DEA).[244]

INTELLIGENCE CYCLE. 1. The process by which information is acquired and converted into intelligence and made available to customers. 2. The process of tasking, collecting, processing, analyzing, and disseminating intelligence is called the *intelligence cycle*. The intelligence cycle drives the day-to-day activities of the Intelligence Community. It starts with the needs of those who are often referred to within the Intelligence Community as intelligence "consumers"—that is, policymakers, military officials, and other decision makers who need intelligence information in conducting their duties and responsibilities. These needs—also referred to as intelligence requirements—are sorted and prioritized within the Intelligence Community, and are used to drive the collection activities of the members of the Intelligence Community that collect intelligence. Once information has been collected it is processed, initially evaluated, and reported to both consumers and so-called all-source intelligence analysts at agencies like the CIA, DIA, and the State Department's Bureau of Intelligence and Research. All-source analysts are responsible for performing a more thorough evaluation and assessment of the collected information by integrating the data obtained from a variety of collection agencies and sources—both classified and unclassified. This assessment leads to a finished intelligence report being disseminated to the consumer. The "feedback" part of the cycle assesses the degree to which the finished intelligence addresses the needs of the intelligence consumer and will determine if further collection and analysis are required.[245] Following are the five steps of the intelligence cycle:

1: Planning and direction. Determining the intelligence requirements, preparing a collection plan, issuing orders and requests to information collection entities, and continuously checking on the productivity of the collection entities.

2: Collection. Acquiring information and providing this information to processing and/or production elements.

3: Processing. Converting collected information into a form more suitable for the production of intelligence.

4: Production. Converting information into finished intelligence through the integration, analysis, evaluation, and interpretation of all available data and the preparation of intelligence products in support of known or anticipated customer requirements.

5: Dissemination. Conveying intelligence in suitable form to customers.

INTELLIGENCE DATA. Extracted from a variety of sensing devices, objects, emanations, documents, and records. *See also* INFORMATION INTELLIGENCE ANALYSIS; INTELLIGENCE (AS A) PRODUCT.

INTELLIGENCE DAY (I-DAY). The day on which the Intelligence Community determines that, within a potential crisis situation, a development occurs which may signal a heightened threat, although the scope and direction of the threat may be ambiguous. The Intelligence Community responds by focusing collection and other resources to monitor and report on the situation as it evolves.

INTELLIGENCE ESTIMATE. An appraisal of elements of intelligence relating to a specific situation or condition in order to determine a target's courses of action, as well as their probable order of adoption; a prediction of future events, developments, or courses of action and their implications and consequences. *See also* NATIONAL INTELLIGENCE ESTIMATE.

INTELLIGENCE FAILURE. Often used to lay blame on the Intelligence Community when an unexpected event or action occurs that may have an impact on U.S. foreign policy; any misunderstanding of a situation that leads a government or its military forces to take actions that are inappropriate and counterproductive to its own interests.[246] However, not all intelligence failures are warning failures. An intelligence failure encompasses all or parts of the intelligence process and system. "Despite our best intentions, the system is sufficiently dysfunctional that intelligence failure is guaranteed. Though the form is less important than the fact, the variations are endless. Failure may be of the traditional variety: we fail to predict the fall of a friendly government; we do not provide sufficient warning of a surprise attack against one of our allies or interests; we are completely surprised by a state-sponsored terrorist attack; or we fail to detect an unexpected country acquiring a weapon of mass destruction. Or it may take a more nontraditional form: we overstate numerous threats leading to tens of billions of dollars of unnecessary expenditures; database errors lead to a politically unacceptable number of casualties in a peace-enforcement operation; or an operation does not go well because the IC is not able to provide the incredibly specific data necessary to support a new generation of weapons. In the end, we may not suffer a Pearl Harbor, but simply succumb to a series of mistakes."[247] "While these surprises have often been cited as intelligence failures [italics added]—and admittedly there were some serious inadequacies in collection and assessment—gross misperceptions and errors in judgment by policymakers and military command were the real causes of failure. There is no better example of the principle that warning is useless unless it results in action to forestall disaster."[248] *See also* WARNING FAILURE.

INTELLIGENCE INFORMATION. 1. Information and knowledge about an adversary obtained through observation, investigation, analysis, or understanding. 2. Information that is under the jurisdiction and control of the Director of Central Intelligence or a member of the Intelligence Community; information on intelligence community protective security programs (e.g., personnel, physical, technical, and information security). 3. Information describing U.S. foreign intelligence and counterintelligence activities, sources, methods, equipment, or methodology used for the acquisition, processing, or exploitation of such intelligence; foreign military hardware obtained for exploitation; and photography or recordings resulting from U.S. intelligence collection efforts.

INTELLIGENCE INFORMATION REPORT (IIR). The primary vehicle to provide human intelligence information to the consumer by using a standardized message format which can easily be included in a database.[249]

INTELLIGENCE JOURNAL. A permanent and official record that lists in chronological order those intelligence activities, reports, and messages that were received and transmitted, that have occurred, and the actions that were taken.

INTELLIGENCE LEVELS. The levels of intelligence correspond to the established levels of war: **strategic**, **operational**, and **tactical**. Like the levels of war, the levels of intelligence serve as a framework in which commanders and MI personnel visualize the logical flow of operations, allocation of resources, and assignment of tasks. The levels of intelligence are not tied to specific echelons but rather to the intended outcome of the operations which they support. The relationship is based upon the political and military objectives of the operation and the commander's needs.[250]

INTELLIGENCE METHOD. The method which is used to provide support to an intelligence source or operation, and which, if disclosed, is vulnerable to counteraction that could nullify or significantly reduce its effectiveness in supporting the foreign intelligence or foreign counterintelligence activities of the United States, or which would, if disclosed, reasonably lead to the disclosure of an intelligence source or operation.[251]

INTELLIGENCE OVERSIGHT BOARD (IOB). Established by President Gerald Ford in 1976 with oversight responsibility for the legality and propriety of intelligence activities. In 1993, the IOB was made a standing committee of the President's Foreign Intelligence Advisory Board. The IOB prepares reports "of intelligence activities that the IOB believes may be unlawful or contrary to Executive order or Presidential directive."[252]

INTELLIGENCE PROCESS. The process by which information is converted into intelligence and made available to users. The process consists of six interrelated intelligence operations: planning and direction, collection, processing and exploitation, analysis and production, dissemination and integration, and evaluation and feedback. *See also* ANALYSIS AND PRODUCTION; COLLECTION; INTELLIGENCE; PROCESSING AND EXPLOITATION.[253]

INTELLIGENCE (AS A) PRODUCT. 1. That which results from the collection, processing, integration, analysis, evaluation, and interpretation of available information. 2. Timely, accurate, and actionable (value-added) information about what other nations or groups, especially potential adversaries, are doing which helps policymakers, decison makers, and military leaders carry out their mission of formulating and implementing national security policy. *See also* INFORMATION; INTELLIGENCE ANALYSIS; INTELLIGENCE DATA.

INTELLIGENCE READINESS. Creation of optimal organizational and procedural conditions to manage security threats, achieved through information management for timely, expert analysis, tailored synthesis, and provision of support to consumers.[254]

INTELLIGENCE REPORT (INTREP). A specific report of information, usually on a single item, made at any level of command in tactical operations and disseminated as rapidly as possible in keeping with the timeliness of the information.[255]

INTELLIGENCE SPECIAL ACCESS PROGRAM (SAP). A program that is primarily designed to protect the planning and execution of especially sensitive intelligence, counterintelligence operations, or collection activities.[256]

INTENTION. An adversary's purpose, plan, commitment, or design for action as possibly exhibited by a leader, decision maker, nation, or a nation's foreign policy. *See also* INDICATION; INDICATOR.

INTERCEPT. Data that is obtained through the passive collection of signals or the process of interrupting access, communication, or the flow of data.

IRAN, FALL OF THE SHAH. It is incontrovertible that in 1978 a major intelligence failure occurred—of great consequence for U.S. interests—when the Intelligence Community did not warn American policymakers that the Shah was about to fall, and that there was significant chance that a fundamentalist, radically anti-Western regime would come to power in Iran. This delinquency was not the monopoly, however, of the National Intelligence Officers, or of the estimative process, or even of the entire U.S. Intelligence Community. Rather, it was a U.S. failure. In short, it was the result of certain mind-sets, shared widely throughout the government, which tended to (1) take the Shah for granted; (2) overestimate Iran's stability; (3) place domestic trends within Iran down the list of U.S. intelligence priorities there; (4) underestimate the disruptive effects of forced modernization in Iran, the growing revolutionary pressures, the increasing grievances against the West, and the embodying of these disruptive forces in a then-exile in Paris, the aged Ayatollah Khomeini; and (5) fail to consider what the enormous consequences for U.S. interests would be in the event America's ally, the Shah, did fall from power.[257]

– J –

JOINT DOCUMENT EXPLOITATION CENTER (JDEC). A physical location for deriving intelligence information from captured adversary documents, including all forms of electronic data and other forms of stored textual and graphic information.

JOINT INFORMATION BUREAU (JIB) (ALSO KNOWN AS COALITION PRESS). Facility established by the joint force commander to serve as the focal point for the interface between the military and the media during the conduct of joint operations. When operated in support of multinational operations, a joint information bureau is called a "combined information bureau" or an "allied press information center."

JOINT INTELLIGENCE OPERATIONS CENTER/COMMAND (JIOC). The USDI defers to the COCOMs on whether it is treated as a command (similar to ground, air, and sea commands) or as a center.

JOINT TERRORISM TASK FORCE (JTTF). The mission of the JTTF is to organize federal, state, and local law enforcement agencies in a coordinated manner for the purpose of detecting, preventing, and responding to domestic and international terrorist organizations and/or individuals who may threaten or attack United States citizens or interests abroad or conduct criminal activity within the United States, and/or any threat or incident involving Weapons of Mass Destruction (WMD) or the proliferation of same directed against the population or interests of the United States.[258] Developed in New York City in 1980 with 11 members from the New York Police Department and 11 FBI investigators whose goal was to be both responsive and proactive. Since September 11, 2001, the FBI has expanded the JTTF initiative from 35 JTTFs to 84 JTTFs nationwide. The FBI reported it had significantly increased the number of its Joint Terrorism Task Forces and, according to the GAO survey, 34 of 40 states and 160 of 228 cities stated that they participated in information-sharing centers.[259] The JTTF concept is widely recognized in the law enforcement community as a good idea, but civil liberty advocates are extremely critical of it.[260] *See also* COUNTERTERRORISM CENTER; INFORMATION ANALYSIS AND

INFRASTRUCTURE PROTECTION; NATIONAL JOINT TERRORISM TASK FORCE; TERRORIST THREAT INTEGRATION CENTER.

JOINT WORLDWIDE INTELLIGENCE COMMUNICATIONS SYSTEM (JWICS). The sensitive, compartmented information portion of the Defense Information Systems Network. It incorporates advanced networking technologies that permit point-to-point or multipoint information exchange involving voice, text, graphics, data, and video teleconferencing.[261]

JUDGMENT. A process of **inference;** the evaluation of one or more possibilities with respect to a specific set of evidence and criteria by which you evaluate the evidence. *See also* INFERENCE.

– K –

KEY ASSUMPTION. Any hypothesis that analysts accept to be true and which form the basis of an assessment. For example, analysts refused to accept the possible collapse of the Soviet Union because their key assumption was that the Communist Party would never relinquish control of their East European allies.

KEY DRIVERS. Variables within a threat scenario that seemingly have a dynamic influence on the environment or the success or failure of the outcome of a particular scenario. For example, as stated in *Global Trends 2015*, over the past 15 months, the National Intelligence Council (NIC), in close collaboration with U.S. government specialists and a wide range of experts outside the government, has worked to identify major *drivers* and trends that will shape the world of 2015. The *key drivers* identified are: (1) Demographics, (2) Natural resources and environment, (3) Science and technology, (4) The global economy and globalization, (5) National and international governance, (6) Future conflict, and (7) The role of the United States. In examining these *drivers*, several points should be kept in mind: No single *driver* or trend will dominate the global future in 2015. Each driver will have varying impacts in different regions and countries. The *drivers* are not necessarily mutually reinforcing; in some cases, they will work at cross-purposes. Taken together, these *drivers* and trends intersect to create an integrated picture of the world of 2015, about which we can make projections with varying degrees of confidence and identify some troubling uncertainties of strategic importance to the United States.[262]

KEY INDICATOR (ALSO KNOWN AS CRITICAL INDICATOR). Those actions or decisions that will immediately and directly affect a threat scenario, constitute a small proportion of the overall indicators, and which can easily be monitored.

KEY JUDGMENTS. Extraction of the overall situation and likely outcome based on an extensive review or research of a given situation; encapsulation of a lengthy estimate, found in the first few pages of an estimate. *See also* KEY QUESTIONS; PRINCIPAL CONCLUSIONS.

KEY QUESTIONS. Basic, "so-what" kernels of the particular estimative situation that should be fashioned at the very outset of any estimate. Framing such key questions is usually a much more difficult task than the novice might assume, and in practice many estimates have been rushed into with no clear picture of what the really essential elements of the situation were in which the policymaker would be most interested.[263] *See also* KEY JUDGMENTS; PRINCIPAL CONCLUSIONS.

KHOBAR TOWERS. A terrorist car bombing of the residence of U.S. military personnel at Khobar Towers complex in Dhahran, Saudi Arabia, on June 25, 1996, killing 19 American military personnel and wounding hundreds more. According to the official congressional report, "It exposed the shortcomings of a U.S. intelligence apparatus that left Americans unprepared for the threat that confronted them." The report raises three points which led to this intelligence failure and operational deficiencies by military leaders and policymakers: (1) intelligence was devoid of specific knowledge of the threat; (2) failures of pro-active analysis (which was mostly reactive); (3) assessments did not acknowledge their own limitations and provided a false sense of confidence in the level of the threat.[264]

KOREAN WAR. A watershed in U.S. national estimating because intelligence failed to ring alarm bells either in June 1950 when the North Koreans were about to invade South Korea, or in November when the Chinese Communists had infiltrated great numbers of combat troops into North Korea in preparation for launching a massive offensive against U.S.-UN forces. This failure to warn led to the creation of the Office of National Estimates and of a system of more effective national intelligence estimating that has endured essentially unchanged to this day.[265]

– L –

LASER INTELLIGENCE (LASINT). Technical and geo-location intelligence derived from laser systems. *See also* SOURCES OF INTELLIGENCE.

LATEST TIME INFORMATION IS OF VALUE. The time by which an intelligence organization or staff must deliver information to the requester in order to provide decision makers with timely intelligence. This must include the time anticipated for processing and disseminating that information, as well as for making the decision.[266]

LEAK. 1. A disclosure of information that has been classified under EO 10501. 2. Coined in the early twentieth century, was applied to inadvertent slips in which information was picked up by reporters. The word quickly acquired a broader, more active meeting: any calculated release of information to reporters with the stipulation that the source remains unidentified. 3. Unauthorized disclosures of classified information; a communication or physical transfer of information to an unauthorized recipient. According to Stephen Hess, there are six types of leaks:

Animus Leak. Used to settle grudges; information is released in order to cause embarrassment to another person.

Ego Leak. Giving information primarily to satisfy a sense of self.

Goodwill Leak. Information offered to "accumulate credit" as a play for a future favor.

Policy Leak. A straightforward pitch for or against a proposal using some document or insider information as the lure to get more attention than might be otherwise justified. The leak of the Pentagon Papers falls into this category.

Trial-Balloon Leak. Revealing a proposal that is under consideration in order to assess its assets and liabilities. Usually proponents have too much invested in a proposal to want to leave it to the vagaries of the press and public opinion. More likely, those who send up a trial balloon want to see it shot down, and because it is easier to generate opposition to almost anything than to build support, this is the most likely effect.

Whistleblower Leak. Usually used by career personnel; going to the press may be the last resort of frustrated civil servants who feel they cannot resolve their dispute through administrative channels. [Hess is careful to point out that whistle-blowing is not synonymous with leaking.][267]

LIMITED DISSEMINATION (LIMDIS). 1. Restrictive controls for classified information established by an original classification authority to emphasize need-to-know measures available within the regular security system. 2. Establishes measures for the protection of information beyond those involving access to classified information per se, but not so stringent as to require the establishment of a Special Access Program. It prohibits use of terminology indicating enhancements to need-to-know, such as Special Need-to-Know (SNTK), MUST KNOW, Controlled Need-to-Know (CNTK), Close Hold, or other similar security upgrade designations and associated unique security requirements such as specialized nondisclosure statements. 3. Used to identify unclassified geospatial information and data which the SECDEF may withhold from public disclosure; may only be used with UNCLASSIFIED.[268]

LINCHPIN ASSUMPTIONS. Premises that hold the argument together and warrant the validity of the conclusion. *See also* KEY DRIVERS; INDICATORS, CRITICAL.

LOCAL INDICATOR LIST. A supplementary collection guide, developed for select activities and specific commands, which can be activated whenever there exists a need to acquire I&W related information during critical periods; this list specifies local activities that can significantly impact a warning problem.

LOW PROBABILITY OF DETECTION. The result of measures used to hide or disguise intentional electromagnetic transmissions.

LOW PROBABILITY OF INTERCEPT. The result of measures to prevent the intercept of intentional electromagnetic transmissions.

– M –

M-TYPE DECEPTION. Achieving a reduction of ambiguity, as perceived by the intended target, by building attractiveness of a wrong alternative; may be more difficult than **A-type deception** because it requires time and carefully orchestrated resources to build a series of misleading false signals. A deception program may start out as an M-type ploy to confirm the adversary's expectations about what is going to happen based on what he or she expects on the basis of logic and experience. However, since most adversaries are prudent enough to consider other possibilities (of which one may be the real solution), the deceiver also may employ an A-type program to increase the number of alternatives. This, if effective, causes the deception target to spread his or her remaining resources over a number of possibilities.[269] *See also* A-TYPE DECEPTION; ACTIVE DECEPTION; DENIAL AND DECEPTION; PASSIVE DECEPTION.

MANIPULATION. A deceptive practice of quoting factual information out of context or reporting only part of a given situation. See also DECEPTION.

MASS EFFECT. Any military or terrorist activity seeking to achieve surprise and momentum on such a scale that the application of a small amount of force will have effects far greater than would be expected from such a force; maximizing the effect of surprise and by selecting a point of application of force that will have the most effect on an adversary. *See also* WEAPONS OF MASS EFFECT.

MEASUREMENT AND SIGNATURE INTELLIGENCE (MASINT). Technically derived intelligence data other than imagery and signals intelligence that locates, identifies, or describes distinctive characteristics of targets. Several disciplines are involved, including nuclear, optical, radio frequency, acoustics, seismic, and materials sciences. "Examples of this might be the distinctive radar signatures of specific aircraft systems or the chemical composition of air and water samples. The MASINT and Technical Collection Directorate, a component of DIA, is responsible for all national and DoD MASINT matters." *See also* SOURCES OF INTELLIGENCE.

MEDICAL INTELLIGENCE (MEDINT). That category of intelligence resulting from collection, evaluation, analysis, and interpretation of foreign medical, bio-scientific, and environmental information that is of interest to strategic planning and military medical planning and operations for the conservation of the fighting strength of friendly forces and the formation of assessments of foreign medical capabilities in both military and civilian sectors.[270]

MEMORANDUM OF AGREEMENT/UNDERSTANDING (MOA/MOU). Establishes a mechanism for cooperation by agreement that describes, often in minute detail, policies, procedures, and specifics. For example, in relation to the Joint Terrorism Task Forces, MOUs and MOAs are signed by lead federal agencies, and spell out the details of state and local activities.[271]

METT-TC. A memory aid used in two contexts: (1) In the context of information management, the major subject categories into which relevant information is grouped for military operations: mission, enemy, terrain and weather, troops and support available, time available, civil considerations. (2) In the context of tactics, the major factors considered during mission analysis. [Note: The Marine Corps uses METT-T: mission, enemy, terrain and weather, troops and support available, time available.][272]

MILITARY INTELLIGENCE. In the context of warning, this term means information that is analyzed, evaluated, and interpreted and that describes and defines a nation's military capabilities for both offensive and defensive postures. Information used to estimate the probable use of military strategy, tactics, and doctrine; provides decision makers, planners, and commanders with data needed to choose courses of action required to counter foreign military threats, and to conduct operations if necessary.

MILITARY STANDARD 882, U.S. Refers to U.S. military document that outlines the probability levels of an undesired event and the severity levels of undesired event consequences as established by the Department of Defense's Military Standard 882C, System Safety Program Requirements. A risk assessment team also assigns values to key assets. Refer to tables 2 and 3. *See also* ESTIMATIVE PROBABILITY.

MIRROR-IMAGING. A belief that leaders of a nation will behave in the same manner as leaders of another nation, particularly in a tense and confusing situation. For example: *mirror-imaging* occurred prior to the bomb-

Table 2.   Probability levels of undesired events.

Probability Level	Specific Event
1. Catastrophic	Death, system loss, or severe environmental damage
2. Critical	Severe injury or occupational illness, major system or environmental damage
3. Marginal	Minor injury or occupational illness, minor system or environmental damage
4. Negligible	Less than minor injury, occupational illness, or system or environmental damage

Table 3. Severity levels of undesired event consequences.

Severity Level	Characteristics
A. Frequent	Likely to occur frequently
B. Probable	Will occur several times
C. Occasional	Likely to occur sometime
D. Remote	Unlikely but possible to occur
E. Improbable	So unlikely it can be assumed that occurrence will not be experienced

ing of the U.S. Naval Base in Pearl Harbor in 1941 when U.S. personnel reasoned that the United States had far greater military, economic, and industrial strength than Japan; thus the Japanese would recognize that they could not win a war against this country. In a sense, U.S. analysts perceived a Japanese attack as irrational based on American perceptions and assumptions.[273]

MISSILE GAP. American perception during the 1960 presidential campaign, fueled by candidate John F. Kennedy, that a gap existed or would soon exist between the number of U.S. intercontinental ballistic missiles (ICBM) and the operational number of Soviet ICBMs. Reportedly, a U.S. Air Force estimate had 600–800 Soviet missiles, CIA had an estimate of 450 missiles, and the U.S. Navy had an estimate of 200 missiles. Proponents of the *missile gap* thesis were able to put public pressure to increase defense spending and a greater procurement of newer ICBMs. Over time the differences in estimates of Soviet ICBM force levels were attributed to differing methodologies, changes in information collection, and varying strategic perceptions by the agencies involved.[274] *See also* CUBAN MISSILE CRISIS.

MISSION CREEP. Any military mission lacking clear goals or objectives that in the continuance of that mission slowly evolves into additional duties and responsibilities. Not to be confused with the term **creeping normalcy.** "National-level orders may contain internal inconsistencies that make a mission especially difficult or even impossible. By analyzing their directives, commanders can (though the literature suggests they rarely do) largely predict what the courses of their operations will be if guidance is not modified. Flawed specifications lead, if not to failure, to changes in missions while they are in progress. The United States has a term for such adjustment to intelligence, policy, planning, and operational shortcomings: *mission creep*.[275] *See also* CREEPING NORMALCY.

MURKY INTELLIGENCE. Of questionable reliability or validity; information that cannot be placed in the context of typical routine analysis to determine its worth. For example,

> United States Deputy Defense Secretary Paul Wolfowitz has said the use of *murky intelligence* is justified in the war on terror, if it prevents future attacks. He was interviewed by several US television networks following a congressional report which concluded the 11 September attacks could have been prevented if security services had shared and acted upon information. "The lesson of 9-11 is that, if you're not prepared to act on the basis of *murky intelligence*, then you're going to have to act after the fact," he said.[276]

See also ACTIONABLE INTELLIGENCE.

– N –

NATIONAL CLANDESTINE SERVICE (NCS). Within the CIA to coordinate U.S. HUMINT (**human intelligence**) efforts; intended to make the CIA Director "national HUMINT manager" for all 15 intelligence agencies; to improve cooperation among the spy agencies, as well as streamline the flow of information to elected officials. The 9/11 Commission ("Kean Commission") also recommended that the CIA Director should emphasize (a) rebuilding the CIA's analytic capabilities; (b) transform the clandestine service by building its human intelligence capabilities; (c) develop a stronger language program, with high standards and sufficient financial incentives; (d) renew emphasis on recruiting diversity among operations officers so they can blend more easily in foreign cities; (e) ensure a seamless relationship between human source collection and signals collection at the operational level; and (f) stress a better balance between unilateral and liaison operations.[277]

NATIONAL COMMUNICATION SYSTEM. Connects the President, the National Security Council, the Director of the Office of Science and Technology Policy, and the Director of the Office of Management and Budget in the implementation of the telecommunications functions and responsibilities, and the coordination of the planning for and provision of national security and emergency preparedness communications for the federal government under crisis or emergency situations.

NATIONAL CRIMINAL INTELLIGENCE SHARING PLAN (NCISP). Developed by the Global Intelligence Working Group (GIWG) and endorsed by U.S. Attorney General John Ashcroft, U.S. Department of Justice (DOJ), the National Criminal Intelligence Sharing Plan ("Plan") is a formal intelligence sharing initiative that addresses the security and intelligence needs recognized after the tragic events of September 11, 2001. It describes a nationwide communications capability that will link together all levels of law enforcement personnel, including officers on the streets, intelligence analysts, unit commanders, and police executives for the purpose of sharing critical data.[278]

NATIONAL DISASTER MEDICAL SYSTEM (NDMS). A national capability to deliver quality medical care to the victims of—and responders to—a domestic (natural or manmade) disaster either at a disaster site, in transit from the impacted area, or into participating definitive care facilities. Located within the Department of Homeland Security, Federal Emergency Management Agency, Response Division, Operations Branch, NDMS is responsible for supporting federal agencies in the management and coordination of the federal medical response to major emergencies and federally declared disasters, including natural disasters, technological disasters, major transportation accidents, and acts of terrorism, including **weapons of mass destruction** events.[279]

NATIONAL ELECTRONIC DISEASE SURVEILLANCE SYSTEM (NEDSS). Seeks to collect and monitor data for disease trends and/or outbreaks to public health personnel nationwide; specifically, to identify and track emerging infectious diseases and potential bioterrorism attacks as well as to investigate outbreaks and monitor disease trends. The vision of NEDSS is to have integrated surveillance systems that can transfer appropriate public health, laboratory, and clinical data efficiently and securely over the Internet; can be found at http://www.cdc.gov/nedss/.

NATIONAL FOREIGN INTELLIGENCE BOARD (NFIB). The senior intelligence community advisory body to the DCI on the substantive aspects of national intelligence. This Board advises the DCI on the production, review, and coordination of national foreign intelligence; the interagency exchanges of foreign intelligence information; arrangements with foreign governments on intelligence matters; the production of intelligence sources and methods; activities of common concern; and such other matters as are referred to it by the DCI. It is composed of the DCI chairman and other appropriate officers of the CIA, Department of State, Department of Defense, Defense Intelligence Agency, and NSA.

NATIONAL FOREIGN INTELLIGENCE PROGRAM (NFIP). Executive order 12333 defines the NFIP as the programs of the CIA, Consolidated Cryptologic Program, General Defense Intelligence Program, specialized DoD reconnaissance activities, and activities of staff elements of the DCI, as well as other programs or agencies within the intelligence community designated jointly by the DCI and the head of the department or by the president as national foreign intelligence or counterintelligence activities. The NFIP provides funds for the bulk of national-level intelligence, counterintelligence, and reconnaissance activities of the CIA, Defense Department, and all civilian federal agencies and departments, as well as those of the intelligence community management structure.

NATIONAL INFORMATION INFRASTRUCTURE (NII). The nationwide interconnection of communications networks, computers, databases, and consumer electronics that make vast amounts of information available to users. The *national information infrastructure* encompasses a wide range of equipment, including cameras, scanners, keyboards, facsimile machines, computers, switches, compact disks, video and audio tape, cable, wire, satellites, fiber-optic transmission lines, networks of all types, televisions, monitors, printers, and much more. The friendly and adversary personnel who make decisions and handle the transmitted information constitute a critical component of the *national information infrastructure*.[280] *See also* DEFENSE INFORMATION INFRASTRUCTURE; GLOBAL INFORMATION INFRASTRUCTURE; INFORMATION.

NATIONAL INTELLIGENCE COUNCIL (NIC). Established within the Office of the Director of Central Intelligence; composed of senior analysts within the intelligence community and substantive experts from the public and private sectors, who shall be appointed by, report to, and serve at the pleasure of, the Director of Central Intelligence. The Council shall (A) produce national intelligence estimates for the government, including, whenever the Council considers appropriate, alternative views held by elements of the intelligence community; and (B) evaluate community-wide collection and production of intelligence by the intelligence community and the requirements and resources of such collection and production.[281] *See also* NATIONAL INTELLIGENCE OFFICER FOR WARNING.

NATIONAL INTELLIGENCE ESTIMATE (NIE). 1. An assessment of a situation which is relevant to the formulation of economic and national security policy, and which projects probable future courses of action and developments; may be structured to illuminate differences of view. 2. A strategic estimate of capabilities, vulnerabilities, and probable courses of action of foreign nations.

NATIONAL INTELLIGENCE OFFICER FOR WARNING (NIO/W). Principal point of contact between the Director of Central Intelligence and intelligence consumers below the cabinet level; primary source of national-level substantive guidance to Intelligence Community planners, collectors, and resource managers; appointed by the Director of Central Intelligence in consultation with the Director of the Defense Intelligence Agency; one of 13 National Intelligence Officers of the **National Intelligence Council**.[282] *See also* NATIONAL INTELLIGENCE COUNCIL.

NATIONAL JOINT TERRORISM TASK FORCE (NJTTF). Co-located in the Strategic Information and Operations Center, Counterterrorism Operational Response Section at FBI headquarters. In part, the NJTTF was created in July 2002 by the FBI to "complement" the JTTFs around the country.[283] NJTTF membership is comprised of representatives from approximately 30 federal, state, and local agencies, and "provides a central fusion point for terrorism information and intelligence to the Joint Terrorism Task Forces, which include state and local law enforcement officers, federal agency officials."[284] The NJTTF also acts as a "point of fusion" for terrorism information by coordinating the flow of information between FBI Headquarters and the other JTTFs located across the country, as well as among the agencies represented on the NJTTF and other government agencies, such as the Department of Homeland Security.[285] *See also* COUNTERTERRORISM CENTER; INFORMATION ANALYSIS AND INFRASTRUCTURE PROTECTION; JOINT TERRORISM TASK FORCE; TERRORIST THREAT INTEGRATION CENTER.

NATIONAL LAW ENFORCEMENT TELECOMMUNICATIONS SYSTEM (NLETS). Created by the principal law enforcement agencies of the states nearly 35 years ago. Since the founding, the role of the NLETS International Justice and Public Safety Information Sharing Network has evolved from being primarily an interstate telecommunications service for law enforcement to a more broad-based network servicing the justice community at the local, state, and federal levels. It is now the pre-eminent interstate law enforcement network in the nation for the exchange of law enforcement and related justice information. The mission of NLETS is to provide, within a secure environment, an international justice telecommunications capability and information services that will benefit the safety, the security, and the preservation of human life and the protection of property. NLETS will assist those national and international governmental agencies and other organizations with similar missions that enforce or aid in enforcing local, state, or international laws or ordinances.[286]

NATIONAL MILITARY JOINT INTELLIGENCE CENTER (NMJIC) ALERT CENTER. Located at the Pentagon, this 24-hour **watch center** monitors incoming current intelligence of national security value.

NATIONAL OPERATIONS SECURITY PROGRAM. Created by Ronald Reagan National Security Decision Directive (NSDD) 298, January 22, 1988. Each executive department and agency assigned or supporting national security missions with classified or sensitive activities shall establish a formal Operational Security (OPSEC) program with the following common features:

- Specific assignment of responsibility for OPSEC direction and implementation
- Specific requirements to plan for and implement OPSEC in anticipation of and, where appropriate, during department or agency activity
- Direction to use OPSEC analytical techniques to assist in identifying vulnerabilities and to select appropriate OPSEC measures
- Enactment of measures to ensure that all personnel commensurate with their positions and security clearances are aware of hostile intelligence threats and understand the OPSEC process
- Annual review and evaluation of OPSEC procedures so as to assist the improvement of OPSEC programs
- Provision for interagency support and cooperation with respect to OPSEC programs
- Agencies with minimal activities that could affect national security need not establish a formal OPSEC program; however, they must cooperate with other departments and agencies to minimize damage to national security when OPSEC problems arise.[287]

NATIONAL POWER. A broad assessment of the means available to a nation in pursuit of its objectives. *See also* ELEMENTS OF NATIONAL POWER.

NATIONAL SECURITY. 1. National defense or foreign relations of the United States. 2. The territorial integrity, sovereignty, and international freedom of action of the United States. Intelligence activities relating to national security encompass all the military, economic, political, scientific, technological, and other aspects of foreign developments that pose actual or potential threats to U.S. national interests.[288]

NATIONAL SECURITY AREA (NSA). An area established on non-federal lands located within the United States, its possessions, or territories, for safeguarding classified and/or restricted data information, or protecting DOE equipment and/or material. Establishment of an NSA temporarily places such non-federal lands under the control of the DOE and results only from an emergency event.[289]

NATIONAL SECURITY COUNCIL (NSC). Established by the National Security Act of 1947 to advise the President with respect to the integration of domestic, foreign, and military policies relating to national security. The NSC is the highest Executive Branch entity providing review of, guidance for, and direction to the conduct of all national foreign intelligence and counterintelligence activities. The statutory members of the NSC are the President, the Vice President, the Secretary of State, and the Secretary of Defense. The Director of National Intelligence and the Chairman of the Joint Chiefs of Staff participate as advisors.

NATIONAL SECURITY INFORMATION (NSI). 1. Data, nuclear and otherwise, classified under the authority of various presidential executive orders. Depending on the degree of harm that unauthorized disclosure could "reasonably be expected to cause," NSI can be classified as Top Secret, Secret, or Confidential. 2. Information that has been determined pursuant to Executive Order 12958 or prior Executive Orders to require protection against unauthorized disclosure and is marked to indicate its classification status when in document form. NSI is referred to as "defense information" in the Atomic Energy Act. Under President George W. Bush, Executive Order 13292 (March 28, 2003) further expands NSI to information related to:

- Military plans, weapons systems, or operations
- Foreign government information
- Intelligence activities (including special activities), intelligence sources or methods, or cryptology
- Foreign relations or foreign activities of the United States, including confidential sources
- Scientific, technological, or economic matters relating to the national security, which includes defense against transnational terrorism

- United States government programs for safeguarding nuclear materials or facilities
- Vulnerabilities or capabilities of systems, installations, infrastructures, projects, plans, or protection services relating to the national security, which includes defense against transnational terrorism
- Weapons of mass destruction[290]

3. Official information or material which requires protection against unauthorized disclosure in the interest of national defense or foreign relations of the United States. The current authority for classifying information as NSI comes from Executive Order (EO) 12356. A declaration of NSI requires prior approval from an authorized person.[291]

NATIONAL SECURITY LETTERS. A type of administrative subpoena which may be issued independently by FBI field offices and not subject to judicial review unless a case comes to court; under Section 505 of the PATRIOT Act which authorized FBI field agents to issue *national security letters* to obtain financial, bank, and credit records of individuals. In certain instances, under 18 U.S.C. 2709, it is possible for the FBI to require the production of records and information pertaining to wire or electronic communications through a *National Security Letter,* where the only requirement is for the agent of the FBI to certify that the records and information sought are "relevant to an authorized investigation."[292]

NATIONAL SECURITY SENSITIVITY LEVELS. Federal employment positions as defined by the U.S. Office of Personnel Management. These levels of federal employment include:

Special-Sensitive. Any positions determined to be in a level higher than Critical-Sensitive because of special requirements under authority other than EO 10450 and EO 12968.

Critical-Sensitive. Potential for exceptionally grave damage to the national security which includes positions that would involve any of the following:

- Access to Top Secret national security information or materials;
- Requirement for a Department of Energy "Q" security clearance for access to DOE national security information, materials, and/or sites
- Development or approval of war plans, plans or particulars of future major or special operations of war, or critical and extremely important items of war
- Investigative duties, the issuance of personnel security clearances, or duty on personnel security boards

- Commissioned law enforcement duties
- Other positions related to national security, regardless of duties, that require the same degree of trust

Noncritical-Sensitive. Potential for serious damage to the national security to include positions involving any of the following:

- Access to Secret or Confidential national security information or materials
- Requirement to obtain a Department of Energy "L" security clearance for access to DOE national security information, materials, and/or sites
- Duties that may directly or indirectly adversely affect the national security operations of the agency[293]

NATIONAL SECURITY SYSTEM. Any telecommunications or information system operated by the United States government, the function, operation, or use of which: 1. involves intelligence activities; 2. involves cryptologic activities related to national security; 3. involves command and control of military forces; 4. involves equipment that is an integral part of a weapon or weapon system; or 5. is critical to the direct fulfillment of military or intelligence missions and does not include a system that is to be used for routine administrative and business applications (including payroll, finance, logistics, and personnel management).

NATIONAL SIGNALS INTELLIGENCE OPERATIONS CENTER (NSOC). Pronounced "n-sock" and located at the National Security Agency, this 24-hour **watch center** monitors incoming intelligence of national security value; not to be confused with NSOC, Navy Satellite Operations Center.

NATIONAL STRATEGY. The art and science of developing and using the diplomatic, economic, and informational powers of a nation, together with its armed forces, during peace and war to secure national objectives. Also called national security strategy or grand strategy.[294, 295]

NEAR-REAL TIME. The reception of data and its analysis that have been processed and communicated close the actual event. *See also* CURRENT INTELLIGENCE; REAL TIME.

NEED-TO-KNOW. 1. A determination made by the possessor of classified information that a prospective recipient has a requirement for access to, knowledge of, or possession of the classified information to perform tasks or services essential to the fulfillment of a classified contract or program. 2. A determination by a person having responsibility for classified information or material, that a proposed recipient's access to such classified information or matter is necessary in the performance of official or contractual duties of employment. 3. The determination by an authorized holder of classified information that a prospective recipient requires access to specific classified information in order to perform or assist in a lawful and authorized governmental function.[296] 4. Executive Order 10501 ("Safeguarding Official Information in the Interests of the Defense of the United States," November 5, 1953) "establishes the basis for the need-to-know concept": "Knowledge or possession of classified defense information shall be permitted only to persons whose official duties require such access in the interest of promoting national defense and if they have been determined to be trustworthy."[297] *See also* ACCESS.

NET ASSESSMENT. Comparative review and analysis of opposing national strengths, capabilities, and vulnerabilities.

NOISE. The quantity of extraneous, irrelevant, or inconsistent signals and signs that could lead to the misinterpretation or masking of a threat. For example,

> The public image of warnings for the impending Pearl Harbor disaster appears to be highly simplified, with outlines clearly marked and with few shadings. The record is full of references to supposedly unambiguous indications of the Japanese plan . . . but, in fact, the signal picture in the limited locale of Honolulu is amazingly complex, and the mass of signals grows increasingly dense and freighted with ambiguities as we move to the larger assemblage of agencies, in Washington. In both places signals announcing the Pearl Harbor attack were always accompanied by competing or contradictory signals, by all sorts of information useless for anticipating this particular disaster. We refer to these competing signals as *noise*. To understand the fact of surprise it is necessary to examine the characteristics of the noise as well as the signals that after the event are clearly seen to herald the attack. If it does nothing else, an understanding of the noise present in any signal system will teach us humility and respect for the job of the information analyst.[298]

See also SIGNAL; PARADOX OF SILENCE.

NONCRITICAL-SENSITIVE (NCS). Potential for serious damage to the national security.

NORMAL THEORY. Projecting an adversary's objectives, capabilities, and propensity to risk based on problematic thinking and making the best possible estimates about numerous instances of behavior over time.[299] *See also* EXCEPTIONAL THEORY.

NOT RELEASABLE TO CONTRACTORS/CONSULTANTS (NO-CONTRACT). This marking may be used only on Intelligence Information that is provided by a source on the express or implied condition that it not be made available to contractors; or that, if disclosed to a contractor, would actually or potentially give him or her a competitive advantage, which could reasonably be expected to cause a conflict of interest with his or her obligation to protect the information.[300]

NOT RELEASABLE TO FOREIGN NATIONALS (NOFORN). This marking is used to identify Intelligence Information that may not be released in any form to foreign governments, foreign nationals, or non-U.S. citizens.[301]

NOVEL INTELLIGENCE FROM MASSIVE DATA (NIMD). A program aimed at focusing analytic attention on the most critical information found within massive data—information that indicates the potential for strategic surprise; actionable information not previously known to the analyst or policy makers. It gives the analyst new insight into a previously unappreciated or misunderstood threat. Massive data has multiple dimensions that may cause difficulty, some of which include volume or depth, heterogeneity or breadth, and complexity. That is, data may be "massive" because of the sheer quantity of similar items, typically a megabyte or more. Some intelligence data sources grow at the rate of four megabytes per month now, and the rate of growth is increasing. A smaller volume of data may nonetheless be considered "massive" because it consists of separately authored information objects in numerous types and formats: structured text in various formats, unstructured text, spoken text, audio, video, tables, graphs, diagrams, images, maps, equations, chemical formulas, etc. Data may also be deemed "massive" because of its inherent complexity, which arises when a single document contains links between multiple information objects, with the meaning of any object dependent on information contained within other objects. Understanding the content of complex data requires being able to process data that has already been fused together, which is beyond the capability of current technology. A deeper level of complexity comes into play when information requires a variety of expertise for full comprehension because of the interconnectedness of the domains.[302]

NUCLEAR INTELLIGENCE (NUCINT). *See* SOURCES OF INTELLIGENCE.

– O –

OCTOBER SURPRISE. The allegation that representatives of the 1980 Ronald Reagan presidential campaign arranged to postpone release of the American hostages held by Iran until after the U.S. presidential election, thus preventing an "October surprise" that would have aided President Jimmy Carter in winning reelection. It was also feared by the Reagan campaign that an *October surprise* could occur should the Carter administration attempt another hostage rescue shortly before the election. Ultimately, the hostages were released—but not until after Reagan's inauguration on January 20, 1981. As events unfolded, the hostages were allowed to leave Iran minutes after Reagan was sworn in as President. *See also* MISSILE GAP.

OFFICE OF NATIONAL ESTIMATES (ONE). Central Intelligence Agency's research office that was to be limited to economic intelligence when it was created in 1950; however, in subsequent years it began dealing with political intelligence. The National Intelligence Council replaced it in 1973. *See also* KOREAN WAR; NATIONAL INTELLIGENCE OFFICER FOR WARNING.

OFFICIAL INFORMATION. Information owned by, produced for or by, or subject to the control of the United States government. All classified information is considered official information. *See also* CLOSED INFORMATION; TWILIGHT INFORMATION.

OFFICIAL USE ONLY (OUO). 1. A designation identifying certain unclassified but sensitive information that may be exempt from public release under the Freedom of Information Act. 2. A security classification marking used during the period July 18, 1949, through October 22, 1951.[303] 3. Any employee, federal or contractor, can determine that an unclassified document contains OUO information if that document is originated within his or her office, or is under the control of his or her office. No special authority or training is required. The first step is for the employee to determine if the information has the potential to damage governmental, commercial, or private interests if given to someone who doesn't need it to perform his or her job.[304]

ONEIROMANCY. A noun (pronounced o-NY-ruh-man-see). The practice of predicting the future by interpreting dreams (not encouraged as a methodology for intelligence analysts). From Greek *oneiros* (dream) and *-mancy* (divination). *See also* FATIDIC.

OPEN INFORMATION. Information in the public domain, in the sense that it does not violate official secrets, national security, or intelligence activities, sources, or methods, and is approved for public **dissemination.** "Sensitive but not classified" scientific and technology (transfer) related information that resides in public libraries, and subscription databases such as Dialog, Lexis-Nexis, and other commercial information products.[305] *See also* CLOSED INFORMATION.

OPEN-SOURCE INTELLIGENCE (OSINT). 1. Information of potential intelligence value that is available to the general public such as from radio, television, newspapers, journals, and the Internet. 2. Publicly available information (for example, any member of the public could lawfully obtain information by request or observation), as well as other unclassified information that has limited public distribution or access; to include any information that may be used in an unclassified context without compromising national security or intelligence sources or methods. If the information is not publicly available, certain legal requirements relating to collection, retention, and dissemination might apply.[306] *See also* SOURCES OF INTELLIGENCE.

OPERATION BARBAROSSA. A German surprise attack on Russia when 3 million German troops poured in from the Arctic Circle to the Black Sea. Although Russian intelligence had uncovered German troop movements eastward, an increase in the number of German aerial surveillance flights over Russia, and the passing of U.S. intelligence to Russian intelligence of Hitler's plans to invade Russia back in 1940, a paranoid Russian government was convinced that similar intelligence leaked to them by the British was really counterintelligence. Nevertheless, Stalin ignored all these warnings and he believed his own intelligence that Hitler would not dare try to fight a war on two fronts. For additional examples of "surprise attacks" *see also* FALKLAND ISLANDS; PEARL HARBOR; SINGAPORE; TET OFFENSIVE; YOM KIPPUR WAR.

OPERATIONAL INTELLIGENCE. Intelligence required for the planning and executing of all types of national security operations. *See also* STRATEGIC INTELLIGENCE; TACTICAL INTELLIGENCE.

OPERATIONAL READINESS. Capability of a unit/formation, ship, weapon system, or equipment to perform the missions or functions for which it is organized or designed. This term may be used in a general sense or to express a level of readiness. *See also* COMBAT READINESS.

OPERATIONAL WARNING. Required for effectively counteracting any major military operation that would hinder the ability to execute those military operations needed to accomplish strategic objectives within theaters or areas of operations.

OPERATIONS SECURITY (OPSEC). 1. A systematic, proven process by which a government, organization, or individual can identify, control, and protect generally unclassified information about an operation/activity and thus deny or mitigate an adversary's ability to compromise or interrupt said operation/activity. 2. A process of identifying critical information and subsequently analyzing friendly actions attendant to military operations and other activities to (a) identify those actions that can be observed by adversary intelligence systems and (b) determine indicators that adversary intelligence systems might obtain and then interpret or piece together to derive critical information in time to be useful to adversaries, and select and execute measures to eliminate or reduce to an acceptable level the vulnerabilities of friendly actions to adversary exploitation.

OPERATIONS SECURITY PROTECTED INFORMATION. Unclassified information concerning Centers for Disease Control and Prevention mission, functions, operations, or programs that require protection in the national interest, security, or homeland defense as iterated in National Security Decision Directive 298, January 1988, which established a National Operations Security Program.[307]

OPINION. A value judgment regarding a future course of action that cannot be directly observed; most heavily relied upon for warning in lieu of factual data. *See also* ANALYSIS; ASSESSMENT.

OPTICAL INTELLIGENCE (OPTINT). Mostly used as a pejorative term for estimates and forecasting based on qualitative or intuitive judgment. The term received widespread use among U.S. intelligence analysts and policymakers during the Vietnam War in the 1960s.[308] *See also* ASSESS-MENT; BEAN-COUNTING ASSESSMENT; SOURCES OF INTELLI-GENCE.

– P –

PARADOX OF COLLECTION. As additional information is collected the analyst becomes inundated with intelligence leading to ambiguity and uncertainty and thus making the person more ignorant; by collecting more intelligence the analyst is exposed to more variables that can lead to more uncertainty.

PARADOX OF EXPERTISE. The belief that the more one becomes an expert in a particular area or field of study, the more likely one will miss changes that would normally be detected by those with less knowledge or experience (i.e., the expert is likely to focus on inconsequential details). The strengths of expertise can also be weaknesses,[309] or as the saying goes, "He wasn't a very good analyst because he kept missing the forest for the trees."

PARADOX OF SILENCE (ALSO KNOWN AS SOUNDS OF SILENCE PARADOX). 1. When the lack of any communications by the enemy may actually be a signal that preparations for war are beginning; the paradox occurs when the enemy uses silence as **noise** to disguise activity. For example, prior to attacking Pearl Harbor on December 7, 1941, the Japanese Fleet had engaged in radio silence, thus making U.S. electronic signal interceptors believe the Imperial Navy had not yet set sail when in fact they were about to attack, thus proving to be the *paradox of silence*; possibly related to the proverb, "the calm before the storm." 2. When a quiescent international environment acts as background noise which, by conditioning observers to a peaceful routine, actually covers preparations for war. *See also* CREEPING NORMALCY; NOISE.

PARADOX OF WARNING (ALSO KNOWN AS WARNING PARA-DOX). 1. The more successful the role of warning in stimulating early and effective counteraction, the less likely it is that the forecast sequence of events will occur. 2. Enemy counteraction based on action taken by the intended victim as a result of a warning that alters the enemy's initially intended course of action. The warning thus appears to be wrong on the basis of the change in enemy action. For example, some businessmen were seeking to sue computer software manufacturers after the expected Y2K computer meltdown scheduled for January 1, 2000. The businessmen were not suing the computer software companies because the newly installed software did not work, but because they had no way of knowing if the Y2K was a real attack on their computers. According to the software companies, the computers continued to function without interruption because the software worked. It could be argued that because of the success of the software, there was no threat. The moral of this story is that good warning sometimes provides countermeasures that may ultimately prove fruitless because the element of surprise is no longer available to the attacker . . . thus, good warning can make liars out of excellent analysts.

PASSIVE ACQUIESCENCE. A term used in the policy, military, and intelligence communities to mean "the acceptance to do nothing." For example, "Over the past few months, with the demise of their safe haven in Afghanistan, some al Qaida operatives have relocated to Iraq. Baghdad's support for international terrorist organizations ranges from explicit and overt support to implicit and *passive acquiescence*."[310]

PASSIVE DECEPTION. Measures designed to mislead a foreign power, organization, or person by causing an object or situation to appear non-threatening when a threat does exist; downplaying capabilities or intentions to look less threatening. "*Passive deception* is primarily based on secrecy and camouflage, on hiding and concealing one's intentions and/or capabilities from the adversary. Some experts view *passive deception* as inferior and not likely to succeed against any competent intelligence organization . . . [which] is not necessarily true [italics added]."[311] A classic example is the Trojan Horse incident in the second millennium. Troy's soldiers accepted a seemingly innocuous gift from their enemy. However, inside the wooden statue of the giant horse were Greek soldiers ready to attack while the city slept. Today, the term "Trojan Horse" resurfaces in the lexicon of cyberwarfare. Most cyber viruses use passive deception to enter a computer's operating system by hiding inside another program or e-mail. *See also* A-TYPE DECEPTION; ACTIVE DECEPTION; DENIAL AND DECEPTION; M-TYPE DECEPTION.

PATENT SECRECY ACT OF 1952. Allows the Secretary of Defense to determine that disclosure of an invention by granting of a patent would be detrimental to national security. A patent application on which a secrecy order has been imposed shall be assigned a classification and be marked and safeguarded accordingly.[312]

PATTERN RECOGNITION. An inductive process of recognizing a commonality or trend in an aggregate of indications from which a plausible explanation or model can be developed.

PEARL HARBOR. Regarded as the worst case of intelligence failure in U.S. history; in 1941, a task force of 33 Japanese ships stationed themselves 200 miles north of Oahu and launched two successive waves of air attack (350 planes) in which the U.S. lost 18 warships, 200 airplanes, and over 2,000 personnel. It was believed by Naval Intelligence that Japan might possibly attack Thailand about that time of year. Although the U.S. lacked any specific human intelligence on Japan, it was intercepting Japanese diplomatic and espionage messages. *See also* FALKLAND ISLANDS; OPERATION BARBAROSSA; SINGAPORE; TET OFFENSIVE; YOM KIPPUR WAR.

PERCEPTION MANAGEMENT. Actions to convey and/or deny selected information and indicators to foreign audiences to influence their emotions, motives, and objective reasoning as well as to intelligence systems and leaders at all levels to influence official estimates, ultimately resulting in foreign behaviors and official actions favorable to the originator's objectives. In various ways, *perception management* combines truth projection, operations security, cover and **deception,** and **psychological operations.**[313] *See also* DECEPTION; PSYCHOLOGICAL OPERATIONS.

PHASES OF WARNING. Stages of a surprise attack that can degrade a nation's defense. The three phases of warning are political, strategic, and tactical, although other analysts label these phases strategic, operational, and tactical. *See also* POLITICAL WARNING; STRATEGIC WARNING; TACTICAL WARNING.

PHOTINT (PHOTO INTELLIGENCE). *See* SOURCES OF INTELLIGENCE.

PHOTOGRAPHIC INTELLIGENCE (PHOTINT). Collected products of photographic interpretation, classified and evaluated for intelligence use, a category of imagery intelligence. *See also* SOURCES OF INTELLIGENCE.

PHYSICAL SECURITY CODES. Security policies and procedures designed for maximum uniformity and standardization. Although these codes were aimed at securing conventional ammunition, they are adaptable to the "special needs of the individual Military Services." The following codes indicate "the degrees of protection required for materials in the interest of national security":

Code A: Confidential Formerly Restricted Data
Code B: Confidential Restricted Data (The lowest classification level applied to information whose unauthorized disclosure could reasonably be expected to cause damage to the national security.)
Code C: Confidential
Code D: Confidential Cryptologic
Code E: Secret Cryptologic
Code F: Top Secret Cryptologic
Code G: Secret Formerly Restricted Data
Code H: Secret Restricted Data
Code K: Top Secret Formerly Restricted Data
Code L: Top Secret Restricted Data
Code S: Secret
Code T: Top Secret
Code U: Unclassified[314]

PLAIN TEXT. Unencrypted communications; specifically, the original message of a cryptogram, expressed in ordinary language.[315]

POCKET LITTER. Seemingly inconsequential items (such as a wallet, driver's license, photographs, matchbooks, and notes) seized upon the arrest of an individual, which may contain important clues to the suspect's past activities and future plans.

POLICY BIAS. Development of analysis to fit established objectives in support of an existing policy or the implementation of a new policy; also known as "finding the facts to fit the conclusion."

> In his view, neither camp can completely avoid the impact of *policy bias* when it comes to dealing with uncertainty. The intelligence side likes to pretend otherwise, but the manner in which it favors certain substantive assumptions over others has predictable implications for US policy debates. The serious policy official recognizes the power of *policy bias* and has a powerful incentive to do all he or she can to insure against the influence of bias and wishful thinking during the working out of analytic assumptions. Policymakers want to succeed and cannot do so without sound assumptions.[316]

POLITICAL INTELLIGENCE. 1. Pertaining to foreign and domestic policies of governments and the activities of political movements. 2. Concerning the dynamics of the internal and external political affairs of foreign countries, regional grouping, multilateral treaty arrangements and organizations, and foreign political movements directed against or affecting established governments or authority.

POLITICAL WARNING. A forecast of increasing tensions between two or more countries that raises the possibility that deterrence can fail, leading to an unforeseen crisis; usually can range over a period of days or months. *See also* STRATEGIC WARNING; TACTICAL WARNING.

POLITICIZED INTELLIGENCE. Any intelligence or analysis that is developed to meet the conclusions or key judgments that have already been predetermined to support policy.

POLLYANNA. One who sees and reports only positive outcomes from current indications, regardless of the message read into the same indications by less-biased analysts. Term originates from the American novel *Pollyanna* (1913) by Eleanor Porter; term is usually capitalized. *See also* CASSANDRA.

POSSIBLE. That which can occur, or may happen, or could come true.[317] Sometimes confused with **probable,** a statement of likelihood. For example, "Their having the capability is *possible,* but the estimate of an opponent's intention to use that capability is not probable." *See also* PROBABLE.

POST-SURPRISE MEASURES. Planned methods and activities to deal with a sudden attack once it has taken place. *See also* BASIC MEASURES OF MILITARY PREPAREDNESS; EMERGENCY MEASURES OF MILITARY PREPAREDNESS.

POTENTIAL THREAT ELEMENTS. Typically classified as left-wing, right-wing, or "special interest"; "any group or individual in which there are allegations or information indicating a possibility of the unlawful use of force or violence in furtherance of a specific motivation or goal, possibly political or social in nature. An actual history of criminal activity increases a group's "point scale" in a threat assessment.[318]

POTOMAC FEVER. A slang term derived from the river that runs adjacent to the Pentagon, this is a pejorative term used to describe those who seek to provide intelligence or information they think senior-level leaders want;

more generally, any **analysis** or **assessment** produced with the guiding principle to please as many and offend as few as possible; warning production used solely to further the ambition and career goals of an individual. *See also* POLITICIZED INTELLIGENCE.

POWER INTANGIBLES. Factors, such as ideology, a government's ability to mobilize resources and manpower, the maintenance of ruling coalitions, or a fear of domestic revolutions or opposition movements, that have an independent impact on political intentions.

PRECAUTIONARY PRINCIPLE. When an activity raises threats of harm to human health or the environment, precautionary measures should be taken even if some cause-and-effect relationships are not fully established scientifically. In this context the proponent of an activity, rather than the public, should bear the burden of proof. The process of applying the *Precautionary Principle* must be open, informed, and democratic and must include potentially affected parties. It must also involve an examination of the full range of alternatives, including no action.[319] Precaution is the basis of some U.S. environmental and food and drug legislation, although the principle is not mentioned by name. These laws incorporate foresight, prevention, and care, and many give regulators authority to take action to prevent possible but unproven harm. For example: As a precautionary measure, the Food and Drug Administration requires all new drugs to be tested before they are put on the market; the Food Quality and Protection Act of 1996 requires pesticides to be proven safe for children or removed— several are being phased out; the National Environmental Policy Act is precautionary in two ways: 1. It emphasizes foresight and attention to consequences by requiring an environmental impact assessment for any federally funded project, and 2. it mandates consideration of alternative plans. NEPA is one of the best national examples of precautionary action.[320]

PRECISION ACQUISITION INTELLIGENCE. Required intelligence needed to create a valid **assessment** in an environment of ambiguity and uncertainty in a given crisis situation or warning problem. For example, data collected on reserve military medical technicians with advanced training in chemical or biological warfare may be the *precision acquisition intelligence* needed to understand a nation's readiness for certain types of warfare. *See also* PRECISION ENGAGEMENT.

PRECISION ATTACK/ENGAGEMENT. Any attack of a target by weapons employing guidance, with sufficient spatial and temporal accuracy that seeks to achieve its required effect with minimum expenditure of munitions and a reduced risk of collateral damage. "It is a scalpel approach to all types of military operations using lethal or non-lethal, kinetic or non-kinetic force. In conventional warfighting, precision engagement is the ability to forgo brute force-on-force tactics and apply discriminate force precisely where required. One B-2 dropping 16 precision-guided weapons and destroying 16 key targets epitomizes precision engagement. It also redefines the traditional military concept of mass. In military operations other than war, precision engagement may be the rapid response of airborne resources, space assets or troops for monitoring peacekeeping operations or the timely airlift of relief supplies for humanitarian operations.[321] *See also* CREEPING NORMALCY; SALAMI TACTICS.

PRECONCEPTION. Also referred to as *self-deception*, an opinion or conception formed in advance of actual knowledge.

PREDICTION. A statement of the expected time, place, and/or magnitude of a future event. *See also* ESTIMATE; FORECAST.

PREDICTIVE INTELLIGENCE. Fulfills the requirement of the need to know what will happen next.

PREEMPTIVE ATTACK. The belief that unless force is initiated first, there will be no time to respond or retaliate as the victim of an opposing attack.

PRESIDENTIAL DECISION DIRECTIVE (PDD). A presidential directive has the same substantive legal effect as an **executive order.** It is the substance of the presidential action that is determinative, not the form of the document conveying that action. Both an executive order and a presidential directive remain effective upon a change in administration, unless otherwise specified in the document, and both continue to be effective until subsequent presidential action is taken.[322] There are several types of PDDs, each determined and expanded on by individual presidential administrations beginning with the Truman administration. PDDs are not publicly disclosed or published (as, for example, executive orders are published in the *Federal Register* and *Code of Federal Regulations*), or revealed to Congress. PDDs remain in effect until they are superseded by a new presidential administration. PDDs may be considered a "presidential secret law."[323] *See also* PRESIDENTIAL DIRECTIVE.

PRESIDENTIAL DECISION DIRECTIVE-56 (PDD-56). After several failed crisis interventions in Somalia, Rwanda, and Haiti, U.S. strategic planners had to improve techniques regarding participation in such missions. President Clinton signed this directive in 1997 to address the need to focus on complex emergencies. Although this document remains classified, in a press release the White House outlined its goals and objectives. The directive orders the National Security Council to work with the National Defense University, Army War College, Pentagon, State Department, Central Intelligence Agency, and other agencies to develop and conduct a multi-agency training and planning program focused on complex emergency issues.[324]

PRESIDENTIAL DIRECTIVE. Substance of a presidential action that has the same substantive legal effect as an **executive order.** Both an executive order and a *presidential directive* remain effective upon a change in administration, unless otherwise specified in the document, and both continue to be effective until subsequent presidential action is taken.[325] *See also* PRESIDENTIAL DECISION DIRECTIVE.

PRESIDENTIAL FINDING. 1. Presidential authorization or directive based on an investigation for covert action, in which the President "finds" covert activities critical to national security. A finding may not authorize or sanction a covert action, or any aspect of any such action, which already has occurred, nor authorize any action that would violate the Constitution or any statute of the United States. 2. Can include political activity, secret use of propaganda, economic disruption, paramilitary operations, formalized covert action by requiring the President to inform Congress in writing (the Hughes-Ryan Act of 1974 which required the President to report any nonintelligence CIA operations such as covert operations to the relevant congressional committee (around 8 congressional committees at the time of the Act) in a timely fashion; the 1980 Intelligence Accountability Act which required only two committees be informed of the President's "finding."[326]

PRESIDENTIAL FOREIGN INTELLIGENCE ADVISORY BOARD (PFIAB). Advises the president on the operation of the intelligence community with emphasis on organization, missions, collection priorities, and coordination among agencies.

PRESIDENT'S DAILY BRIEF (PDB). CIA classified national security information and analysis sent to the President daily. It is "inherently privileged," according to the CIA, and therefore cannot be publicly disclosed, regardless of age or content.[327]

PRESIDENT'S FOREIGN INTELLIGENCE ADVISORY BOARD (PFIAB). This board provides advice to the President concerning the quality and adequacy of intelligence collection, of analysis and estimates, of counterintelligence, and of other intelligence activities. The PFIAB, through its Intelligence Oversight Board, also advises the President on the legality of foreign intelligence activities. The PFIAB usually has 16 members selected from among distinguished citizens outside the government who are qualified on the basis of achievement, experience, independence, and integrity. Unique within the government, the PFIAB traditionally has been tasked with providing the President with an independent source of advice on the effectiveness with which the intelligence community is meeting the nation's intelligence needs. *See also* INTELLIGENCE OVERSIGHT BOARD.

PREVENTION, HUMANITARIAN. Activities to provide outright avoidance of the adverse impact of hazards and means to minimize related environmental, technological, and biological disasters.[328]

PREVENTIVE ATTACK. When senior-level leaders believe that an armed confrontation is not imminent, although it is likely to occur at a later date, and it is decided that by attacking now they would seize the initiative. *See also* PREEMPTIVE ATTACK.

PREVENTIVE DIPLOMACY. Diplomatic actions taken in advance of a predictable crisis to prevent or limit violence before it occurs. When a nation acts with political and economic tools, in concert with others, to head off conflict before it reaches the threshold of mass violence or military intervention. "The UN mission in Macedonia has been used as a part of a strategy of *preventive diplomacy* [italics added], and it is perhaps best known within a range of different preventive efforts undertaken within a longer period in this country."[329]

PRIDE OF PREVIOUS POSITION. When an analyst has already expressed a viewpoint and is extremely reluctant to change it for fear of admitting error. *See also* CLIENTITIS; DOUBLE BLIND.

PRINCIPAL CONCLUSIONS. Those conclusions of a report or estimate that are emphasized to elicit a specific action or point to a clear understanding of a potential threat or action; based on basic intelligence. If done poorly or with bias, it can have a disastrous effect. Prior to the Korean War in 1950, General MacArthur's own estimates by his G-2, Major General

Charles Willoughby, were purposely slanted. "MacArthur did not want the Chinese to enter the war in Korea. Anything MacArthur wanted, Willoughby produced intelligence for. . . . In this case, Willoughby falsified the intelligence reports."[330] *See also* ASSESSMENT; KEY JUDGMENTS; KEY QUESTIONS.

PRIVACY ACT OF 1974. According to the law, "Each agency that maintains a system of records shall . . . upon request by any individual to gain access to his record or to any information pertaining to him which is contained in the system, permit him and upon his request, a person of his own choosing to accompany him, to review the record and have a copy made of all or any portion thereof in a form comprehensible to him, except that the agency may require the individual to furnish a written statement authorizing discussion of that individual's record in the accompanying person's presence." [Sources: 5 U.S.C. § 552a(d)(1), "Overview of the Privacy Act of 1974, 2004 Edition, http://www.usdoj.gov/04foia/1974 indrigacc.htm; and EPIC, The Privacy Act of 1974, http://www.epic.org/privacy/1974act/]

PRIVILEGE. Specialized information that has controlled access to ensure confidentiality or impose secrecy. There are several types of privilege that the intelligence analyst should know:

Attorney-Client Privilege: Confidential, open communication between a client and attorney so the attorney is completely informed of all facts in a legal matter.

Attorney Work Product Doctrine Privilege: It is not designed to protect client confidences but, rather, to shelter the "mental processes" of the attorney; considered an independent source of immunity from discovery.

Executive Privilege: Allows the President and other high officials of the executive branch to keep certain communications private if disclosing those communications would disrupt the functions or decision-making processes of the executive branch. As demonstrated by the Watergate hearings, this privilege does not extend to information germane to a criminal investigation; presidential claims of a right to preserve the confidentiality of information and documents.

Least Privilege: Requires that someone be granted the most restrictive set of privileges needed for the performance of a set of authorized tasks.

Privileged Information: An exemption from the Freedom of Information Act.

State Secrets Privilege: Allows the government to deny information to be used in court because of military secrets. Between the years 1953 and 1976, the privilege was used four times; since 2001, the state secrets privilege has been invoked 23 times. In *United States v. Reynolds* (1953), the Supreme Court defined the process through which the government can claim the state secrets privilege; it "is not to be lightly invoked."[331]

PRIVILEGED INFORMATION. Exemption from the Freedom of Information Act which has been utilized by some courts as an alternative for protecting nonconfidential commercial or financial information.[332]

PROBABLE. Likely to occur or prove true; supported generally but not conclusively by the evidence.[333] Commonly confused with *possibility.* According to a U.S. national warning estimate of 1966, "Intelligence is not likely to give warning of *probable* Soviet intent to attack until a few hours before the attack, if at all. Warning of increased Soviet readiness, implying a possible intent to attack, might be given somewhat earlier."[334] *See also* POSSIBLE.

PROCESSING. The manipulation of collected raw information to make it useable in analysis to prepare for data storage or retrieval.

PROCESSING AND EXPLOITATION. In intelligence usage, the conversion of collected information into forms suitable to the production of intelligence.[335]

PRODUCTION. 1. An intelligence product (e.g., estimates, memoranda, and other reports) produced from the analysis of available information. 2. Preparation of reports based on an analysis of information to meet the needs of the intelligence users within and outside the Intelligence Community.[336]

PROOF. Justifying an argument through the process of logical analysis. It involves analyzing the relationship between given facts (evidence) and a theory (hypothesis) with the claim that it explains these facts in terms of the observational data and context. Problems arise when the analyst has to reason from the known to the unknown or from probable, possible, hypothesized, or stipulated factual (evidence) to further inferred facts.[337] *See also* EVIDENCE.

PROPRIETARY INFORMATION. Material and information relating to or associated with a company's products, business, or activities, including but not limited to financial information, data or statements; trade secrets; product research and development; existing and future product designs and performance specifications; marketing plans or techniques; schematics; client lists; computer programs; process; and know-how that have been clearly identified and properly marked by the company as proprietary information, trade secrets, or company confidential information.

PROPRIETARY INFORMATION INVOLVED (PROPIN). This marking is used, with or without a security classification, to identify information provided by a commercial firm or private source under an express or implied understanding that the information will be protected as a trade secret or proprietary data believed to have actual or potential value. This marking may be used in conjunction with the "NOCONTRACT" marking to preclude dissemination to any contractor.[338]

PROTECTED CRITICAL INFRASTRUCTURE INFORMATION (PCII). The Protected CII Program Manager or the Protected CII Program Manager's designees shall mark Protected CII materials as follows: "This document contains Protected CII. In accordance with the provisions of 6 CFR part 29, it is exempt from release under the Freedom of Information Act (5 U.S.C. 552(b)(3)). Unauthorized release may result in civil penalty or other action. It is to be safeguarded and disseminated in accordance with Protected CII Program requirements."[339]

PROTECTION FOR INTELLIGENCE. Two levels exist for the protection of intelligence: both the *product* (i.e., the finished report) and the *sources and methods* (i.e., how the intelligence was collected) will determine the classification of the intelligence. See also CLASSIFICATION LEVELS; CLASSIFICATION MARKINGS.

PSYCHOLOGICAL OPERATIONS (PSYOP). Planned operations to convey selected information and indicators to foreign audiences to influence their emotions, motives, objective reasoning, and ultimately the behavior of foreign governments, organizations, groups, and individuals. The purpose of psychological operations is to induce or reinforce foreign attitudes and behavior favorable to the originator's objectives.[340]

PUBLIC AFFAIRS GROUND RULES. Conditions established by a military command to govern the conduct of news gathering and the release and/or use of specified information during an operation or during a specific period of time.[341]

PUBLIC AFFAIRS GUIDANCE (PAG). Normally, a package of information to support the public discussion of defense issues and operations. Such guidance can range from a telephonic response to a specific question to a more comprehensive package. Included could be an approved public affairs policy, contingency statements, answers to anticipated media questions, and community relations guidance. The *public affairs guidance* also addresses the method(s), timing, location, and other details governing the release of information to the public. *Public affairs guidance* is approved by the Assistant to the Secretary of Defense for Public Affairs.[342]

– Q –

QUERYING. The exchange of information between analysts of different organizations with a common mission; also, requesting additional or amplifying information on specific collection activities.

– R –

RADAR INTELLIGENCE (RADINT). Intelligence information derived from data collected by radar. *See also* SOURCES OF INTELLIGENCE.

RADIATION INTELLIGENCE (RINT). The functions and characteristics derived from information obtained from unintentional electromagnetic energy emanating from foreign devices, excluding nuclear detonations and radioactive sources.

RAW INTELLIGENCE. 1. Information that has been collected but that has not been processed for validity. According to U.S. Army Personnel Command, "MI [military intelligence] Officers lead, manage, and direct intelligence planning and operations at the tactical, operational, and strategic levels across the operational continuum. At all levels, MI Officers plan, supervise, and conduct collection and analysis of *raw intelligence* information. From this information, MI officers produce and **disseminate** finished **all-source intelligence** products for commanders and other intelligence consumers."[343] 2. Information that has been obtained from generally reliable sources; however, it is not necessarily corroborated. It is deemed valid not only because of the sources but also because it coincides with other known information; usually time sensitive and its value is perishable in a relatively short period.[344] *See also* FINISHED INTELLIGENCE.

REACH-BACK CAPABILITY. An organization's ability to provide additional detailed analysis to deployed units. Example: In an attempt to help the Russians rescue their sunken submarine, the U.S. Secretary of Defense said, "We have proposed having teams of experts who have a so-called *reach-back capability* [italics added] to well-organized mission specific expertise."[345]

READINESS. The level of capability within a predetermined time period with which an actor can adequately respond to an attack. Historically, *readiness* of U.S. military forces at the unit level has been measured using the Status of Resources and Training System (SORTS), under the sponsorship of the JCS. Under SORTS, units report their overall *readiness* status as well as the status of four resource areas (personnel, equipment and supplies on hand, equipment condition, and training). The *readiness* status of a unit is reported by assigning capability, or "C," ratings as follows:

C1: Unit can undertake the full wartime missions for which it is organized or designed.

C2: Unit can undertake the bulk of its wartime missions.

C3: Unit can undertake major portions of its wartime missions.

C4: Unit requires additional resources and/or training to undertake its wartime missions, but if the situation dictates, it may be required to undertake portions of the missions with resources on hand.

C5: Unit is undergoing a service-directed resource change and is not prepared to undertake its wartime missions.

While SORTS still provides the basic underpinning to readiness assessments, both OSD and JCS have established senior oversight groups in recent years to focus on readiness issues at a higher level and provide a more comprehensive assessment of *readiness* [italics added].[346]

REAL TIME. Pertaining to the timeliness of data or information which has been delayed only by the time required for electronic communication. This implies that there are no noticeable delays.[347] *See also* CURRENT INTELLIGENCE; NEAR-REAL TIME.

RECIPROCAL FEAR (OF SURPRISE ATTACK). 1. The strong incentive to initiate the first action or launch a preemptive attack because to not do so would cause irreparable vulnerability. 2. The possibility that crisis conditions may trigger automatic mobilization responses, loss of control, and preemptive attacks, resulting in a self-fulfilling prophecy. Understanding this concept is best exhibited by the following phrase: "We fear they fear we fear they will strike; so they may strike . . . so we must."

RECONNAISSANCE. A mission undertaken to obtain information about the activities, resources, or intentions of a threat or potential threat.

RECOVERY, HUMANITARIAN. Decisions and actions taken after a disaster with a view to restoring or improving the pre-disaster living conditions of the stricken community, while encouraging and facilitating necessary adjustments to reduce disaster risk.[348]

RED. In information processing context, denotes encrypted/classified data, text, equipment, processes, systems, or installations associated with information that requires emanations security protection. For example, wiring that carries unencrypted classified information either exclusively or mixed with unclassified is termed *red*.[349] See also BLACK.

RED TEAM ANALYSIS. Understanding the behavior of an individual or group by modeling a replica of how this adversary would think about a particular issue; forecasting how a foreign leader or group may behave.

REDUNDANT EVIDENCE. The association of two or more items of evidence that increasingly favor the same conclusion. There are two types: *corroborative redundancy* (e.g., when an item of evidence is repeatedly sent) and *cumulative redundancy* (e.g., when the value of two items for estimation is greater than either item alone).[350] *See also* CONVERGENT EVIDENCE; DIVERGENT EVIDENCE.

RELIEF RESPONSE. The provision of assistance or intervention during or immediately after a disaster to meet the life preservation and basic subsistence needs of those people affected. It can be of an immediate, short-term, or protracted duration.[351]

REQUIREMENT. 1. General or specific request for intelligence information made by a member of the Intelligence Community. 2. A statement of information needed and which is directed to the intelligence community, agency, or source.

RESTRICTED. An active security classification marking used by some foreign governments and international organizations.[352]

RINT (RADIATION INTELLIGENCE-UNINTENTIONAL). *See* SOURCES OF INTELLIGENCE.

RISK. Probability that a particular threat will exploit a particular vulnerability of the nation's security that will result in damage to life, health, property, or the environment. *See also* RISK ASSESSMENT; RISK MANAGEMENT.

RISK ASSESSMENT. A deliberate, analytical approach to identify which threats can exploit which vulnerabilities in an organization's specific assets. Variables should be ranked according to predetermined criteria, such as the probability of a threat targeting a specific asset or the impact of a vulnerability being exploited by a specific threat in which the results in a prioritized list of risks that can be used to select safeguards to reduce vulnerabilities by creating levels of protection.

RISK ASSESSMENT (IN SUPPORT OF HUMANITARIAN OPERATIONS). The probability of harmful consequences, or expected losses (deaths, injuries, property, livelihoods, economic activity disrupted, or environment damaged) resulting from interactions between natural or human-induced hazards and vulnerable conditions. Conventionally risk is expressed by the notation Risk = Hazards × Vulnerability. Some disciplines also include the concept of exposure to refer particularly to the physical aspects of vulnerability. Beyond expressing a possibility of physical harm, it is crucial to recognize that risks are inherent or can be created or exist within social systems. It is important to consider the social contexts in which risks occur and that people therefore do not necessarily share the same perceptions of risks and their underlying causes.[353]

RISK MANAGEMENT. The decision-making process involving considerations of political, social, and economic factors with relevant assessments relating to a potential threat so as to develop, analyze, and compare options and to select the optimal response to mitigate that threat. *See also* RISK; RISK ASSESSMENT.

RISK MANAGEMENT PRINCIPLES. The three principles include (1) while risk generally cannot be eliminated, it can be reduced by enhancing protection from validated and credible threats; (2) although many threats are possible, some are more likely to occur than others; and (3) all assets are not equally critical.

– S –

SALAMI TACTICS. The incremental attainment of an objective in a slow, methodical way by reducing capabilities in one location, while increasing capabilities in another location. Recently, this term appeared in the editorial pages: "The selling of [President] George Bush's tax cut relies heavily on *salami tactics* [italics added]—slicing away opposition a bit at a time. To understand how fundamentally misleading that sales pitch is, we must look at the whole salami."[354] *See also* CREEPING NORMALCY; PRECISION ATTACK.

SANITIZATION. The process of editing, or otherwise altering, intelligence or intelligence information to protect sensitive sources, methods, and analytical capabilities so as to permit greater dissemination of the data.[355] *See also* SANITIZE.

SANITIZE. Process to remove information from media such that data recovery is not possible. It includes removing all classified labels, markings, and activity logs.[356] *See also* SANITIZATION.

SCENARIO. A narrative, timeline estimate of one significant path or development that may be followed by opposing or friendly strategic forces, offering key indicators for intelligence and actionable threats or opportunities for supported decision makers. *See also* THREAT SCENARIO.

SCIENTIFIC AND TECHNICAL INTELLIGENCE. Information on foreign scientific advancements and technologies. *See also* COMBAT INTELLIGENCE; CURRENT OPERATIONAL INTELLIGENCE; ESTIMATIVE INTELLIGENCE; WARNING INTELLIGENCE

SECURITY DILEMMA. Any action by a nation or a decision by that nation's leadership to enhance security that may also lead to a shift in a systemic power balance that could be perceived to endanger other nations.[357]

SENSITIVE BUT UNCLASSIFIED (SBU) INFORMATION. Information for which disclosure, loss, misuse, alteration, or destruction could adversely affect national security or governmental interests. National security interests are those unclassified matters that relate to the national defense or foreign relations of the U.S. government. Governmental interests are those related, but not limited to, the wide range of government or government-derived economic, human, financial, industrial, agricultural, technological, and law-enforcement information, as well as the privacy or confidentiality of personal or commercial proprietary information provided to the U.S.

government to its citizens.[358] The following Department of Homeland Security information categories fall under SBU:

- For Official Use Only (FOUO)
- Official Use Only (OUO)
- Sensitive Homeland Security Information (SHSI)
- Limited Official Use (LOU)
- Law Enforcement Sensitive (LES)
- Safeguarding Information (SGI)
- Unclassified Nuclear Information (UCNI)

SENSITIVE BY AGGREGATION. Refers to the fact that information on one site may seem unimportant, but when combined with information from other websites, it may form a larger and more complete picture that was neither intended nor desired. Similarly, the compilation of a large amount of information together on one site may increase the sensitivity of that information and make it more likely that site will be accessed by those seeking information that can be used against the government.[359]

SENSITIVE COMPARTMENTED INFORMATION (SCI). Special controls that indicate restricted access is required to handle this information because of the programs that were used to collect the information and the intelligence that was produced.

SENSITIVE COMPARTMENTED INFORMATION FACILITY (SCIF). An accredited area, room, group of rooms, or installation where sensitive compartmented information (SCI) may be stored, used, discussed, and/or electronically processed. *Sensitive compartmented information facility* (SCIF) procedural and physical measures prevent the free access of persons unless they have been formally indoctrinated for the particular SCI authorized for use or storage within the SCIF.[360]

SENSITIVE HOMELAND SECURITY INFORMATION (SHSI). Established in the Homeland Security Act of 2002, it is information which "calls for us to identify and safeguard homeland security information that is sensitive, but unclassified." The regulations governing this category have not been completed.[361]

SENSITIVITY ANALYSIS. A process of determining the significance of changes or variations in the base level of identical, similar, or related types of activity over a period of time; trends are shifts in base level over an extended time period, while anomalies are sudden variations or nonsequential types of changes in the base level. *See also* CREEPING NORMALCY.

SIGNAL. Information accurately interpreted as evidence that points to an adversary's future action or intention. *See also* NOISE.

SIGNALS INTELLIGENCE (SIGINT). *See* SOURCES OF INTELLIGENCE.

SIGNPOSTS. Intermediate developments indicating that events may not be unfolding as expected; also known as indicators of change.

SINGAPORE. A Japanese surprise attack against the British during World War II in 1942 that resulted in 130,000 well-equipped British, Australian, and Indian troops surrendering to 35,000 ill-equipped Japanese soldiers; considered one of the greatest military defeats by Britain. For additional examples of surprise attacks, *see also* FALKLAND ISLANDS; OPERATION BARBAROSSA; PEARL HARBOR; TET OFFENSIVE; YOM KIPPUR WAR.

SINGLE-POINT CONCLUSION. A threat scenario that considers no other alternative. For example, U.S. intelligence has been criticized for developing all their weapons of mass destruction scenarios for Iraq, before the war, on the assumption that Iraq had that capability.

SITUATION ASSESSMENT. 1. An assessment produced by analyzing various indicators to provide a comprehensive projection of a current situation (with the understanding that additional or unknown variables can immediately change any outcomes from a situation assessment). 2. The perception of the quality and quantity of variables in the environment, that comprehending their meaning and the projection of their status into the near future will result in analysis of how various actions will occur in the future.[362]

SITUATION AWARENESS. *See* SITUATION ASSESSMENT.

SLAM DUNK. Disclosed in Bob Woodward's book *Plan of Attack*, DCI George Tenet had assured President Bush of the existence of Iraqi WMD using this phrase to imply 100-percent certainty. Reportedly, Tenet admitted that these were the two stupidest words he ever uttered. Iraqi WMD have never been found.

SOUNDS OF SILENCE PARADOX. *See* PARADOX OF SILENCE.

SOURCE. 1. A person, thing, or activity from which information is obtained. 2. In clandestine activities, a person (agent), normally a foreign national, in the employ of an intelligence activity for intelligence purposes. 3. In interrogation activities, any person who furnishes information, either with or without the knowledge that the information is being used for intelligence purposes. In this context, a controlled source is in the employment or under the control of the intelligence activity and knows that the information is to be used for intelligence purposes. An uncontrolled source is a voluntary contributor of information and may or may not know that the information is to be used for intelligence purposes.[363]

SOURCES OF INTELLIGENCE. The means or systems used to observe, sense, and record or convey information of conditions, situations, and events.[364] There are seven primary source types, ten secondary source types, and three tertiary source types. The *primary* source types are counterintelligence (CI), human intelligence (HUMINT), imagery intelligence (IMINT), measurement and signature intelligence (MASINT), open source intelligence (OSINT), signals intelligence (SIGINT), technical intelligence (TECHINT). The *secondary* source types are acoustical intelligence (ACINT), communications intelligence (COMINT), electronic intelligence (ELINT), electro-optical intelligence (ELECTRO-OPTINT), infrared intelligence (IRINT), nuclear intelligence (NUCINT), radiation intelligence-unintentional (RINT). The *tertiary* source types under ELINT are foreign instrumentation and signals intelligence (FISINT), telemetry intelligence (TELINT), and radar intelligence (RADINT).[365] *See also* ATTRIBUTES OF INTELLIGENCE QUALITY.

SPECIAL ACCESS PROGRAM (SAP). Any program that imposes need-to-know or access controls beyond those normally required for access to Confidential, Secret, or Top Secret information. Examples of such controls include, but are not limited to, special clearance, adjudication, or investigative requirements; special designation of officials authorized to determine need-to-know; or special lists of persons determined to have a need-to-know. Special access controls may be applied to "an extremely sensitive activity requiring special protection from disclosure to prevent significant damage to national security or the reputation or interests of the United States." 2. Any program imposing a need-to-know or access controls beyond those normally provided for access.[366] *See also* SENSITIVE COMPARTMENTED INFORMATION.

SPECIAL INFORMATION OPERATIONS (SIO). Information operations that, by their sensitive nature and due to their potential effect or impact, security requirements, or risk to the national security, require a special review and approval process.[367]

SPECIAL NATIONAL INTELLIGENCE ESTIMATE (SNIE). Specific policy problems that need to be addressed in the immediate future; generally unscheduled and prepared more quickly than national intelligence estimates. Some cynics of the intelligence process have said, "an SNIE is an NIE that was never written beforehand." *See also* NATIONAL INTELLIGENCE ESTIMATE.

SPLIT KNOWLEDGE. Separation of data and information into two or more parts, each part constantly kept under control of authorized individuals or teams so no one individual or team will know the whole data.[368]

SPOT REPORT. A brief narrative report of essential information covering events or conditions that may have an immediate and significant effect on current planning and operations. A spot report is accorded the fastest means of transmission to the watch officer.

STATIC INFORMATION/INTELLIGENCE. Statistical and historical information on an enemy's capabilities; associated with "basic" intelligence. "[Prior to World War II] the question of who sent what to the operating forces was of course partly a matter of prestige. The static information was dull, safe, old, long term and primarily based on public sources. Directives were usually based on top-secret sources that concerned either the intentions of the U.S. government or of the enemy and were usually exciting and up to the minute."[369]

STOPLIGHT CHART. A graphical representation depicting the different levels of warning or activity within a country or region. The term originates from the typical warning chart found in most military command headquarters. For example, countries that are color coded green represent normal military activity within the country, yellow coded countries represent unusual military activity within the country, and red coded countries represent extremely unusual military activity that is occurring within a country. However, "the often-used but crude *'stoplight' charts* [italics added]—red-amber-green 'metrics' of easily observable variables—may be useless or even counterproductive if they oversimplify complex situations, inaccurately and incompletely measure key variables or address peripheral ones, or stimulate unwarranted confidence about how well the situation 'outside the wire' is understood."[370]

STOVEPIPE WARNING. An administrative process that transmits information through a predetermined set of guidelines and that does not allow the information to be shared outside the organization or within the organization among departments. For example, in response to NATO's accidental bombing of the Chinese Embassy in Belgrade, "House Intelligence Committee Chairman Porter Goss (R-Florida) suggested the problem might be what he called *stovepiping*. Goss, a former CIA employee, told CNN: 'In the Intelligence Community, everyone does his job and you don't share the information unless there is a need to know. This could be a case where the right compartments didn't talk to each other.'"[371] *See also* BOOTLEGGING.

STRATEGIC DEPTH. The elements of space and time, which when accommodated by intelligence analysis, provide a means for timely warning.

STRATEGIC INFORMATION AND OPERATIONS CENTER (SIOC). Located in the Federal Bureau of Investigation (FBI) headquarters building in Washington, DC, this crisis center is the agency's worldwide connection to the Department of Defense, other governmental agencies, and the FBI's network of field offices in the U.S. and abroad. In operation since 1998, the center can handle four international crises at once.

STRATEGIC INFORMATION WARFARE. Intersection of information and strategic warfare.

STRATEGIC INTELLIGENCE. Intelligence required for the formation of policy and military plans at national and international levels. Its components include such characteristics as biographic data, economic, sociological, transportation, telecommunications, geography, political, and scientific and technical intelligence. *See also* TACTICAL INTELLIGENCE.

STRATEGIC PLAN, DEPARTMENT OF HOMELAND SECURITY. Seven goals are identified to support the components of risk from any threat, if and when it should occur, as outlined in *Securing Our Homeland* published in 2004. Those seven goals include awareness, prevention, protection, response, recovery, service, and organizational excellence.[372]

STRATEGIC WARNING. A forecast of a probable attack or a forecast that enemy-initiated hostilities may be imminent; warning must be received early enough to permit decision makers to undertake countermeasures (military, political, or diplomatic) prior to actual hostilities; usually can range from a few weeks to several days. "For strategic warning, the key problem is not when attack may occur, but whether the enemy is preparing to attack at all. . . . *Strategic warning* is not a forecast of imminent attack. *Strategic warning is a forecast of probable attack* [original italics] and it is this above all which the policy official and commander need to know."[373] *See also* POLITICAL WARNING; TACTICAL WARNING.

STRATEGIC WARNING LEAD TIME. That time between the receipt of strategic warning and the beginning of hostilities. This time may include strategic warning pre-decision time and post-decision time. Refer to table 2. *See also* STRATEGIC WARNING POST-DECISION TIME; STRATEGIC WARNING PRE-DECISION TIME.

STRATEGIC WARNING POST-DECISION TIME. That time after a decision is made in response to strategic warning and the order is executed. This time ends with the start of hostilities or termination of the threat. Refer to table 2. *See also* STRATEGIC WARNING LEAD TIME; STRATEGIC WARNING PRE-DECISION TIME.

STRATEGIC WARNING PRE-DECISION TIME. That time which begins upon receipt of strategic warning and ends when a decision is ordered and executed. Refer to figure 1. *See also* STRATEGIC WARNING LEAD TIME; STRATEGIC WARNING POST-DECISION TIME.

SURGE CAPABILITY. (This definition is as it appears in a study by the House of Representatives Permanent Select Committee on Intelligence.) Defined very broadly, it is the ability to move intelligence resources quickly to address immediate, usually ad hoc, needs; augment existing resources from outside the Intelligence Community; and improve responsiveness of resources by building in more flexible options for collection and analysis. Taken together, these capabilities should provide for the development and maintenance of some level of knowledge on all countries and issues providing an intelligence base. This "surge" capability needs to be flexible, dynamic and well-planned—one that can be relied upon both day-to-day and during crises.[374]

Figure 1.   Strategic warning lead time, post-decision time, and pre-decision time.

SURVEILLANCE. The systematic observation of aerospace, surface or subsurface areas, places, people, or things by visual, aural, photographic, or other means.

SWOT ANALYSIS. Acronym for Strengths, Weaknesses, Opportunities, and Threats (SWOT); an analytic tool to assist in determining resource priorities, capitalizing on opportunities, thwarting enemy initiatives, identifying and exploiting advantages over the enemy, and shoring up defensive vulnerabilities and weaknesses; summarizes the most potent and essential knowledge about a situation in relation to the threat and environment; a relatively straightforward way to institutionalize knowledge so that it is readily accessible to others who have a **need-to-know** and who can help advance the quality of knowledge it imparts; has the effect of organizing a lot of critical thinking about a situation in a straightforward and simple manner.

SYNTHESIS. The assembly of essential facts, data, opinions, and other elements of information into a whole or plausible intelligence explanation or model in a form suitable for a particular consumer.

– T –

TACIT KNOWLEDGE. Intangible, internal, intuitive knowledge that is undocumented and maintained in the human mind; has typically been characterized by intangible factors such as perception, belief, values, skill, intuition, "know-how," and "gut feeling." *See also* EXPLICIT KNOWLEDGE.

TACTICAL INTELLIGENCE. Intelligence that is required for the planning and conduct of tactical operations. Essentially, *tactical intelligence* and **strategic intelligence** differ only in scope, point of view, and level of employment. Seeks to gather and manage diverse information to facilitate a successful prosecution of the intelligence target. TI is also used for specific decision making or problem solving to deal with an immediate situation or crisis.[375] *See also* OPERATIONAL INTELLIGENCE; STRATEGIC INTELLIGENCE.

TACTICAL INTELLIGENCE AND RELATED ACTIVITIES (TIARA). Comprised of the array of reconnaissance and target acquisition programs that are a functional part of the basic military force structure and provide direct information support to military operations.

TACTICAL WARNING. Short-term warning that an attack is imminent or that forces are in motion; primarily intended for military commanders who must respond to it with usually no time to redeploy defensively; primarily the responsibility of operational forces. Detection of the initial movements of the attack itself, before combat occurs; time can range from minutes to hours depending on the distance from the ground force assembly area or missile launch site to target. *See also* POLITICAL WARNING; STRATEGIC WARNING.

TARGET. An individual, operation, or activity that an adversary has determined possesses information that might prove useful in attaining his or her objective.

TASKING. The levying of specific requirements on intelligence collection assets.

TEAR LINE. A physical line that appears on a message or document which separates information that has been approved for foreign/public disclosure and information which must not be released. Usually, that information below the tear line is releasable and that above the tear line remains classified and/or nonreleasable. 2. In a classified report there may be a summary of critical information, without a description of sources and methods that is below a designated line on the report. This portion is "torn off" of the report making it Sensitive But Unclassified (SBU) and may be disseminated to law enforcement personnel who do not have a security clearance as "Law Enforcement Sensitive."[376]

TECHNICAL INTELLIGENCE (TECHINT). *See* SOURCES OF INTELLIGENCE.

TECHNICAL SUPPORT WORKING GROUP (TSWG). The U.S. national forum that identifies, prioritizes, and coordinates interagency and international research and development (R&D) requirements for combating terrorism. The TSWG rapidly develops technologies and equipment to meet the high-priority needs of the combating terrorism community, and addresses joint international operational requirements through cooperative R&D with major allies. The TSWG continues to focus its program development efforts to balance investments across the four pillars of combating terrorism:

Antiterrorism. Defense measures taken to reduce vulnerability to terrorist acts.

Counterterrorism. Offensive measures taken to prevent, deter, and respond to terrorism.

Intelligence Support. Collection and dissemination of terrorism-related information taken to oppose terrorism throughout the entire threat spectrum; to include terrorist use of chemical, biological, radiological, and nuclear materials or high-yield explosive devices.

Consequence Management. Preparation for and response to the consequences of a terrorist event.[377]

TECHNOLOGICAL ASYMMETRY. The unequal sophistication or distribution of technology within a country that could possibly lead to the overestimation of an enemy's capability. For example, country A has the ability to build a nuclear bomb but may lack the ability to weaponize it into a delivery system, which would result in *technological asymmetry* (assuming the country was seeking a nuclear missile capability).

TECHNOLOGICAL DEVELOPMENT. Five stages to be monitored to determine the threat capability of a real (or potential) enemy. The 5 stages are basic research (to develop a theoretical understanding); item fabrication (translating a theory into practice by developing experimental confirmation); production prototype (to demonstrate feasibility); full production (item is available and can or could possibly be mass produced) and maturity (minor changes are made to production). *See also* TECHNOLOGICAL SURPRISE.

TECHNOLOGICAL SURPRISE. The unilateral advantage gained by the introduction of a new weapon or by the use of a known weapon in an innovative way against an adversary who is either unaware of its existence or not ready with effective countermeasures. For example,

> The post-Cold War political climate does not guarantee any army's arsenal to come from a single supplier state. S2's [intelligence officers] cannot template capabilities based on a single (normally Russian) model. Such diversity not only complicates Order of Battle study; it also provides opportunities for technological surprise. *Technological surprise* is the bogeyman for TECHINT [technical intelligence] analysis: the specter of U.S. commanders encountering optics, weapons ranges, or armor more sophisticated than they thought an opponent possessed. The key to preventing technological surprise is training soldiers ahead of time to look for, recognize, and report on new or modified weapons on the battlefield. The 203rd MI Battalion responds to such spot reports with a TECHINT Collection Team, which photographs and often retrieves the new systems off of the battlefield for further study. This cycle of recognition, reporting, retrieval, and analysis is fundamental to avoiding *technological surprise* [italics added].[378]

TELEMETRY INTELLIGENCE (TELINT). Information derived from the intercept, processing, and analysis of foreign telemetry. *See also* SOURCES OF INTELLIGENCE.

TERMS OF REFERENCE. Those elements that define the subject matter of a report or estimate to include: context, scope, and timeframe. According to Sherman Kent, considered one of the standard-bearers of intelligence analysis at CIA, *terms of reference* "focus the forthcoming estimate on the new major points which were discerned as the principal concern of the requestor; aimed to ask the questions (irrespective of anyone's ability to supply factual answers) which would direct research and cogitation to the general area of these major points. In a word, it was a statement of precisely what was wanted and a polite message to the community's expert research analysts, telling what was wanted of them."[379]

TERRORISM INFORMATION AWARENESS. 1. "Previously known as Total Information Awareness, this name created in some minds the impression that TIA was a system to be used for developing dossiers on U.S. citizens. That is not DoD's intent in pursuing this program. Rather, DoD's purpose in pursuing these efforts is to protect U.S. citizens by detecting and defeating foreign terrorist threats before an attack. To make this objective absolutely clear, DARPA has changed the program name to Terrorism Information Awareness. 2. A research and development program that will integrate advanced collaborative and decision support tools; language translation; and data search, pattern recognition, and privacy protection technologies into an experimental prototype network focused on combating terrorism through better analysis and decision making. If successful, and if deployed, this program of programs would provide decision- and policy-makers with advance actionable information and knowledge about terrorist planning and preparation activities that would aid in making informed decisions to prevent future international terrorist attacks against the United States at home or abroad. In short, DoD's aim is to make a significant leap in technology to help those working to "connect the dots" of terrorist-related activity as identified in the aftermath of the attacks against the United States on September 11, 2001, and that are related to improving information analysis in our continuing war against terrorism."[380]

TERRORISM INFORMATION PREVENTION SYSTEM (ALSO KNOWN AS OPERATION TIPS). 1. The program was announced in concept in January 2002 for the stated purpose of creating a national information sharing system for specific industry groups to report suspicious, publicly observable activity that could be related to terrorism. The program was scheduled to be operational in the fall of 2002 as one of the new Citizen Corps programs.

> The initiative's design is based on existing programs, such as Highway Watch and Coast Watch, which allow truckers and ship captains to report dangerous conditions along their routes. In response to significant demand among industry groups, Operation TIPS would make these programs available nationwide by providing specific industry groups a single phone number for reporting potentially terrorist-related activities occurring in public areas. Specifically, industry groups have looked to the Justice Department to offer a reliable and cost-effective system that their workers could use to report information to state, local, and federal law enforcement agencies about unusual activities they might observe in the normal course of their daily routines. Any and all activities of the Federal Government to implement the proposed component program of the Citizen Corps known as Operation TIPS (Terrorism Information and Prevention System) are hereby prohibited.[381]

TERRORIST THREAT INTEGRATION CENTER (TTIC). Consists of 5 equal partners (CIA, FBI, DHS, DoD, DOS) to fuse and analyze all-source information relating to terrorism; conducts no collection activities of its own, but has access to all intelligence products, from raw to finished, available in the U.S. government; TTIC analysts produce analysis, they play no role in the support of counterterrorism operations. TTIC produces the daily threat matrix, the daily situation report, and community threat advisories, all of which were formerly produced by the Counter Terrorism Center. TTIC hopes to extend the dissemination of intelligence products to the "sensitive but unclassified" level with spot commentaries and other products. TTIC is intended to provide one-stop shopping for terrorist threats, both home and abroad. Personnel size (end strength) is approximately 300 analysts. *See also* COUNTERTERRORISM CENTER; INFORMATION ANALYSIS AND INFRASTRUCTURE PROTECTION; JOINT TERRORISM TASK FORCE.

TET OFFENSIVE. A nationwide surprise assault on January 30–31, 1968, during the Tet Holiday occurred when North Vietnamese attacked U.S. troops in South Vietnam. Although considered a failed tactical military defeat, it is considered a strategic political victory since this led to public pressure for withdrawal of U.S. forces by the American public. *See also* FALKLAND ISLANDS; OPERATION BARBAROSSA; PEARL HARBOR; SINGAPORE; YOM KIPPUR WAR.

THIRD-AGENCY RULE. The governing rule that states that except as provided in section 102, National Security Act of 1947, classified information originating in one U.S. agency (e.g., DoD) will not be disseminated by another agency to which the information has been made available without the consent of the originating agency.[382]

THREAT. 1. The extant military, economic, and political capability of a foreign country with aggressive intentions to use such capability to undertake any action whose consequences will be detrimental to another country. 2. In the context of surprise, *threat* is the culmination of a country's capabilities and intentions. 3. In the security technology context, the likelihood that attempts will be made to gain unauthorized access to information or facilities.[383] *See also* RISK.

THREAT ANALYSIS. Examination of information to identify the elements comprising a threat.[384]

THREAT CONDITION (THREATCON). A designated scale used to convey a situation in a particular country or region as it pertains to terrorist activity. *Threat conditions* are measured by military commanders in the field based on intelligence reports and local conditions. There are five *threat condition* levels, each of which carries suggestions about vehicle inspections, personnel alerts, and identity checks. Local commanders decide what to do under each condition. The five levels of *threat condition* are:

Threat Condition Normal. No threat of terrorist activity is present.

Threat Condition Alpha. There is a general threat of possible terrorist activity against installations, building locations, and/or personnel, the nature and extent of which are unpredictable.

Threat Condition Bravo. There is an increased and more predictable threat of terrorist activity even though no particular target has been identified.

Threat Condition Charlie. An incident has occurred or intelligence has been received indicating some form of terrorist action is imminent.

Threat Condition Delta. A terrorist attack has occurred or intelligence has been received indicating that action against a specific location is likely. "Threat Condition Delta is appropriate 'if you really do have information that you think is specific and credible and presents a real possibility of danger to your forces at the local level,' Rear Adm. Craig Quigley told journalists this afternoon [coming after the attack on the USS *Cole* off the coast of Yemen]."[385]

See also DEFENSE CONDITION; WATCH CONDITION.

THREAT MANAGEMENT. Provides warning of war and instability to support planning and the development of contingency measures to deter, avoid, deflect, and manage threats before they inflict damage on persons or a country's interests and to support early readiness measures so as to minimize the damage should deterrence fail; to provide warning support throughout the duration of the crisis management phases, through to the restoration of normal conditions.

THREAT PERCEPTION. Derived from another nation's behavior, and is a function of both estimated capabilities and intentions.

THREAT SCENARIO. A sequence of events that when completed represent an unambiguous threat; provides the basis for the formulation of an indicator list.

TRANSIENT ELECTROMAGNETIC PULSE SURVEILLANCE TECHNOLOGY (TEMPEST). An unclassified short name referring to investigations and studies of compromising emanations. Compromising emanations are unintentional intelligence-bearing signals that, if intercepted and analyzed, will disclose classified information when they are transmitted, received, handled, or otherwise processed by any information processing equipment. Because the details of many TEMPEST issues are classified and controlled under strict conditions of need-to-know, unclassified discussions must be somewhat general.[386]

TWILIGHT INFORMATION. "Lies somewhere between deep concealment and full disclosure." Competing elements of secrecy and partial disclosure are the bipolar elements of twilight information. *Twilight information* may be partially released through (redacted) Freedom of Information Act requests, consist of information previously considered classified, sensitive, or proprietary, or simply be omitted due to regulatory allowances such as categorical exclusion. *Twilight information* has its roots in the Reagan Administration National Security Defense Directive (NSDD)-145, which authorized the National Security Agency (NSA) to develop means to protect "unclassified sensitive information." NSDD-145 permitted NSA to control the dissemination of government, government-derived, and nongovernment information that might "adversely affect the national security." NSDD-145 has had a powerful impact on librarians, publishers, and citizens who argued that national security classification already existed that "partitioned" to protect sensitive information.[387]

– U –

UNAUTHORIZED DISCLOSURE. Communication or physical transfer of classified information to an unauthorized recipient; the compromise of classified information by communication or physical transfer to an unauthorized recipient. It includes the unauthorized disclosure of classified information in a newspaper, journal, or other publication where such information is traceable to an agency because of a direct quotation or other uniquely identifiable fact.[388]

UNCLASSIFIED INTELLIGENCE. "Intelligence is information, which has been discovered, discriminated, distilled, and disseminated in a form tailored to the needs of a specific policymaker at a specific time and place."[389] Information, a document, or material that has been determined not to be classified or that has been declassified by a proper authority; also defined as a limited distribution category applied to the wide range of unclassified types of official information, not requiring protection as National Security Information, but limited to official use and not publicly releasable.

UNDERCOVER OPERATION. A phrase usually associated with the law enforcement community that describes an operation so planned and executed as to conceal the identity of or permit plausible denial by the sponsor. It is synonymous with *covert operation*.

UNKNOWN. 1. A code meaning "information not available." 2. An unidentified target. An aircraft or ship that has not been determined to be hostile, friendly, or neutral using identification friend or foe and other techniques, but that must be tracked by air defense or naval engagement systems.[390]

UPGRADING. The determination that certain classified information requires, in the interests of national security, a higher degree of protection against unauthorized disclosure than currently provided, coupled with a changing of the classification designation to reflect the higher degree.[391]

– V –

VALIDATION OF INFORMATION. Procedures governing the periodic review of criminal intelligence information to assure its continuing compliance with system submission criteria established by regulation or program policy.[392]

VALUE ADDED. Additional analysis or commentary in a report that significantly redirects or confirms an assessment for a warning effort. For example, an individual who has lived in a target country recently may have input that would impart *value added* to current intelligence operations.

VOICE-IN-THE-WILDERNESS. A forecast or warning given within the context of receptive ambiguity, negligence, or denial by the consumer; an assessment or report that is contradictory to an overwhelming consensus.

VULNERABILITY. The susceptibility of information to exploitation by an adversary.

VULNERABILITY ANALYSIS. A process that examines a friendly operation or activity from the point of view of an adversary, seeking ways to determine critical information in time to disrupt or defeat the operation or activity.

VULNERABILITY, HUMANITARIAN. Those conditions that are determined by physical, social, economic, and environmental factors or processes, which increase the susceptibility of a community to the impact of hazards.

– W –

WARDEN SYSTEM. An informal method of communication used to pass information to U.S. citizens during emergencies.[393]

WARN EXPOSED. Vulnerability of friendly forces to nuclear weapon effects in which personnel are assumed to be in a position that all skin is covered with minimal thermal protection provided by a "two-layer summer uniform." However, this has been used as a pejorative term to indicate a victim's false sense of security and insulation from a perceived threat. *See also* WARN PROTECTED.

WARN PROTECTED. Vulnerability of friendly forces to nuclear weapon effects in which personnel are assumed to be in a position against heat, blast, and radiation afforded in closed armored vehicles or crouched in foxholes with improvised overhead shielding. However, this has been used as a pejorative term to indicate a victim's false sense of security and insulation from a perceived threat. *See also* WARN EXPOSED.

WARNING. A notification of impending activities that may, or may be perceived to, adversely affect U.S. national security interests or military forces; for the U.S. Intelligence Community, it is those measures taken, and the intelligence information produced, by the Intelligence Community to avoid surprise to the President, the NSC, and the Armed Forces of the United States by foreign events of major importance to the security of the United States. It includes strategic but not tactical warning.[394]

WARNING, STRATEGIC. Intelligence information or intelligence regarding the threat of the initiation of hostilities against the U.S. or in which U.S. forces may become involved; it may be received at any time prior to the initiation of hostilities. It does not include tactical warning.[395]

WARNING, TACTICAL. Notification that the enemy has initiated hostilities. Such warning may be received at any time from the launching of the attack until it reaches its target.[396]

WARNING CENTER. A site where strategic intelligence assessments are made in support to, and as a part of, a larger warning system. *See also* ALERT CENTER, INDICATIONS CENTER; WATCH CENTER.

WARNING DAY (W-DAY). The day on which the Intelligence Community judges that a potential adversary's preparations (political, economic, and military) suggest that a decision to initiate hostilities occurred. This term may also be used to designate a specific day when conditions represent a growing threat.

WARNING FAILURE. An unanticipated action or event or a decision by a foreign leader that results in detrimental consequences to another nation's national security. Often related to the failure to forecast events before they happen. However, not all *warning failures* are solely the responsibility of the Intelligence Community. Intelligence is used to influence decisions that may result in a specific action. For example, if a policymaker receives intelligence that a specific act will likely occur, and the policymaker implements no preventative action, is that a warning failure? "On 14 April 1997 the following letter was sent to William Daley, the secretary of commerce, expressing concerns about the proposed cuts in the budget of the National Weather Service:

> Dear Mr. Secretary:
> The recent announcement of significant cuts in the budget of the National Weather Service and their impact on the Weather Service's capability to warn of severe weather and flood hazards to protect life and property is cause for deep concern. The effect of the budget reductions has been to force the Service to hold a large number of vacancies as well as reduce the number of key employees. This thinning of the Weather Service staffing increases the risk of *warning failures* with potentially tragic consequences. There is no need to cite the aftermath of Hurricane Andrew, the blizzard of 1996, the recent tornadoes in Arkansas and the flooding in the Ohio River valley to illustrate the importance of timely warnings. While nobody can specifically identify when and where a warning will fail, we can say, with assurance, that the risk of *warning failure* is now substantially increased. As maintenance of critical equipment degrades because of a lack of personnel and spare parts, the chances of failure increase. As meteorologists and other professionals are eliminated, or positions remain vacant, the forecast and warning load on those that remain becomes excessive.[397]

See also INTELLIGENCE FAILURE.

WARNING INTELLIGENCE. Notice that something urgent might happen that may require immediate attention; an intelligence product upon which to base a notification of impending activities on the part of foreign powers, including hostilities, which may adversely affect military forces or security interests.[398] *See also* COMBAT INTELLIGENCE; CURRENT INTELLIGENCE; ESTIMATIVE INTELLIGENCE; SCIENTIFIC AND TECHNICAL INTELLIGENCE.

WARNING INTELLIGENCE APPRAISAL. Provides in-depth analysis and assessment. It is prepared, printed, and disseminated on an urgent basis whenever a short assessment of imminent development is of considerable interest to high-level officials. An alerting document on a developing intelligence and warning situation.[399]

WARNING JUDGMENT. A forecast of the anticipated course of action that a threat will take; an appraisal of a future course of anticipated events or estimate of the likelihood (probability) of occurrence of a current or potential threat.

WARNING LEAD TIME (WLT). 1. A point in time deemed necessary to adequately prepare prior to an attack or an outbreak of hostilities. 2. The time between the receipt of warning and the beginning of hostilities. This time may include two action periods: warning pre-decision time and warning post-decision time. For example, the TET cease-fire (by North Vietnam), its subsequent cancellation, and the difficulty of reaching commanders going off for holiday leave compounded the problem of disseminating intelligence warnings. In the words of one U.S. communications officer, "Really we needed 36 to 48 hours [*warning lead time*] to get a message down to everybody [U.S. military forces in Vietnam]. The U.S. had just 18 hours to alert the whole of MACV [Military Assistance Command in Vietnam]. As a result the majority of units were surprised by the attack when it came on the night of 31 January 1968."[400] Refer to table 3. *See also* STRATEGIC WARNING LEAD TIME; STRATEGIC WARNING POST-DECISION TIME; STRATEGIC WARNING PRE-DECISION TIME.

WARNING NET. A communications system established for the purpose of disseminating warning information of enemy movements to all affected commands.

WARNING NOTICES (AS IT RELATES TO CLASSIFICATION). Appear on classified documents to alert the reader that special precautions are required in the handling and releasing of information. When required, the warning notices appear in their full form on the front cover, title page, or first page of a document. A shorter form also appears at the top or bottom center of applicable pages, on telegram caption lines, and on tables, figures, charts, etc. Examples include:

Not Releasable to Foreign Nationals (NoForn/NF). When information is limited only to U.S. government employees.

Not Releasable to Contractors or Contractor Consultants (No Contract/NC). When information has been provided to the United States by a foreign government or international organization, or information is generated by the United States pursuant to a joint arrangement with a foreign government or international organization, use the notice.

Foreign Government Information (FGI): If the information is foreign government information that must be concealed, do not use the marking and mark the document as if it were entirely of U.S. origin.

Warning Notice—Intelligence Sources or Methods Involved (WNINTEL/WN). When the originator must have continuing knowledge and supervision of the use of information, use the following notice:

Dissemination and Extraction of Information Controlled by Originator (OrCon/OC). For classified material containing Restricted Data or Formerly Restricted Data, as defined by the Atomic Energy Act of 1954 as amended (which concerns the design, manufacture, or utilization of atomic weapons; the production of special nuclear material; or the use of special nuclear material in the production of energy).

WARNING OF ATTACK. A warning to national policymakers that an adversary is not only preparing its armed forces for war, but intends to launch an attack in the near future. According to Presidential Decision Directive 63, which discusses the newly formed National Infrastructure Protection Center (NIPC), "All executive departments and agencies shall cooperate with the NIPC and provide such assistance, information and advice that the NIPC may request, to the extent permitted by law. All executive departments shall also share with the NIPC information about threats and *warning of attacks* and about actual attacks on critical government and private sector infrastructures, to the extent permitted by law.[401] *See also* WARNING OF WAR.

WARNING OF WAR. A warning to national policymakers that a state or alliance intends war or is on a course that substantially increases the risks of war and is taking steps to prepare for war. "The 1938 Nazi Party Congress put the might of Hitler's fearsome Wehrmacht on full display to the world and made clear what a forceful hold the Fuhrer had on his people.

Delivering his fiery speeches to the well rehearsed formations, he gave Europe an implicit *warning of war* [italics added] which would erupt one year later."[402] *See also* WARNING OF ATTACK.

WARNING ORDER. A preliminary notice of an order or an action that is to follow; designed to give subordinates time to make the necessary plans and preparations; commonly referred to as a "heads up" notice. According to some Department of Defense documents, this term may also refer to "a crisis action planning directive issued by the Chairman of the Joint Chiefs of Staff that initiates the development and evaluation of courses of action by a supported commander and requests that a commander's estimate be submitted."

WARNING PARADOX. Enemy counteraction based on friendly action taken as a result of a warning; alters the enemy's initially intended course of action. The warning thus appears to be wrong on the basis of the change in enemy action. *See also* CRY-WOLF SYNDROME.

WARNING PROBLEM. An identified potential threat that when translated into threat scenario(s) postulates a sequence of events, which, when this process is completed, represents an unambiguous threat. *Warning problems* are usually never eliminated but are considered inactive, once the threat no longer exists, to foster an "institutional memory."

WARNING SYNTHESIS. The building of a plausible threat model from specific (indications intelligence) facts and opinions and the development of a warning judgment based upon this threat model; an inductive process wherein the warning judgment on the threat model is refined as new intelligence becomes available or when the validity of existing intelligence options is upgraded.

WARNING SYSTEMS. Arrangements to rapidly **disseminate** information concerning imminent disaster threats to government officials, institutions, and the population at large in the areas at immediate risk.

WARNING THRESHOLD. A level of activity, specific action(s), or decision(s) by key personnel that result in the implementation of a heightened sense of awareness and action. *See also* WATCH CONDITION.

WARNING TIME. *See* WARNING LEAD TIME.

WATCH CENTER. A location for the review of all incoming intelligence information and which possesses, or has access to, extensive communications for alerting local intelligence personnel and contacting appropriate external reporting sources and other nodes in the indications and warning system. *See also* ALERT CENTER; INDICATIONS CENTER; WARNING CENTER; WATCH OFFICER.

WATCH CONDITION (WATCHCON). 1. An operational and intelligence alerting mechanism that provides a shorthand expression of the reporting organization's degree of intelligence concern regarding a particular warning problem. Often confused with **Defense Conditions (DEFCONS)** and **Threat Conditions (THREATCONS)**. 2. Intelligence interest and concern relative to the potential outlined in a warning problem. A warning problem for a country or region is a set of detectable events that might lead to a crisis and threaten U.S. citizens, interests, and operating forces. WATCHCON IV is defined as a "potential threat," WATCHCON III is "increased threat," WATCHCON II is "significant threat," and WATCHCON I is "clear immediate threat." For example,

> Through the summer of 1990, the US Defense Intelligence Community followed Iraq's dispute with Kuwait with increasing alarm. Through July, DIA tracked Iraq's military buildup along the border with Kuwait and the mediation efforts in the region. During the second half of July, US Defense Intelligence officials began to warn policy officials of the possibility of an Iraqi attack on Kuwait. DIA's crisis support organizations and ties to the commands proved crucial in providing intelligence support to CENTCOM and policymakers during the Gulf crisis and war that followed. Both DIA and CENTCOM had established the Iraq regional warning problem and assumed *watch condition* (WATCHCON) level IV in April 1990. DIA raised its WATCHCON to level III on 21 July and to level II on 24 July based on the concentration of Iraqi troops on the Kuwaiti border and the failure of diplomatic initiatives. DIA declared WATCHCON level I on 1 August, the first time any command or agency had assumed this highest level watch condition in advance of a conflict.[403]

See also DEFENSE CONDITION; THREAT CONDITION.

WATCH OFFICER. A person, usually assigned to a command's intelligence unit, trained to identify indications of hostilities that require immediate attention; a senior officer who is the duty representative of the commander in intelligence matters.

WEAPONEERING. The process of determining the quantity of a specific type of lethal or nonlethal weapons required to achieve a specific level of damage to a given target. Considering target vulnerability, weapon effect, munitions, delivery accuracy, damage criteria, probability of kill, and weapon reliability.[404]

WEAPONS OF MASS DESTRUCTION (WMD). Generally defined as any nuclear, biological, or chemical weapon; specifically, under U.S. law, any weapon or device that is intended, or has the capability, to cause death or serious bodily injury to a significant number of people through the release, dissemination, or impact of:

- toxic or poisonous chemicals or their precursors
- a disease organism
- radiation or radioactivity[405]

WEAPONS OF MASS EFFECT (WME). The ability of a person, group, or nation-state to threaten the use of weapons of mass destruction, regardless of whether it possesses them, to affect another person, group, or nation-state(s) decision-making and policy process. For example, a *weapon of mass effect* could be cyber attacks on U.S. commercial information systems or attacks against transportation networks, which would have a greater economic or psychological effect than a relatively small release of a lethal agent. *See also* MASS EFFECT.

WEBSITES, ACTIVE EARLY WARNING SYSTEMS. See the following classifications:

Country Indicators for Foreign Policy (CIFP). A geopolitical database, developed by the Canadian Department of National Defense in 1991, has since operated under the guidance of principal investigator at Carleton University in Canada. The CIFP database currently includes statistical data in issue areas, in the form of over 100 performance indicators for 196 countries, spanning 15 years (1985 to 2000) for most indicators which are drawn from a variety of open sources. Located at http://www.carleton.ca/cifp.

International Crisis Group (ICG). An independent, nonprofit, nongovernmental organization, with over 110 staff members on five continents, working through field-based analysis and high-level advocacy to prevent and resolve deadly conflict. Located at http://www.crisisgroup.org/home/.

Global Information and Early Warning System (GIEWS). Operated under the Food and Agriculture Organization of the United Nations, this warning system reviews the world food supply and the demand for food, by issuing reports on the world food situation and by providing early warnings of impending food crises in individual countries. Located at http://www.fao.org/giews/english/index.htm.

Humanitarian Early Warning Service (HEWS). An interagency partnership project aimed at establishing a common platform for humanitarian early warnings and forecasts for natural hazards and sociopolitical developments worldwide. Located at http://www.hewsweb.org/home_page/default.asp.

International Strategy for Disaster Reduction (ISDR), United Nations. Promotes disaster resilient communities by promoting increased awareness of the importance of disaster reduction as an integral component of sustainable development, with the goal of reducing human, social, economic, and environmental losses due to natural hazards and related technological and environmental disasters; additional sites include Tsunami early warning, and a terminology of disaster risk reduction. Located at http://www.unisdr.org.

National Oceanic and Atmospheric Administration, United States. Contains links to National Oceanic and Atmospheric Administration websites that contain information about *weather related warnings and watches.* Located at http://weather.gov/warnings.php.

South Eastern Europe (SEE) Early Warning System, United Nations Development Programme. The objective of this project is to promote the process of democratization and aid transition in South Eastern Europe through the provision of an Early Warning System (EWS) that will assist Non-Government organizations and governments in forecasting regional crises. The EWSs are intended to prevent conflict or crisis stemming from instability or tension, to facilitate strategic national policymaking, and to promote international assistance or investment. The main strength of an EWS lies in its ability to enable governments to identify situations of potential conflict by providing a tool to design appropriate policies for the situation at hand. Located at http://earlywarning.undp.sk/Home.

WORKING FILES (ALSO CALLED WORKING PAPERS). Documents that could be used in a finished product to include rough notes, calculations, or drafts assembled or created and used to prepare or analyze other documents.[406]

– X –

X*n*. Signifies an exemption of declassification of a document within 10 years because disclosure of its contents could reasonably be expected to cause damage to the national security beyond the 10-year limit; *n* is the exemption category number as listed in section 1.6 of Executive Order 12958.[407]

– Y –

YANKEE WHITE. A rigorous, special security investigation and background check for (military) personnel working with the President. The 89 U.S. Air Force Security Police Squadron administers the Yankee White clearance program.[408]

YES/NO WARNING. A theoretical system that provides a clear understanding for intelligence services to tell them that there will either be an attack or not so that appropriate counter-mobilization actions can be taken or not taken. While this is a warning system that policymakers can rely upon so that all uncertainty is removed from the decision-making process and thus is attractive, it is unfortunately not a realistic goal. Except in hindsight the theoretical problem with this system is that while there will inevitably be indications of the other side's intentions to attack, these can easily be lost in the noise of contrary or ambiguous indications. Mostly, successful surprise attacks occur "not out of the blue, but out of a murky grey which did not fit well into the *Yes/No warning* model."[409]

YOM KIPPUR WAR (ALSO KNOWN AS THE 1973 ARAB-ISRAELI WAR). Fought from October 6 (Yom Kippur, a day of fasting and the holiest day in the Jewish calendar) to October 24, 1973, when Egypt and Syria opened a coordinated surprise attack against Israel. On the Golan Heights, approximately 180 Israeli tanks faced an onslaught of 1,400 Syrian tanks, while fewer than 500 Israeli troops were attacked by 80,000 Egyptians along the Suez Canal. Israel mobilized its reserves and eventually defended itself by taking the war deep into Syria and Egypt. The Arab states were resupplied by sea and air from the Soviet Union, which rejected U.S. efforts to work toward an immediate ceasefire. As a result, the United States belatedly began its own airlift to Israel. Two weeks later, Egypt was saved from a disastrous defeat by UN Security Council Resolution 338 calling for "all parties to the present fighting to cease all firing and terminate all military activity immediately." The vote came on the day that Israeli forces cut off and isolated the Egyptian Third Army and were in a position to destroy it. Despite the Israel Defense Forces' ultimate success on the battlefield, the war was considered a diplomatic and military failure. For additional examples of surprise attacks, *see also* FALKLAND ISLANDS; OPERATION BARBAROSSA; PEARL HARBOR; SINGAPORE; TET OFFENSIVE.

NOTES

1. This concept is discussed in more detail in a report by the Senate Select Committee on Intelligence, *A Report: The Intelligence Estimates A-B Team Episode Concerning Soviet Strategic Capability and Objectives,* 95th Congress, 2d sess., 1978.

2. Used throughout by Michael Dewar, *The Art of Deception in Warfare* (Newton, Abbot, Devon, UK: David & Charles, 1989), see Donald C. Daniel, and Katherine L. Herbig, eds., *Strategic Military Deception* (New York: Pergamon Press, 1982); Betty Glad, ed., *Psychological Dimensions of War* (Newbury Park, CA: SAGE Publications, Inc., 1990); Klaus Knorr, and Patric Morgan, eds., *Strategic Military Surprise: Incentives and Opportunities* (New Brunswick, NJ: National Strategy Information Center, Inc., 1983); Stuart Sutherland, *Irrationality: Why We Don't Think Straight* (New Brunswick, NJ: Rutgers University Press, 1992); Ola Svenson, and A. John Maule, eds., *Time Pressure and Stress in Human Judgment and Decision Making* (New York: Plenum Press, 1993).

3. John Hughes-Wilson, *Military Intelligence Blunders* (New York: Carroll & Graf, 1999), 329.

4. "U.S. & Canadian Jet Fighters Move to Counter Probes by Russian Bombers," *Sierra Times,* 6 March 2001, http://www.sierratimes.com/arafp120100.htm, accessed 6 March 2001.

5. Statement not associated with any specific document or report.

6. United Nations International Strategy for Disaster Reduction, http://www.unisdr .org/eng/library/lib-terminology-eng%20home.htm.

7. National Security Act of 1947, Title VI, Protection of Certain National Security Information, SEC 606 [50 U.S.C. 426].

8. Committee for National Security Systems (CNSS). Instruction 4009. National Information Assurance Glossary, May 2003, http://www.nsa.gov/ia/index.cfm.

9. President Bush to reporters at Fort Hood, Texas, on Monday, April 12, 2004, as reported by Cable News Network.

10. *USA Today,* p. 1, April 8, 2004.

11. Michael I. Handel, "Intelligence and Deception," in John Gooch and Amos Perlmutter (eds.), *Military Deception and Strategic Surprise* (Newark, NJ: Frank Cass & Co, 1982), 134.

12. U.S. Department of State, *Foreign Affairs Manual,* 12FAM090, "Definitions of Diplomatic Security Terms," November 13, 2003, http://foia.state.gov/REGS/Search.asp.

13. DoD, *The Department of Defense Dictionary of Military and Associated Terms,* JP 1-02, May 9, 2005, http://www.dtic.mil/doctrine/jel/new_pubs/jp1_02.pdf.

14. Final Report, Senate Select Committee on Intelligence, 26 April 1976.

15. Mark G. Ewig, "Surprise from Zion: The 1982 Israeli Invasion of Lebanon," *Airpower Journal* 35, no. 6 (September–October 1984): 48–57, http://www.airpowamaxwell .afmil/airchronicledaureview/1984/sep-oct/ewig.html, accessed 11 February 2001.

16. DoD. *The Department of Defense Dictionary of Military and Associated Terms.* Joint Pub 1-02.

17. Richard J. Heuer, *The Psychology of Intelligence Analysis,* Center for the Study of Intelligence (Washington, DC: 1999).

18. United States. Department of Justice. Justice Management Division. Information Security Policy Group. Classified national security information. Washington, DC: U.S.

Dept. of Justice, Justice Management Division, Security and Emergency Planning Staff: Information Security Policy Group, 1998.

19. Final Report, Senate Select Committee on Intelligence, 26 April 1976.

20. Joint Pub 2-0, *Joint Doctrine for Intelligence Support to Operations*, October 1993.

21. Committee for National Security Systems (CNSS). Instruction 4009. *National Information Assurance Glossary*, May 2003, http://www.nsa.gov/ia/index.cfm.

22. DoD. National Industrial Security Program Operating Manual (NISPOM). DoD 5220.22-M. Chapter 9. January 1995, http://www.fas.org/sgp/library/nispom/chap_09.htm.

23. Department of the Army. Marine Corps Combat Development Command. Department of the Navy. *Operational Terms and Graphics*. FM 1-02 (FM 101-5). September 21, 2004.

24. Office of Public Affairs, Central Intelligence Agency. *A Consumer's Guide to Intelligence: Gaining Knowledge and Foreknowledge of the World around Us*. Washington, DC, and Springfield, VA: National Technical Information Service, [1999].

25. Richard Ashley, "Bayesian Decision Analysis in International Relations Forecasting: The Analysis of Subjective Processes," in *Forecasting in International Relations,* ed. Nazli Choucri (Cambridge, MA: M.I.T. Press, 1978), 149–171.

26. Sam Adams, *War of Numbers: An Intelligence Memoir* (Vermont: Steerforth Press, 1994). This term is discussed throughout the book symbolizing the misuse and abuse of quantitative analysis to meet political domestic goals by U.S. politicians.

27. Press conference held on 16 September 1999 on the results of the NATO air campaign against Serb military and police forces in Kosovo and in southern Serbia.

28. U.S. Department of State. Foreign Affairs Manual. 12FAM090 "Definitions of Diplomatic Security Terms." November 13, 2003, http://foia.state.gov/REGS/Search.asp.

29. Mary M. Chen. "The Progressive Case and the Atomic Energy Act: Waking to the Dangers of Government Information Controls." *George Washington Law Review* 48 no. 2 (1979–1980): 163–311.

30. Department of the Army. Marine Corps Combat Development Command. Department of the Navy. *Operational Terms and Graphics*. FM 1-02 (FM 101-5). September 21, 2004.

31. Office of Public Affairs. Central Intelligence Agency. *A Consumer's Guide to Intelligence: Gaining Knowledge and Foreknowledge of the World around Us*. Washington, DC, and Springfield, VA: National Technical Information Service, [1999].

32. Richard Betts, *Military Readiness: Concepts, Choices, Consequences* (Washington, DC: The Brookings Institution, 1995), 53.

33. National Imagery and Mapping Agency. "NIMA Guide to Marking Classified Documents." October 4, 2001, http://www.fas.org/sgp/othergov/DoD/nimaguide.pdf.

34. Loch Johnson, "Spies," *Foreign Policy* 20 (September/October 2000): 22.

35. John Hughes-Wilson, *Military Intelligence Blunders*, 251.

36. Douglas Jehl and Eric Schmitt. "Reports on Pentagon's New Spy Units Set Off Questions in Congress," *New York Times*, January 25, 2005.

37. DOE. *Understanding Classification*. Washington, DC: U.S. Dept. of Energy, Assistant Secretary for Defense Programs, Office of Classification, 1987. E 1.15:0007/1. ISOO. Executive Order 12958 "Classified National Security Information," Amended.

38. DoD. *The Department of Defense Dictionary of Military and Associated Terms.* Joint Pub 1-02.

39. National Imagery and Mapping Agency. "NIMA Guide to Marking Classified Documents." October 4, 2001, http://www.fas.org/sgp/othergov/DoD/nimaguide.pdf.

40. United States. Department of Justice. Justice Management Division. Information Security Policy Group. Classified national security information. Washington, DC: U.S. Dept. of Justice, Justice Management Division, Security and Emergency Planning Staff: Information Security Policy Group, 1998.

41. Office of Justice Programs. Department of Justice. The National Criminal Intelligence Sharing Plan v.1.0. October 2003. http://it.ojp.gov/documents/200507_ncisp.pdf. Department of Energy. Office of Security Affairs. Office of Safeguards and Security. "Safeguards and Security Glossary of Terms." December 18, 1995, http://www.directives .doe.gov/references/; NARA. Reagan EO 12356 "National Security Information," http:// www.archives.gov/federal-register/executive-orders/1982.html; and Executive Order 13292 "Further Amendment to Executive Order 12958, as Amended, Classified National Security Information," http://www.archives.gov/federal-register/executive-orders/2003.html. Source: ISOO. Executive Order 12958 "Classified National Security Information," Amended. http://www.archives.gov/isoo/policy-documents/eo-12958-amendment.html#1.2, Los Alamos National Lab. "Definitions." http://www.hr.lanl.gov/SCourses/All/Portion Marking/define.htm, Federation of American Scientists. http://www.fas.org/irp/DoDdir/ doe/o5631_2c/o5631_2ca2.htm and Energy. 10 CFR 1045 http://www.gpoaccess.gov/ CFR/index.html.

42. A uniform method of marking classified information is reflected in DCID 1/7, which also called for a "control markings register" that lists all the markings authorized to classify a document. DoD. *Intelligence Community Classification and Control Markings Implementation*, http://ww.fas.org/sgp/othergov/icmarkings.ppt. "Preliminary Draft— Minimum Standards for the Handling and Transmission of Classified Information in Executive Departments and Agencies of the Federal Government." Issued pursuant EO 9835, United States. Congress. House. Committee on Expenditures in the Executive Departments. Subcommittee on Extra Legal Activities in the Departments. Investigation of Charges that Proposed Security Regulations Under Executive Order 9835 Will Limit Free Speech and a Free Press: hearings before the United States House Committee on Expenditures in the Executive Departments, Subcommittee on Extra Legal Activities in the Departments, Eightieth Congress, first session, on Nov. 14, 1947.

43. U.S. Department of State. *Foreign Affairs Manual.* 12FAM090 "Definitions of Diplomatic Security Terms."

44. Warren Christopher statement at the Senate Confirmation Hearing of Secretary-Designate Warren Christopher before the Senate Foreign Relations Committee, in Washington, DC, on 13 January 1993.

45. Susan L. Maret. The Channel of Public Papers: Control of Government Information and Its Relation to an Informed Citizenry. Dissertation. Union Institute and University, 2002, and Sheldon Cohen. Security Clearances and the Protection of National Security Information Law and Procedures. Defense Personnel Security Research Center, (DTIC) Technical Report 00-4. November, 2000.

46. U.S. Commission on National Security 21st Century, Seeking a National Strategy: A Concept for Preserving Security and Promoting Freedom-Phase II Report (Washington, DC: U.S. Commission on National Security 21st Century, April 2000)

47. John A. Gentry, "Complex Civil-Military Operations: A U.S. Military-Centric Perspective," *Naval War College Review* 53, no. 4 (Autumn 2000): 60.

48. Central Intelligence Agency. Center for the Study of Intelligence. "Critique of the Codeword Compartment of the CIA." March 1977 and EO 11652, March 8, 1972. DoD. *The Department of Defense Dictionary of Military and Associated Terms.* JP 1-02. May 9, 2005.

49. Central Intelligence Agency. Center for the Study of Intelligence. "Critique of the Codeword Compartment of the CIA." March 1977.

50. Harold Ford, *Estimate Intelligence: The Purposes and Problems of National Intelligence Estimating* (Lanham, MD: University Press of America, 1993), 330.

51. Department of the Army. Marine Corps Combat Development Command. Department of the Navy. *Operational Terms and Graphics.* FM 1-02 (FM 101-5). September 21, 2004.

52. Office of Public Affairs. Central Intelligence Agency. *A Consumer's Guide to Intelligence: Gaining Knowledge and Foreknowledge of the World around Us.* Washington, DC, and Springfield, VA: National Technical Information Service, [1999].

53. Department of the Army. Marine Corps Combat Development Command. Department of the Navy. Operational Terms and Graphics. FM 1-02 (FM 101-5). September 21, 2004.

54. DoD. *The Department of Defense Dictionary of Military and Associated Terms.* Joint Pub 1-02.

55. Committee for National Security Systems (CNSS). Instruction 4009. *National Information Assurance Glossary.*

56. Office of Public Affairs. Central Intelligence Agency. *A Consumer's Guide to Intelligence: Gaining Knowledge and Foreknowledge of the World around Us.* Washington, DC, and Springfield, VA: National Technical Information Service, [1999].

57. Final Report, Senate Select Committee on Intelligence, 26 April 1976.

58. Committee for National Security Systems (CNSS). Instruction 4009. National Information Assurance Glossary, May 2003.

59. United States Agency for International Development, *Conflict Early Warning Systems: Terms and Concepts.* (News Orleans, LA: Tulane Institute for International Development, May 1999), under the term "complex emergency."

60. Bill Lambrecht, "After Iraq Visit, Bond Warns of Compromised Intelligence," *St. Louis Post-Dispatch*, January 20, 2006.

61. Centers for Disease Control. "Manual Guide—Information Security CDC-02." Office of Security and Emergency Preparedness.

62. U.S. Army Regulation 220-1, June 1981.

63. ISOO. Executive Order 12958 "Classified National Security Information," Amended. and Executive Order 13292 "Further Amendment to Executive Order 12958, as Amended, Classified National Security Information."

64. Committee for National Security Systems (CNSS). Instruction 4009. *National Information Assurance Glossary.*

65. DoD. *The Department of Defense Dictionary of Military and Associated Terms.* Joint Pub 1-02.

66. Swedish Ministry for Foreign Affairs, "Preventing Violent Conflict: The Search for Political Will, Strategies and Effective Tools," seminar held 19–20 June 2000 in Sweden.

67. U.S. Department of Defense Directive 3025.15, "Military Assistance to Civil Authorities," 18 February 1997, paragraph E2.

68. Jonathan B. Tucker and Amy Sands, "An Unlikely Threat," *Bulletin of the Atomic Scientists* 55, no. 4 (July/August 1999): 46–52.

69. Integrated C⁴ I Architecture Division. *C⁴ISR Handbook for Integrated Planning* (Washington, DC: Defense Intelligence Agency Publications Division).

70. Centers for Disease Control. "Manual Guide—Information Security CDC-02." Office of Security and Emergency Preparedness "Sensitive But Unclassified Information."

71. Executive Order 13292 "Further Amendment to Executive Order 12958, as Amended, Classified National Security Information." 22 CFR 171. "Foreign Relations, Department of State." (a detailed list of records that are exempt under 5 U.S.C. 552a(k)(1). "The reason for invoking this exemption is to protect material required to be kept secret in the interest of national defense and foreign policy.")

72. U.S. Department of State. *Foreign Affairs Manual.* 12FAM090 "Definitions of Diplomatic Security Terms." November 13, 2003.

73. DoD. Army Regulation AR381-45. "Investigative Records Repository." August 25, 1989.

74. DoD. *The Department of Defense Dictionary of Military and Associated Terms.* Joint Pub 1-02.

75. Department of the Army. Army Regulation 380-10, "Foreign Disclosure and Contacts with Foreign Representatives," June 22, 2005, and FAS. International Programs Security Handbook Chapter 4. Office of the Deputy to the Under Secretary of Defense (Policy) for Policy Support, 1993.

76. J. David Singer and Paul F. Diehl, *Measuring the Correlates of War* (Ann Arbor, MI: University of Michigan Press, 1990), 11.

77. Department of the Air Force. *Cornerstones of Information Warfare.* 1995.

78. Department of the Army. Marine Corps Combat Development Command. Department of the Navy. *Operational Terms and Graphics.* FM 1-02 (FM 101-5). September 21, 2004. Executive Order 12333 and U.S. Department of Defense. *DoD Counterintelligence Functional Services*, DoD Instruction 5240.16.

79. "Counterintelligence to the Edge." and DoD Directive 5105.67, "Department of Defense Counterintelligence Field Activity (DoD CIFA)."

80. Taken in part from Robert Gellman. "Public Records: Access, Privacy, and Public Policy: A Discussion Paper" and David S. Sanson. "The Pervasive Problem of Court-Sanctioned Secrecy and the Exigency of National Reform." 53 Duke L. J. 807.

81. Global Security, http://www.globalsecurity.org/military/world/dprk/army.htm.

82. Judicial Administration. 28 CFR 23, http://www.gpoaccess.gov/CFR/index.html.

83. Department of Justice. "Criminal Intelligence Information Operating Systems." 28 CFR 23.3(b)(1) http://www.gpoaccess.gov/CFR/index.html.

84. DoD. *The Department of Defense Dictionary of Military and Associated Terms.* Joint Pub 1-02.

85. Department of the Army. Marine Corps Combat Development Command. Department of the Navy. Operational Terms and Graphics. FM 1-02 (FM 101-5).

86. Department of Energy. Office of Security Affairs. Office of Safeguards and Security. "Safeguards and Security Glossary of Terms."

87. Department of Energy. Office of Security Affairs. Office of Safeguards and Security. "Safeguards and Security Glossary of Terms."

88. Department of Homeland Security, Critical Infrastructure Information Act of 2002 (Title II Subtitle B, Homeland Security Act of 2002, 6 U.S.C. 131-134) and Coalition of Journalists for Open Government.

89. Office of Public Affairs. Central Intelligence Agency. *A Consumer's Guide to Intelligence: Gaining Knowledge and Foreknowledge of the World around Us.* Washington, DC, and Springfield, VA: National Technical Information Service, [1999].

90. *Defense Special Security Communications System Operating Instructions System Procedures* (U), NSA, 6 Feb 1973.

91. Coalition of Journalists for Open Government.

92. Committee for National Security Systems (CNSS). Instruction 4009. National Information Assurance Glossary, May 2003, http://www.nsa.gov/ia/index.cfm.

93. Committee for National Security Systems (CNSS). Instruction 4009. *National Information Assurance Glossary*, May 2003.

94. This quote pertains to the 1968 Tet offensive; Adams, xiii.

95. DoD. *The Department of Defense Dictionary of Military and Associated Terms.* Joint Pub 1-02.

96. U.S. Department of State. *Foreign Affairs Manual.* 12FAM090 "Definitions of Diplomatic Security Terms." November 13, 2003, http://foia.state.gov/REGS/Search.asp.

97. Department of State. Foreign Affairs Manual. 10 FAM 413.2 "Office of Research," http://foia.state.gov/REGS/fams.asp?level = 2&id = 11&fam = 0.

98. Department of the Army. Marine Corps Combat Development Command. Department of the Navy. Operational Terms and Graphics. FM 1-02 (FM 101-5). September 21, 2004.

99. National Imagery and Mapping Agency. "NIMA Guide to Marking Classified Documents."

100. ISOO. Executive Order 12958 "Classified National Security Information," Amended. and Executive Order 13292 "Further Amendment to Executive Order 12958, as Amended, Classified National Security Information."

101. "New Democrat Watch #8: Clinton Bungee Jumping on Nuclear Testing Endangers National Security," *Decision Brief* No. 93-D58. (Washington, DC: The Center for Security Policy, 6 July 1993).

102. Department of the Army. Marine Corps Combat Development Command. Department of the Navy. Operational Terms and Graphics. FM 1-02 (FM 101-5).

103. Committee for National Security Systems (CNSS). Instruction 4009. National Information Assurance Glossary.

104. National Archives and Records Administration. 36 CFR 1234.2.

105. Jeffrey W. Seifert. "Data Mining: An Overview." CRS Report for Congress December 16, 2004. http://www.fas.org/irp/crs/RL31798.pdf. General Accounting Office. Data Mining: Federal Efforts Cover a Wide Range of Uses. GAO-04-548, May 4, 2004. http://www.gao.gov/htext/d04548.html.

106. Barry R. Schneider, "Principles of War for the Battlefield of the Future," New Era Warfare? A Revolution in Military Affairs, http://www.airpower.maxwell.afmil/air chronicles/battle/ov-2.html.

107. Michael Handel, "Intelligence and Deception," in *Military Deception and Strate-*

gic Surprise, ed. John Gooch and Amos Perlmutter (London, UK: Frank Cass & Co., 1982), 124–125.

108. Department of the Army. Marine Corps Combat Development Command. Department of the Navy. *Operational Terms and Graphics.* FM 1-02 (FM 101-5). September 21, 2004.

109. Alvin S. Quist. Secrecy News. March 13, 2003.

110. John Pike, *Defense Intelligence Agency Products,* http://wwwfas.org/irp/dia/ product.

111. Department of the Army. Marine Corps Combat Development Command. Department of the Navy. Operational Terms and Graphics. FM 1-02 (FM 101-5).

112. DoD. AR 381-12. January 15, 1993. "Subversion and Espionage Directed against the U.S. Army."

113. 18 U.S.C. 798. "Disclosure of Classified Information."

114. This explanation comes from one of the designers of this method, Olaf Helmer, "The Use of Expert Opinion in International Relations Forecasting," *Forecasting in International Relations,* ed. Nazli Choueri (Massachusetts: MIT Press, 1978), 116–123.

115. U.S. Congressional Commission, Report of the U.S. Congressional Commission to Assess the Ballistic Missile Threat to the United States, 15 July 1998, paragraph F.

116. Department of Defense. Washington Headquarters. "DoD Issuances."

117. Centers for Disease Control. "Manual Guide—Information Security CDC-02." Office of Security and Emergency Preparedness "Sensitive But Unclassified Information." 07/22/2005.

118. Alvin S. Quist. "Security Classification of Information." Chapter 1.

119. Specific types of derogatory information are listed in 10 CFR 710 (below) and Executive Order 10450, [59 FR 35185, July 8, 1994, as amended at 66 FR 47063, Sept. 11, 2001]. Energy. 10 CFR 710.8.

120. Department of the Air Force. "Cornerstones of Information Warfare." 1995.

121. United Nations International Strategy for Disaster Reduction, http://www.unisdr .org/eng/library/lib-terminology-eng%20home.htm.

122. UN Department of Humanitarian Affairs (UNHA), *The Use of Military and Civil Defense Assets in Relief Operations Reference Manual* (New York: United Nations Press, 1995), under "disaster alert."

123. UNHA, under "disaster preparedness."

124. UNHA, under "disaster prevention."

125. UNHA, under "disaster relief."

126. UNHA, under "disaster response."

127. United Nations International Strategy for Disaster Reduction, http://www.unisdr .org/eng/library/lib-terminology-eng%20home.htm.

128. UNHA, under "disaster team."

129. Francis J. Hughes and David Schum, unpublished manuscript, *The Art and Science of the Process of Intelligence Analysis,* Washington, DC: Joint Military Intelligence College.

130. Federal Rules of Civil Procedure.

131. United States Intelligence Community, http://www.intelligence.gov/2-counterint _f.shtml. Source: Department of the Army. Marine Corps Combat Development Command. Department of the Navy. Operational Terms and Graphics. FM 1-02 (FM 101-5).

132. Todd Leyenthal, "Disinformation Integral Part of Iraqi Strategy," Backgrounder from USIA, 4 February 1991, http://www.fas.org/news/iraq/1991J91O204-171055.htm.

133. Department of the Army. Marine Corps Combat Development Command. Department of the Navy. Operational Terms and Graphics. FM 1-02 (FM 101-5). September 21, 2004.

134. DoD. National Industrial Security Program Operating Manual (NISPOM). DoD 5220.22-M. Chapter 9. January 1995. U.S. Department of Commerce. Manual of Security Policies and Procedures. Chapter 20.

135. U.S. Department of State. *Foreign Affairs Manual.* 2FAM070 "Dissent Channel." (F2AM071.2).

136. For complete information see FactsCanada.ca, http://www.factscanada.ca/friday/friday-2000-07-10-06.shtml.

137. Department of the Army. Marine Corps Combat Development Command. Department of the Navy. Operational Terms and Graphics. FM 1-02 (FM 101-5).

138. DoD. Army Regulation AR381-45. "Investigative Records Repository."

139. Executive Order 13292 "Further Amendment to Executive Order 12958, as Amended, Classified National Security Information."

140. Lawrence K. Gershwin, National Intelligence Officer for Science and Technology (as prepared for delivery) Statement for the Record for the Joint Economic Committee Cyber Threat Trends and U.S. Network Security, 21 June 2001, http://www.cia.gov/cial publicajfairs/speeches/gershwin_speech_O6222001.html.

141. DoD. DOD 5200.1-R Information Security Program. Appendix C.

142. Department of State. *Foreign Affairs Manual.* 10 FAM 413.2 "Office of Research."

143. United Nations International Strategy for Disaster Reduction, http://www.unisdr .org/eng/library/lib-terminology-eng%20home.htm.

144. Department of the Army. Marine Corps Combat Development Command. Department of the Navy. *Operational Terms and Graphics.* FM 1-02 (FM 101-5).

145. Final Report, Senate Select Committee on Intelligence, 26 April 1976.

146. UNHA, under "emergency."

147. UNHA, under "emergency medical system."

148. UNHA, under "emergency medicine."

149. UNHA, under "emergency operations center."

150. For further information go to http://www.cdc.gov/eis.

151. DoD. AR 381-12. January 15, 1993. "Subversion and Espionage Directed against the U.S. Army." See also 18 U.S.C. and Article 106a, Uniform Code of Military Justice.

152. Department of Defense. DoD Dictionary of Military and Associated Terms. May 2005.

153. Office of Public Affairs. Central Intelligence Agency. *A Consumer's Guide to Intelligence: Gaining Knowledge and Foreknowledge of the World around Us.* Washington, DC, and Springfield, VA: National Technical Information Service.

154. Sherman Kent, "Words of Estimated Probability," in Sherman Kent and the Board of National Estimates: Collected Essays, ed. Donald P. Steury (Washington, DC: Center for the Study of Intelligence, 1994), 132–139.

155. [Nolo] Everybody's Legal Dictionary, http://www.nolo.com/dictionary/dictionary_alpha.cfm?wordnumber = 662&alpha = E.

156. Hughes and Schum, *Process of Intelligence Analysis*.

157. DOE. Chief Information Officer. "Records Management Definitions."

158. Richard Betts, "Warning Dilemmas: Normal Theory vs. Exceptional Theory," *Orbis 26* (Winter 1983): 828–833.

159. Department of the Army. Marine Corps Combat Development Command. Department of the Navy. *Operational Terms and Graphics*. FM 1-02 (FM 101-5). September 21, 2004.

160. Arthur Schlesinger. *The Imperial Presidency*. New York: Atlantic Monthly, 1973.

161. Paul Begala, former Clinton advisor. *New York Times*, July 5, 1998.

162. Tor Nørretranders. *The User Illusion: Cutting Consciousness Down to Size*. Trans. Jonathan Sydenham. New York: Viking Penguin, 1998.

163. Department of the Army. Marine Corps Combat Development Command. Department of the Navy. *Operational Terms and Graphics*. FM 1-02 (FM 101-5).

164. Federal Emergency Management Agency (FEMA), Department of Homeland Security. "Production or Disclosure of Information." 44 CFR 5.3.

165. *Federal Register* July 12, 2005 (Volume 70, Number 132), and Center for Strategic and International Studies (CSIS) "Security Controls on Scientific Information and the Conduct of Scientific Research."

166. John Pike, "Security and Classification," http://www.ostgate.com/classification.html.

167. Department of the Army. Marine Corps Combat Development Command. Department of the Navy. *Operational Terms and Graphics*. FM 1-02 (FM 101-5).

168. David Kahn, *The Code-Breakers: The Comprehensive History of Secret Communications from Ancient Times to the Internet* (New York: Scribner Press, 1996), 508–509.

169. U.S. Department of State, Memorandum Prepared in the Central Intelligence Agency, Washington, 19 January 1961. (Planning an invasion of Cuba), *Foreign Relations of the United States,* 1961–1963, Vol. X, Cuba, 1961–1962.

170. Executive Order 12958 "Classified National Security Information," Amended. http://www.archives.gov/isoo/policy-documents/eo-12958-amendment.html#1.2 and Source: Executive Order 13292 "Further Amendment to Executive Order 12958, as Amended, Classified National Security Information." http://www.archives.gov/federal-register/executive-orders/2003.html.

171. National Archives and Records Administration. 36 CFR 1220 "Federal Records, General," http://www.gpoaccess.gov/cfr/index.html.

172. David L. Carter. *Law Enforcement Intelligence: A Guide for State, Local, and Tribal Law Enforcement Agencies*. Dept. of Justice, Office of Community Oriented Policing Services, 2004, http://www.cops.usdoj.gov/default.asp?Item=1404.

173. Helmer, 117.

174. Stephen Glover, "The Serbs are still being presented as the bad guys. So what's new in the news from Kosovo?" *The Spectator* 284, no. 8952 (4 March 2000): 28.

175. Defense Advanced Research Project Agency (DARPA). "Urban Sunrise." February 2004, http://www.fas.org/man/eprint/urban.pdf, and Department of the Army Field Manual 3-07 (at globalsecurity.org), http://www.globalsecurity.org/military/library/policy/army/fm/3-07/.

176. FAS. "White House Conference Call Briefing," http://www.fas.org/sgp/news/2003/03/wh032503.html.

177. National Security Act of 1947, as amended (50 U.S.C. Chapter 15, 401(a)) and Executive Order 12333, 3.4. "United States Intelligence Activities." Uniting and Strengthening America by Providing Appropriate Tools Required to Intercept and Obstruct Terrorism (USA Patriot) Act of 2000.

178. Homeland Security Presidential Directive-2, October 29, 2001. "Combating Terrorism Through Immigration Policies." and "Attorney General Ashcroft Outlines Foreign Terrorist Tracking Task Force." October 31, 2001.

179. Committee for National Security Systems (CNSS). Instruction 4009. National Information Assurance Glossary.

180. Section 142d of the Atomic Energy Act, Los Alamos National Lab. "Definitions," DOE. Understanding Classification. Washington, DC: U.S. Dept. of Energy, Assistant Secretary for Defense Programs, Office of Classification, 1987, and 10 CFR 1016 §1016.3 "Definitions."

181. David L. Carter. *Law Enforcement Intelligence: A Guide for State, Local, and Tribal Law Enforcement Agencies.* Dept. of Justice, Office of Community Oriented Policing Services, 2004. Department of Homeland Security Management Directive 11042 "Safeguarding Sensitive But Unclassified (For Official Use Only) Information," May 11, 2004. DoD. Defense Personnel Security Research Center. "Employees Guide to Security Responsibilities."

182. United States Congress. Senate Committee on Governmental Affairs. Report of the Commission on Protecting and Reducing Government Secrecy: Hearing before the Committee on Governmental Affairs, United States Senate, One Hundred Fifth Congress, First Session, May 7, 1997. Washington: Government Printing Office, 1997; Paul E. Kostyu. "Nothing More, Nothing Less: Case Law Leading to the Freedom of Information Act." *American Journalism* 12, no. 4 (1995): 464–476; Herbert N. Foerstel. *Freedom of Information and the Right to Know: The Origins and Applications of the Freedom of Information Act.* Westport, CT: Greenwood Press, 1999, and the John Moss Foundation website.

183. Department of Justice "Freedom of Information Guide." May 2004. Gina Marie Stevens, "Homeland Security Act of 2002: Critical Infrastructure Information Act." CRS Report for Congress February 28, 2003, http://www.fas.org/sgp/crs/RL31762.pdf, Freedom of Information Guide, May 2004, http://www.usdoj.gov/oip/exemption2.htm#homeland, and DOJ. Office of Information and Privacy. FOIA Post. "New Attorney General FOIA Memorandum Issued," http://www.usdoj.gov/oip/foiapost/2001foiapost19.htm.

184. United States. Advisory Commission on Intergovernmental Relations. Citizen Participation in the American Federal System. Washington: Advisory Commission on Intergovernmental Relations, 1980.

185. Gil Baldwin. "Fugitive Documents: On the Loose or On the Run," http://www.lib.umich.edu/govdocs/adnotes/2003/241003/an2410d.htm.

186. National Imagery and Mapping Agency. "NIMA Guide to Marking Classified Documents."

187. Department of the Army. Marine Corps Combat Development Command. Department of the Navy. Operational Terms and Graphics. FM 1-02 (FM 101-5). September 21, 2004.

188. U.S. Army Field Manual 100-6, "Information Operations," 1996.

189. DoD. DoD Directive 3020.40. Defense Critical Infrastructure Program (DCIP). August 19, 2005, http://www.fas.org/irp/doddir/dod/d3020_40.pdf.

190. Instruction 4009. National Information Assurance Glossary, May 2003, http://www.nsa.gov/ia/index.cfm.

191. Department of Energy. Office of Security Affairs. Office of Safeguards and Security. "Safeguards and Security Glossary of Terms."

192. Irving, Janis. (1972). *Victims of groupthink.* Boston: Houghton Mifflin; Irving, Janis. (1982). *Groupthink: Psychological studies of policy decisions and fiascos.* 2nd ed. Boston: Houghton Mifflin.

193. Centers for Disease Control. "Manual Guide—Information Security CDC-02." Office of Security and Emergency Preparedness "Sensitive But Unclassified Information."

194. U.S. Department of Justice. Freedom of Information Act Guide. May 2004.

195. Department of Homeland Security. Homeland Security Advisory Council Home Page, http://www.dhs.gov/dhspublic/display?theme = 9&content = 3386, and HSCA Charter, http://www.dhs.gov/interweb/assetlibrary/HSAC_Charter.pdf.

196. This entire entry comes from the White House website: http://www.whitehouse.gov/news/releases/2002/03/20020312-5.html.

197. Library of Congress. "Laws and Regulation Governing the Protection of Sensitive But Unclassified Information," http://www.loc.gov/rr/frd/pdf-files/sbu.pdf.

198. Matthew E. Broderick, Director Homeland Security Operations Center. Statement before the House Committee on Homeland Security, Intelligence, Information Sharing, and Terrorism Risk Assessment Subcommittee, July 20, 2005.

199. William Shakespeare, *Hamlet,* Act IV, Scene V, lines 83–87.

200. Shim Jae-yun, "Seoul Banks Ask Gov't to Repay Russian Debts," *Korea Times,* 19 December 2000, B 1.

201. Department of the Army. Marine Corps Combat Development Command. Department of the Navy. *Operational Terms and Graphics.* FM 1-02 (FM 101-5). September 21, 2004.

202. United Nations General Assembly, "Strengthening of the Coordination of Emergency Humanitarian Assistance of the United Nations," *Report of the Secretary-General* (2 September 1994): A/49/177.

203. Bruce Watson, Susan Watson, and Gerald Hopple, *United States Intelligence: An Encyclopedia* (New York: Garland Publishing, Inc., 1990), 594. Hereafter cited as: Watson.

204. Watson, 286.

205. Watson, 287.

206. U.S. Department of State, Bureau for International Narcotics and Law Enforcement Affairs, *U.S. Department of State International Narcotics Control Strategy Report,* March 1995, http://dosfan.llb.ulc.edu/ERC/law/INC/1995/09.html, accessed 17 February 2001.

207. Edward J. Laurence, "Light Weapons and Intrastate Conflict Early Warning Factors and Preventative Action," *Carnegie Commission on Preventing Deadly Conflict Report* (1998), http://www.ccpdc.org/pubs/weap/weap.html.

208. World Bank website, http://web.worldbank.org/WBSITE/EXTERNAL/TOPICS/EXTPOVERTY/EXTPAME/0,,contentMDK:20191410~menuPK:435489~pagePK:148956~piPK:216618~theSitePK:384263,00.html. Cited hereafter as World Bank.

209. World Bank.

210. World Bank.

211. World Bank.

212. Edward Waltz, *Knowledge Management: In the Intelligence Enterprise* (Norwood, MA: Artech House, 2003), 11–12. He refers to four different types of inferential analyses which are those that explain past events, the structure of an organization, current behaviors, and foreknowledge which forecast future attributes.

213. DoD Joint Pub 2-0, *Joint Doctrine for Intelligence Support to Operations*, October 1993.

214. Office of Management and Budget, Circular No. A-130, "Management of Federal Information Resources." February 8, 1996. ISOO. Executive Order 12958 "Classified National Security Information," Amended. March 28, 2003. and Executive Order 13292 "Further Amendment to Executive Order 12958, as Amended, Classified National Security Information."

215. Department of the Air Force. "Cornerstones of Information Warfare." 1995.

216. U.S. Army Field Manual 100-6, "Information Operations," 1996.

217. Committee for National Security Systems (CNSS). Instruction 4009. National Information Assurance Glossary, May 2003. Department of the Army. Marine Corps Combat Development Command. Department of the Navy. Operational Terms and Graphics. FM 1-02 (FM 101-5). September 21, 2004.

218. Department of the Army. Marine Corps Combat Development Command. Department of the Navy. *Operational Terms and Graphics*. FM 1-02 (FM 101-5).

219. Defense Acquisition University. Glossary: Defense Acquisition Acronyms and Terms. 11th ed.

220. F. Woody Horton. "Government Information Life Cycle Management." Appendix 16 Comprehensive Assessment of Public Information Dissemination. National Commission on Libraries and Information Science, June 2000–March 2001. OMB. "Management of Federal Information Resources." Circular A-130. February 1996.

221. Department of the Army. Marine Corps Combat Development Command. Department of the Navy. Operational Terms and Graphics. FM 1-02 (FM 101-5).

222. Defense Acquisition University. Glossary: Defense Acquisition Acronyms and Terms. 11th ed., 2003, http://www.dau.mil/pubs/Glossary/preface.asp, Department of the Air Force. "Cornerstones of Information Warfare." 1995. Department of the Army. Marine Corps Combat Development Command. Department of the Navy. *Operational Terms and Graphics*. FM 1-02 (FM 101-5).

223. Committee for National Security Systems (CNSS). Instruction 4009. *National Information Assurance Glossary.*

224. Department of the Army. Marine Corps Combat Development Command. Department of the Navy. Operational Terms and Graphics. FM 1-02 (FM 101-5). September 21, 2004.

225. OMB. "Management of Federal Information Resources." Circular A-130. February 1996.

226. U.S. Army Field Manual 100-6, "Information Operations," 1996. "Public Printing and Documents." 44 U.S.C. 35 Subchapter II § 3532. Department of the Army. Marine Corps Combat Development Command. Department of the Navy. Operational Terms and Graphics. FM 1-02 (FM 101-5).

227. ISOO, http://www.archives.gov/isoo/about/, and ISOO 2004 Report to the President, http://www.archives.gov/isoo/reports/2004-annual-report.html.

228. Commission on the Intelligence Capabilities of the United States Regarding Weapons of Mass Destruction ("Silberman-Robb Commission"). March 31, 2005, http://www.wmd.gov/report/report.html.

229. Department of Homeland Security. "Protected Critical Infrastructure Information." 6 CFR 29.2, http://www.gpoaccess.gov/cfr/index.html.

230. Defense Acquisition University. Glossary: Defense Acquisition Acronyms and Terms. 11th ed., 2003. http://www.dau.mil/pubs/Glossary/preface.asp. Department of the Army. Marine Corps Combat Development Command. Department of the Navy. Operational Terms and Graphics. FM 1-02 (FM 101-5). September 21, 2004, https://atiam.train.army.mil/soldierPortal/atia/adlsc/view/public/4876-1/FM/1-02/toc.htm.

231. Defense Acquisition University. Glossary: Defense Acquisition Acronyms and Terms. 11th ed., 2003. http://www.dau.mil/pubs/Glossary/preface.asp. Department of the Army. Marine Corps Combat Development Command. Department of the Navy. Operational Terms and Graphics. FM 1-02 (FM 101-5).

232. Defense Acquisition University. Glossary: Defense Acquisition Acronyms and Terms. 11th ed., 2003. Department of the Air Force. "Cornerstones of Information Warfare." 1995.

233. Martin Libicki, "The Mesh and the Net: Speculations on Armed Conflict in an Age of Free Silicon." National Defense University, March 1994, and "What Is Information Warfare?" National Defense University ACIS Paper 3, August 1995.

234. "Entry of Merchandise." 19 U.S.C. Section 1484.

235. "Protection of Human Subjects." 21 CFR 50. The National Commission for the Protection of Human Subjects of Biomedical and Behavioral Research. "Ethical Principles and Guidelines for the Protection of Human Subjects of Research." ("Belmont Report"). April 18, 1979.

236. John Arquilla, and David Ronfeldt. *The Emergence of Noopolitik: Toward an American Information Strategy*. Santa Monica, CA: Rand, 1999.

237. Kent Anderson, *Intelligence-Based Threat Assessments for Information Networks and Infrastructures: A White Paper* (Portland, OR: Global Technology Research, Inc., 1998): 4.

238. DoD. *The Department of Defense Dictionary of Military and Associated Terms.* Joint Pub 1-02.

239. General Accounting Office (GAO). Information Security: Computer Attacks at Department of Defense Pose Increasing Risks. GAO/AIMD-96-84, 1996. Office of Management and Budget (OMB). "Guidelines for Ensuring and Maximizing the Quality, Objectivity, Utility, and Integrity of Information Disseminated by Federal Agencies." Executive Order 13292 "Further Amendment to Executive Order 12958, as Amended, Classified National Security Information." and Department of Energy. Office of Security Affairs. Office of Safeguards and Security. "Safeguards and Security Glossary of Terms." December 18, 1995.

240. Globalsecurity.org. "Intelink," http://www.globalsecurity.org/intell/systems/intelink.htm.

241. Department of Energy. Office of Security Affairs. Office of Safeguards and Security. "Safeguards and Security Glossary of Terms." December 18, 1995, http://www.directives.doe.gov/references/.

242. Department of State. 22 CFR 9. Appendix A, http://www.gpoaccess.gov/cfr/index.html.

243. Department of Energy. Office of Security Affairs. Office of Safeguards and Security. "Safeguards and Security Glossary of Terms." December 18, 1995.

244. United States Intelligence Community, http://www.intelligence.gov/1who.shtml.

245. Office of Public Affairs. Central Intelligence Agency. *A Consumer's Guide to Intelligence: Gaining Knowledge and Foreknowledge of the World around Us.* Washington, DC, and Springfield, VA: National Technical Information Service, [1999]. Commission on the Intelligence Capabilities of the United States Regarding Weapons of Mass Destruction ("Silberman-Robb Commission"). March 31, 2005.

246. Schulsky, A. and Schmitt, G. *Silent Warfare: Understanding the World of Intelligence* (Washington, DC: Brassey's, 2002).

247. Russ Travers, "The Coming Intelligence Failure," *Unclassified Studies in Intelligence* 1, no. 1 (1997).

248. Cynthia M. Grabo, "Warning Intelligence," The Intelligence Profession Series, no. 4 (McLean, VA: Association of Former Intelligence Officers, 1987).

249. DoD Counterintelligence Collection Reporting." Department of Defense 5240.17. October 26, 2005.

250. Department of the Army. FM 34-1. "Fundamentals of IEW Operations." Chapter 2. *Intelligence and Electronic Warfare Operations.* September 1994.

251. U.S. Department of State. Foreign Affairs Manual. 12FAM090 "Definitions of Diplomatic Security Terms." November 13, 2003.

252. Central Intelligence Agency. "Executive Oversight of Intelligence." *Factbook on Intelligence.*

253. DoD. *The Department of Defense Dictionary of Military and Associated Terms.* Joint Pub 1-02.

254. Russell G. Swenson, *An Office Manager's Guide to Intelligence Readiness.* Occasional Paper Number Three (Washington, DC: Joint Military Intelligence College, June 1996).

255. DoD. *The Department of Defense Dictionary of Military and Associated Terms.* Joint Pub 1-02.

256. Department of the Army. "Special Access Programs (SAPs) and Sensitive Activities." AR 380–381.

257. Ford, 121.

258. FBI. "War on Terrorism Counterterrorism," http://www.fbi.gov/terrorinfo/counterrorism/partnership.htm.

259. General Accounting Office. "U.S. Attorneys: Performance-Based Initiatives Are Evolving." May 2004. GAO-04-422.

260. General Accounting Office. "Homeland Security: Information Sharing Responsibilities, Challenges, and Key Management Issues." September 17, 2003. GAO-03-1165T.

261. DoD. *The Department of Defense Dictionary of Military and Associated Terms.* Joint Pub 1-02.

262. National Intelligence Council, *Global Trends 2015: A Dialogue about the Future with Nongovernmental Experts* (U.S. Government: NIC 2000–02, December 2000), 8.

263. Ford, 36.

264. U.S. House National Security Committee Staff Report, August 14, 1996.

265. Ford, 44.

266. Department of the Army. Marine Corps Combat Development Command. Department of the Navy. *Operational Terms and Graphics.* FM 1-02 (FM 101-5).

267. NARA. Eisenhower EO 10501, November 5, 1953 "Safeguarding Official Information in the Interests of the Defense of the United States." Richard Kielbowicz. (58) "Leaks to the Press as a Communication within and between Organizations." *Newspaper Research Journal* 1, no. 2 (1979/1980): 53–58. Stephen Hess. *The Government/Press Connection: Press Officers and Their Offices*. Washington, DC: Brookings Institution, 1984. 77–79. Department of Defense. DoD Directive 5210.50 July 22, 2005, "Unauthorized Disclosure of Classified Information to the Public."

268. Department of Energy. Office of Security Affairs. Office of Safeguards and Security. *Safeguards and Security Glossary of Terms*. December 18, 1995. John Pike. "Security and Classification." National Imagery and Mapping Agency. "NIMA Guide to Marking Classified Documents." October 4, 2001.

269. Dewar. The Art of Deception in Warfare, 84.

270. DoD. *The Department of Defense Dictionary of Military and Associated Terms*. Joint Pub 1-02.

271. A list of MOU/MOAs between federal, state, and local governments for JTTFs can be found at http://faculty.maxwell.syr.edu/asroberts/foi/jttf.html.

272. Department of the Army. Marine Corps Combat Development Command. Department of the Navy. Operational Terms and Graphics. FM 1-02 (FM 101-5).

273. Ladislas Fargo, *The Broken Seal: The Story of "Operation Magic" and the Pearl Harbor Disaster* (New York: Random House, 1967), 284.

274. Edgar M Bottoms, *The Missile Gap* (Rutherford: Fairleigh Dickenson University Press, 1971), 155.

275. Gentry, 61.

276. BBC News, July 28, 2003, accessed at http://news.bbc.co.uk/1/hi/world/middle_east/3102409.stm.

277. National Commission on Terrorist Attacks Upon the United States. Chapter 13, http://www.9-11commission.gov/report/911Report_Ch13.htm; Joint Inquiry Staff Statement Proposals for Reform within the Intelligence Community. October 3, 2002. *San Jose Mercury News*, October 13, 2005; Senator Pat Roberts, Chair of the Senate Intelligence Committee; and John B. Roberts II. Op-Ed. "Chinese Mole Hunt at CIA." *Washington Times*.

278. Department of Justice. Bureau of Justice Assistance, http://it.ojp.gov/topic.jsp?topic_id=93.

279. For more information, go to http://www.oep-ndms.dhhs.gov.

280. DoD. *The Department of Defense Dictionary of Military and Associated Terms*. Joint Pub 1-02.

281. War and National Defense. 50 U.S.C. 15 Subchapter I § 403–3.

282. Director of Central Intelligence Directive No. 1/5, National Intelligence Warning, 23 May 1979.

283. The Federal Bureau of Investigation's Efforts to Improve the Sharing of Intelligence and Other Information. Audit Report 04-10, https://www.justice.gov/oig/audit/fbi/0410/final.pdf (Redacted and Unclassified).

284. General Accounting Office. "Homeland Security." GAO 04 453.

285. FBI Director Robert Mueller, March 3, 2003, testimony to the Senate Committee on the Judiciary, War Against Terrorism: Working Together to Protect America (S. Hrg. 108–137).

286. National Law Enforcement Telecommunication System, http://www.nlets.org/general.html.

287. FAS. NSDD—National Security Decision Directives, Reagan Administration, http://www.fas.org/irp/offdocs/nsdd298.htm.

288. Executive Order 13292 "Further Amendment to Executive Order 12958, as Amended, Classified National Security Information," http://www.archives.gov/federal-register/executive-orders/2003.html. Office of Public Affairs. Central Intelligence Agency. *A Consumer's Guide to Intelligence: Gaining Knowledge and Foreknowledge of the World around Us.* Washington, DC, and Springfield, VA: National Technical Information Service.

289. DoD. Directive 5100.52, "DoD Response to an Accident or Significant Incident Involving Radioactive Materials." December 21, 1989, http://www.fas.org/nuke/guide/usa/doctrine/dod/5100-52m/chap2.pdf (replaced by DoD Directive 3150.8, "DoD Response to Radiological Accidents," 06/13/1996).

290. FAS. Executive Orders. Executive Order 12065, http://www.fas.org/irp/offdocs/eo/eo-12065.htm and http://www.archives.gov/federal-register/executive-orders/1978.html; Executive Order 13292 "Further Amendment to Executive Order 12958, as Amended, Classified National Security Information," http://www.archives.gov/federal-register/executive-orders/2003.html; Alvin S. Quist. "Security Classification of Information." http://www.fas.org/sgp/library/quist2/chap_3.html; and Alexander DeVolpi et al. *Born Secret: The H-bomb, the Progressive Case and National Security.* New York: Pergamon Press, 1981.

291. DOE. Understanding Classification. Washington, DC: U.S. Dept. of Energy, Assistant Secretary for Defense Programs, Office of Classification, 1987. E 1.15:0007/1. David L. Carter. *Law Enforcement Intelligence: A Guide for State, Local, and Tribal Law Enforcement Agencies.* Dept. of Justice, Office of Community Oriented Policing Services, 2004.

292. Congressional Research Service. "Administrative Subpoenas and National Security Letters in Criminal and Foreign Intelligence Investigations: Background and Proposed Adjustments." April 15, 2005, http://www.fas.org/sgp/crs/natsec/RL32880.pdf, and American Civil Liberties Union (ACLU). "Challenging the Constitutionality of the National Security Letter."

293. U.S. Office of Personnel Management. "National Security Positions." 5 CFR 732.

294. DoD. *The Department of Defense Dictionary of Military and Associated Terms.* Joint Pub 1-02.

295. Committee for National Security Systems (CNSS). Instruction 4009. National Information Assurance Glossary, May 2003.

296. As determined that such persons shall possess an appropriate security clearance and access approval granted pursuant to Executive Order 12968, Access to Classified Information. DoD. Defense Personnel Security Research Center. "Employees Guide to Security Responsibilities." DOE. Department of Energy Directive DOE-5631.2c. U.S. Department of Justice. United States Marshals Service. Office of Inspections. Internal Security Division. Information Security. Washington, DC: 1991. J 25.2:In 3. Executive Order 13292 "Further Amendment to Executive Order 12958, as Amended, Classified National Security Information." Director of Central Intelligence "Directive 1/7 Security Controls on the Dissemination of Intelligence Information." 3.6 June 30, 1998.

297. Need-to-know is defined by DoD Directive 5200.1 Subsection VII.D, Enclosure 1 as discussed from C. Donald Garrett. "The Role of 'Need-to-Know' in Releasing Classified Information." *Defense Industry Bulletin* 5, no. 2 (February 1969): 1–3.

298. Roberta Wohlstetter, *Pearl Harbor: Warning and Decision* (CA: Stanford University Press), 3.

299. Betts, 828–833.

300. DoD. *National Industrial Security Program Operating Manual* (NISPOM). DoD 5220.22-M. Chapter 9. January 1995.

301. DoD. *National Industrial Security Program Operating Manual* (NISPOM). DoD 5220.22-M. Chapter 9. January 1995.

302. Intelligence Community Advanced Research and Development Activity (ARDA). NIMD, http://ic-arda.org/Novel_Intelligence/index.html.

303. Department of Energy. Office of Security Affairs. Office of Safeguards and Security. "Safeguards and Security Glossary of Terms." December 18, 1995.

304. DOE Manual 471.3-1 and DOE Communiqué. vol. 20, no. 1, February 2004.

305. Susan L. Maret. The Channel of Public Papers: Control of Government Information and Its Relation to an Informed Citizenry. Dissertation. Union Institute and University, 2002.

306. Office of Public Affairs. Central Intelligence Agency. *A Consumer's Guide to Intelligence: Gaining Knowledge and Foreknowledge of the World around Us.* Washington, DC, and Springfield, VA: National Technical Information Service, [1999].

307. Centers for Disease Control. "Manual Guide—Information Security CDC-02." Office of Security and Emergency Preparedness "Sensitive But Unclassified Information."

308. Discussed at length in Sam Adams's *War of Numbers.*

309. C. Camerer and E. Johnson, "The Process-Performance Paradox in Expert Judgment: How Can Experts Know So Much and Predict So Badly?" K. Ericsson and J. Smith, eds., *Toward a General Theory of Expertise: Prospects and Limit* (Cambridge, UK: Cambridge University Press, 1991).

310. Prepared Statement of General Richard B. Myers, Chairman, Joint Chiefs of Staff, to the House Armed Services Committee on September 18, 2002.

311. Handel, 133.

312. DoD Directive 5535.2. "Delegations of Authority to the Secretaries of the Military Departments-Inventions and Patents." and FAS. "Invention Secrecy Activity" statistics from the U.S. Patent and Trademark Office.

313. DoD. *The Department of Defense Dictionary of Military and Associated Terms.* Joint Pub 1-02.

314. DoD 5160.65-M "Single Manager for Conventional Ammunition (Implementation Joint Conventional Ammunition Policies and Procedures)," 04/1989. Chapter 12 Table 12-11.

315. Final Report, Senate Select Committee on Intelligence, 26 April 1976.

316. Jack Davis, "The Challenge of Managing Uncertainty: Paul Wolfowitz on Intelligence Policy-Relations," *Studies in Intelligence*, Vol. 39, No. 5, 1996, http://www.cia.gov/csi/studies/96unclass/davis.htm.

317. *Random House Dictionary* (NY: Ballantine Books, 1980), 697.

318. Dreyfuss, Robert. The Cops Are Watching You. *The Nation*, June 3, 2002.

319. Wingspread Conference on the Precautionary Statement. January 26, 1998, http://www.sehn.org/wing.html.

320. Science and Environmental Health Network. "Precautionary Principle FAQ," http://www.sehn.org/ppfaqs.html.

321. Colonel Ronald Baughman, USAF, "The United States Air Force Perspective," *Rusi Journal* 145, no. 6 (December 2000): 75–76.

322. Department of Justice. "Legal Effectiveness of a Presidential Directive, as Compared to an Executive Order." January 29, 2000.

323. FAS Project on Government Secrecy, http://www.fas.org/irp/offdocs/direct.htm.

324. U.S. President, Presidential Directive-56, "The Clinton Administration's Policy on Managing Complex Contingency Operations," 20 May 1997, AI–A7.

325. Department of Justice. "Legal Effectiveness of a Presidential Directive, as Compared to an Executive Order." January 29, 2000.

326. Leonard W. Levy and Louis Fisher, eds., *Encyclopedia of the American Presidency*. New York: Simon & Schuster, 1994. War and National Defense. 50 U.S.C. Sec. 413b, http://www.gpoaccess.gov/U.S.C.ode/.

327. "Professor Sues CIA for President's Daily Brief," December 23, 2004, http://www2.gwu.edu/~nsarchiv/pdbnews/index.htm.

328. United Nations International Strategy for Disaster Reduction, http://www.unisdr.org/eng/library/lib-terminology-eng%20home.htm.

329. Biljana Vankovska-Cvetkovska, "Between Preventive Diplomacy and Conflict Resolution: The Macedonian Perspective on the Kosovo Crisis," paper presented at the International Studies Association 40th Annual Convention, 17–20 February 1999 (Washington, DC, 1999).

330. Clay Blair, *The Forgotten War: America in Korea, 1950–1953* (New York: Times Books, 1987), 377.

331. *Federal Rules of Civil Procedure* at R. 26 and the *Federal Rules of Evidence* at R. 501; *Federal Rules of Civil Procedure* at R. 26 and the *Federal Rules of Evidence* at R. 501; Nolo Press Legal Glossary; Morton Rosenberg. "Presidential Claims of Executive Privilege: History, Law, Practice and Recent Developments." *CRS Report for Congress*, September 21, 1999; *United States v. Nixon* 418 U.S. 683 (1974); also see Arthur Schlesinger. *The Imperial Presidency*. New York: Atlantic Monthly, 1973, for a historical discussion of the privilege; Source: U.S. Department of State. Foreign Affairs Manual. 12FAM090 "Definitions of Diplomatic Security Terms." November 13, 2003; U.S. Department of Justice. Freedom of Information Act Guide, May 2004: FAS. *Secrecy News* April 21, 2004, http://www.fas.org/sgp/jud/index.html#reynolds. Rick Blum. *Secrecy Report Card 2005*. OpenTheGovernment.org. September 2005, http://www.openthegovernment.org/otg/SRC2005.pdf.

332. U.S. Department of Justice. *Freedom of Information Act Guide*, May 2004.

333. Random House Dictionary, 712.

334. Cynthia M. Grabo, "Strategic Warning: The Problem of Timing," *Studies in Intelligence* 16 (Spring 1972), 79.

335. DoD. *The Department of Defense Dictionary of Military and Associated Terms*. Joint Pub 1-02.

336. Executive Order No. 12036, 26 January 1978 and Final Report, Senate Select Committee on Intelligence, 26 April 1976.

337. Hughes and Schum, *Process of Intelligence Analysis.*

338. DoD. *National Industrial Security Program Operating Manual* (NISPOM). DoD 5220.22-M. Chapter 9. January 1995.

339. Department of Homeland Security. *Protected Critical Infrastructure Information*, 6 CFR 29.6.

340. DoD. *The Department of Defense Dictionary of Military and Associated Terms.* Joint Pub 1-02.

341. DoD. *The Department of Defense Dictionary of Military and Associated Terms.* Joint Pub 1-02.

342. DoD. *The Department of Defense Dictionary of Military and Associated Terms.* Joint Pub 1-02.

343. U.S. Army Personnel Command, Military Intelligence Branch, http://www.fas .org/i1p/agencylarmylperscomlopmdlmil, accessed 17 April 2001.

344. David L. Carter. Law Enforcement Intelligence: A Guide for State, Local, and Tribal Law Enforcement Agencies. Dept. of Justice, Office of Community Oriented Policing Services, 2004.

345. Robert Suro, "Up In Arms: The Defense Department; Zeroing In on Zero Casualty Syndrome," *Washington Post*, 2, August 2000, A19.

346. Mark E. Gebicke, Director, Military Operations and Capabilities Issues, National Security and International Affairs Division, appearance before the Subcommittee on Military Readiness, Committee on National Security, House of Representatives on 1 March 1997, published as GAO/T-NSIAD-97-107.

347. Department of the Army. Marine Corps Combat Development Command. Department of the Navy. Operational Terms and Graphics. FM 1-02 (FM 101-5).

348. United Nations International Strategy for Disaster Reduction, http://www.unisdr .org/eng/library/lib-terminology-eng%20home.htm.

349. U.S. Department of State. Foreign Affairs Manual. 12FAM090 "Definitions of Diplomatic Security Terms."

350. For examples, see Richard Clark, *Intelligence Analysis: A Target-Centric Approach* (Washington, DC: CQ Press, 2004), 118–119.

351. United Nations International Strategy for Disaster Reduction, http://www.unisdr .org/eng/library/lib-terminology-eng%20home.htm.

352. Eisenhower EO 10501, November 5, 1953 "Safeguarding Official Information in the Interests of the Defense of the United States" eliminated the "Restricted" level leaving only Top Secret, Secret, and Confidential. Made a differentiation between national security and national defense. Source: National Archives and Records Administration (NARA) and Department of Energy. Office of Security Affairs. Office of Safeguards and Security. "Safeguards and Security Glossary of Terms." December 18, 1995.

353. United Nations International Strategy for Disaster Reduction, http://www.unisdr .org/eng/library/lib-terminology-eng%20home.htm.

354. Paul Krugman, "Slicing the Salami," *New York Times,* Outlook Section, February 2001, 17.

355. DoD. Instruction 5210.52. "Security Classification of Airborne Sensor Imagery and Imaging Systems." May 18, 1989.

356. Committee for National Security Systems (CNSS). Instruction 4009. *National Information Assurance Glossary*, May 2003, http://www.nsa.gov/ia/index.cfm.

357. This definition is expanded upon in Kenneth N. Waltz, *Theory of International Politics* (New York: Random House, 1979) and Joseph M. Grieco, *Cooperation among Nations: Europe, America, and Non-Tariff Barriers* (Ithaca: Cornell University Press, 1990), 28–29.

358. Department of Energy. Office of Security Affairs. Office of Safeguards and Security. "Safeguards and Security Glossary of Terms." December 18, 1995.

359. Centers for Disease Control. "Manual Guide—Information Security CDC-02." Office of Security and Emergency Preparedness "Sensitive But Unclassified Information." Part B. 07/22/2005, http://www.fas.org/sgp/othergov/cdc-sbu.pdf.

360. Department of Defense. *DoD Dictionary of Military and Associated Terms.* Amended. JP 1-02.

361. Remarks by Secretary Ridge to the Association of American Universities, http://www.dhs.gov/dhspublic/display?content = 558; Alice R. Buckhalter, John Gibbs, and Marieke Lewis. "Laws and Regulation Governing the Protection of Sensitive But Unclassified Information." Federal Research Division, Library of Congress. September 2004, http://www.loc.gov/rr/frd/pdf-files/sbu.pdf; Andrew Card ("The Card Memo"), "Guidance on Homeland Security Information Issued." March 21, 2002, http://www.usdoj.gov/oip/foiapost/2002foiapost10.htm.

362. This definition is based on Mica Endsley's definition, which can be found in "Toward a Theory of Situation Awareness in Dynamic Systems," SA Technologies Inc. Human Factors, 1995, 37(1), 32–64.

363. Department of the Army. Marine Corps Combat Development Command. Department of the Navy. Operational Terms and Graphics. FM 1-02 (FM 101-5). September 21, 2004.

364. Joint Pub 2-0, *Joint Doctrine for Intelligence Support to Operations,* October 1993.

365. Defense Security Service, http://www.dss.mil/isec/chapter9.htm#Section 3, *DoD Dictionary of Military and Associated Terms.* DODD 5100.20. "The National Security Agency and the Central Security Service," December 23, 1971, ASD(I), thru Ch 4, June 24, 1991.

366. Army Regulation 380–381, 12 October 1998, section 1-4(6), DoD 5200.1-M, and Army Regulation 380–381, 21 April 2004.

367. DoD. *The Department of Defense Dictionary of Military and Associated Terms.* Joint Pub 1-02.

368. Committee for National Security Systems (CNSS). Instruction 4009. National Information Assurance Glossary, May 2003, http://www.nsa.gov/ia/index.cfm.

369. Roberta Wohlstetter, *Pearl Harbor: Warning and Decision* (CA: Stanford University Press, 1962), 318.

370. Gentry, 71.

371. Cable News Network broadcast on 11 May 1999.

372. U.S. Department of Homeland Security, *Strategic Plan: Securing Our Homeland,* 2004, 9.

373. Grabo, *Strategic Warning,* 92.

374. U.S. House of Representatives Permanent Select Committee on Intelligence. *IC21: The Intelligence Community in the 21st Century* (Washington, DC: U.S. Government Printing Office).

375. David L. Carter. Law Enforcement Intelligence: A Guide for State, Local, and Tribal Law Enforcement Agencies. Dept. of Justice, Office of Community Oriented Policing Services, 2004.

376. David L. Carter. Law Enforcement Intelligence: A Guide for State, Local, and Tribal Law Enforcement Agencies. Dept. of Justice, Office of Community Oriented Policing Services, 2004. 85 n.118, http://www.cops.usdoj.gov/default.asp?Item=1404.

377. TSWG Technical Support Working Group, http://www.tswg.gov/tswg/about/about.htm.

378. Richard H.M. Outzen, "Technical Intelligence: Added Realism at the NTC," *Technical Intelligence* newsletter of the National Ground Intelligence Center (Aberdeen Proving Ground, MD: Technical Intelligence Unit) 4, no. 1 (January–February 1999), 11.

379. Sherman Kent. "The Law and Custom of the National Intelligence Estimate," *DCI Miscellaneous Studies,* MS-12 (February 1976): 43; declassified February 1994.

380. DARPA. "Executive Summary." Report to Congress regarding the Terrorism Information Awareness Program, http://www.eff.org/Privacy/TIA/TIA-report.html.

381. Deleted TIPS "Citizen Corps" Webpages cached @ The MemoryHole. Source: Homeland Security Act of 2002. Section 880, http://www.fas.org/sgp/congress/2002/hr5710-111302.html and http://www.thememoryhole.org/policestate/tips-deleted.htm.

382. DoD. Army Regulation AR381-45. "Investigative Records Repository." August 25, 1989, http://www.army.mil/usapa/epubs/pdf/r381_45.pdf, and National Security Act of 1947, http://www.intelligence.gov/0-natsecact_1947.shtml#s102.

383. U.S. Department of State. Foreign Affairs Manual. 12FAM090 "Definitions of Diplomatic Security Terms." November 13, 2003, http://foia.state.gov/REGS/Search.asp.

384. Committee for National Security Systems (CNSS). Instruction 4009. National Information Assurance Glossary, May 2003, http://www.nsa.gov/ia/index.cfm.

385. Barbra Starr, "US Military on High Alert," ABCNews.com, http://abcnews.go.com/sections/world/DailyNews/terror001024.html, accessed 12 April 2001.

386. FAS Project on Intelligence Reform, http://www.fas.org/irp/program/security/tempest.htm and http://www.fas.org/sgp/library/nispom/chap_11.htm.

387. Remarks of Senator John Kerry in speaking of Senate colleague Daniel Moynihan: "Our vast intelligence apparatus, built to sustain America in the long twilight struggle of the Cold War, continues to grow at an exponential rate." *Congressional Record* May 1, 1997, http://www.fas.org/sqp/congress/kerry.html; Susan L. Maret. The Channel of Public Papers: Control of Government Information and Its Relation to an Informed Citizenry. Dissertation. Union Institute and University, 2002, United States. National Commission on Libraries and Information Science (NCLIS). Hearing on Sensitive But Not Classified Information, Washington, DC: 1988, and Herbert N. Foerstel. *Secret Science: Federal Control of American Science and Technology.* Westport, CT: Praeger, 1993 (especially Chapter 5, "Secret But Not Classified").

388. Executive Order 13292 "Further Amendment to Executive Order 12958, as Amended, Classified National Security Information" and DoD Directive 5210.50. U.S. Department of State. *Foreign Affairs Manual.* 12FAM090 "Definitions of Diplomatic Security Terms." November 13, 2003.

389. Robert David Steele. "Virtual Intelligence: Conflict Avoidance and Resolution Through Information Peacekeeping," http://www.usip.org/virtualdiplomacy/publications/papers/virintell.html.

390. Department of the Army. Marine Corps Combat Development Command. Department of the Navy. *Operational Terms and Graphics*. FM 1-02 (FM 101-5). September 21, 2004, https://atiam.train.army.mil/soldierPortal/atia/adlsc/view/public/4876-1/FM/1-02/toc.htm.

391. National Imagery and Mapping Agency. "NIMA Guide to Marking Classified Documents." October 4, 2001, http://www.fas.org/sgp/othergov/DoD/nimaguide.pdf.

392. Judicial Administration. 28 CFR 23, http://www.gpoaccess.gov/CFR/index.html.

393. DoD. *The Department of Defense Dictionary of Military and Associated Terms*. JP 1-02. May 9, 2005, http://www.dtic.mil/doctrine/jel/new_pubs/jp1_02.pdf.

394. Director of Central Intelligence (DCI) Directive No. 1/5, National Intelligence Warning, 23 May 1979.

395. DCI Directive No. 1/5.

396. DCI Directive No. 1/5.

397. "Past Presidents of AMS Voice Concern about Cuts in the National Weather Service Budget," *American Meteorological Society (AMS) Newsletter* 18, no. 4 (April 1997), 1.

398. Watson, 594.

399. Watson, 594.

400. Hughes-Wilson, 214.

401. Prepared testimony of Ronald L. Dick, Director, National Infrastructure Protection Center, Federal Bureau of Investigation, before the House Committee on Commerce Subcommittee on Oversight and Investigations on Thursday, 5 April 2001.

402. World War II Nazi Rally photograph, quotation, *Electric Library Plus*, http://www.elibrary.cornm/sp/plus, accessed 1 May 2001.

403. Brian G. Shellum, *Defense Intelligence Crisis Response Procedures and the Gulf War*, DIA website http://www.dia.mil/history/histories/response.html.

404. Department of Defense. *DoD Dictionary of Military and Associated Terms. Amended*. JP 1-02.

405. U.S. Law: Title 50, Chapter 40, Code § 2302.

406. DOE. Chief Information Officer. "Records Management Definitions."

407. Los Alamos National Lab. "Definitions," http://www.hr.lanl.gov/SCourses/All/PortionMarking/define.htm.

408. DoD. DoDI 5210.87 "Selection of DoD Personnel and Civilian Personnel and Contractor Employees for Assignment to Presidential Support Activities (PSAs)," 11/30/1998, http://www.dtic.mil/whs/directives/corres/html/521087.htm, Global Security .org, http://www.globalsecurity.org/wmd/systems/nuclear-football.htm and http://www.e-publishing.af.mil/pubfiles/89aw/90/89awi90-101/89awi90-101.pdf.

409. Richard Brody, "The Limits of Warning," *The Washington Quarterly*, Summer 1983.

Appendix

Essential Intelligence Websites

U.S. Intelligence Community and Associated Members

Air Intelligence Agency: http://aia.lackland.af.mil/aia/site.cfm
Army Intelligence: https://icon.army.mil
Army Intelligence and Security Command: http://www.inscom.army.mil
Central Intelligence Agency: http://www.cia.gov
Coast Guard: http://www.uscg.mil
Congressional Oversight (House of Representatives Permanent Select Committee on Intelligence: http://intelligence.house.gov; Senate Select Committee on Intelligence: http://intelligence.senate.gov/index.htm)
Department of Defense: http://www.defenselink.mil
Department of Homeland Security: http://www.dhs.gov/dhspublic (Federal Emergency Management Agency: http://www.fema.gov)
Defense Intelligence Agency: http://www.dia.mil
Department of Justice: http://www.usdoj.gov (National Drug Intelligence Center: http://www.usdoj.gov/ndic)
Department of State Bureau of Intelligence and Research: http://www.state.gov/s/inr
Department of Treasury Office of Intelligence: http://www.treas.gov (Secret Service: http://www.treas.gov/usss/index.shtml)
Director of National Intelligence: http://www.odni.gov
Drug Enforcement Administration: http://www.usdoj.gov/dea
Federal Bureau of Investigation: http://www.fbi.gov
Marine Corps Intelligence: http://hqinet001.hqmc.usmc.mil/DirInt
National Geo-Spatial Intelligence Agency: http://www.nga.mil
National Intelligence Council: http://www.cia.gov/nic
National Reconnaissance Office: http://www.nro.gov
National Security Agency: http://www.nsa.gov
Naval Intelligence: http://www.nmic.navy.mil

President's Foreign Intelligence Advisory Board
United States Intelligence Community: http://www.intelligence.gov

International Intelligence

Australian Defence Intelligence Organisation: http://www.defence.gov.au/
dio
Australian Secret Intelligence Service: http://www.asis.gov.au/index.html
Australian Security Intelligence Organisation: http://www.asio.gov.au
British Security Service, MI5: http://www.mi5.gov.uk
British Secret Intelligence Service, MI6: http://www.sis.gov.uk/output/Page
2.html
Canadian Security Intelligence Service: http://www.csis-scrs.gc.ca
France (unoffical) Intelligence Stratégique (site is in French): http://www.in
telligence-strategique.fr.st
German Bundesnachrichtendienst (BND, site is in German): http://www
.bnd.bund.de/DE/Home_Vorschaltseite/home_node_mit_javaSkript.html
German Militärischer Abschirmdienst (MAD, site is in German): http://
www.bundeswehr.de/C1256EF4002AED30/CurrentBaseLink/N264HLD
2829MMISDE
Hungarian National Security Office: http://www.nbh.hu/english/index.htm
Interpol (international police): http://www.interpol.int
Israel (nongovernment) Intelligence & Terrorism Center: http://www.inter
pol.int
Italian Intelligence and Democratic Security Service: http://www.sisde.it
Jordanian General Intelligence Department: http://www.gid.gov.jo
New Zealand Security Intelligence Service: http://www.nzsis.govt.nz
Organization for Security and Cooperation in Europe: http://www.osce.org
Polish Foreign Intelligence Agency: http://www.aw.gov.pl/
Polish Internal Security Agency: http://www.abw.gov.pl
Portuguese Strategic and Defense Intelligence Service: http://www.sied.pt
Portuguese Security Intelligence Service: http://www.sis.pt
Russian Language Site on Intelligence: http://www.sis.pt
Russian Intelligence: http://www.fsb.ru
Russian Foreign Intelligence: http://svr.gov.ru
Spanish National Intelligence Center: http://www.cni.es/castellano/index
.html
Turkish National Intelligence Organization: http://www.mit.gov.tr/main.html

Education and Research (Noncommerical)

Amnesty International: http://www.amnesty.org
Army War College: http://www.carlisle.army.mil

Brookings Institute: http://www.brook.edu

Center for Army Lessons Learned: http://call.army.mil

Center for the Study of Intelligence: http://www.odci.gov/csi/index.html

Computer Emergency Response Team (CERT) Coordination Center: http://www.cert.org

Federation of American Scientists: http://www.fas.org

Foreign Military Studies Office, Joint Reserve Intelligence Center: http://fmso.leavenworth.army.mil

Heritage Foundation: http://www.heritage.org

Human Rights Watch: http://www.hrw.org

Institute for Policy Studies: http://www.ips-dc.org

International Intelligence Ethics Association: http://www.intelligence-ethics.org

Joint Military Intelligence College (DIA): http://www.dia.mil/jmic

Loyola College (Maryland), political science department-strategic intelligence: http://www.loyola.edu/dept/politics/intel.html

Military Education Research Library Network (MERLN): http://merln.ndu.edu

Naval Postgraduate School Center for Contemporary Conflict: http://www.ccc.nps.navy.mil/index.asp

Naval War College: http://www.nwc.navy.mil/defaultf.htm

National Memorial Institute for the Prevention of Terrorism: http://www.mipt.org

Nuclear Control Institute: http://www.nci.org

Nuclear Threat Initiative: http://www.nti.org

Potomac Institute: http://www.potomacinstitute.org

Rand Corporation: http://www.rand.org

University of Haifa (Israel): http://www.terrorismexperts.org

University of Pittsburg Center for Biosecurity: http://www.upmc-biosecurity.org

U.S. Institute of Peace: http://www.usip.org

General Reference (Commercial)

Refdesk.com: http://www.refdesk.com

SearchMil.com: http://www.searchmil.com

About the Author

Jan Goldman is a professor at the Joint Military Intelligence College in Washington, D.C. He has been working in the intelligence community, focusing on strategic warning and threat management, for almost 25 years, and has contributed to the development of several intelligence warning and crisis centers. He is the author or editor of several publications, including *Ethics of Spying: A Reader for the Intelligence Community* (2006) and the recently declassified textbook by Cynthia Grabo, *Anticipating Surprise: Analysis for Strategic Warning*.